YALE LAW LIBRARY SERIES
IN LEGAL HISTORY AND REFERENCE

POWER
AND JUSTICE
IN MEDIEVAL
ENGLAND

THE LAW OF PATRONAGE AND
THE ROYAL COURTS

Joshua C. Tate

Yale
UNIVERSITY PRESS

New Haven & London

Published with support from the Lillian Goldman Law Library,
Yale Law School.

Yale University Press books may be purchased in quantity for
educational, business, or promotional use. For information, please email
sales.press@yale.edu (U.S. office) or sales@yaleup.co.uk (U.K. office).

Set in MT Baskerville & MT Bulmer type by IDS Infotech Ltd.,
Chandigarh, India.
Printed in the United States of America.

Library of Congress Control Number: 2021944507
ISBN 978-0-300-16383-4 (hardcover: alk. paper)

A catalogue record for this book is available from the British Library.

This paper meets the requirements of ANSI/NISO
Z39.48-1992 (Permanence of Paper).

10 9 8 7 6 5 4 3 2 1

For Lisa

CONTENTS

CONTENTS

ACKNOWLEDGMENTS

This book has been a long time in coming, and it has benefited from the support of many colleagues. Above all, I must thank Charles Donahue Jr., who first suggested that I look at the advowson writs and has been a mentor throughout my career, and Paul Brand, who has taught me more than anyone else about how to interpret the English plea rolls. I am most obliged to Robert Palmer for digitizing the royal court records through the AALT project and for helping me resolve some doubtful points in the rolls discussed herein. Susanne Brand, Harry Dondorp, Paul Freedman, Richard Helmholz, Jim Whitman, Anders Winroth, and the two anonymous reviewers who read my manuscript submission also provided important insight on certain points. I am grateful for the input of the scholars who attended my presentations at various conferences and workshops, including the British Legal History Conference, the International Congress of Medieval Canon Law, the SMU Law Faculty Forum, and multiple meetings of the American Society for Legal History. Greg Ivy and the staff of the Underwood Law Library have been very helpful in making sources available to me in the challenging circumstances of the COVID-19 pandemic.

This project began with my Yale PhD dissertation, "Advowson Law and Litigation in the English Royal Courts, 1154–1250," directed by Anders Winroth. Chapter 2 of this book expands on "The Third Lateran Council and the *Ius Patronatus* in England," my contribution to the *Proceedings of the Thirteenth International Congress of Medieval Canon Law,* as well as my article "The Origins of *Quare Impedit,*" published in the *Journal of Legal History* in 2004. (Text from the latter is reprinted by permission of the publisher, Taylor and Francis Ltd., http://www.tandfonline.com.) Some of the ideas in chapter 3 were first presented in "Ownership and Possession in the Early Common Law," published in the *American Journal of Legal History*. Portions of chapter 5 first appeared in "Royal Privilege and Episcopal Rights in the Later Thirteenth Century: The Case of the Ashbourne Advowson, 1270–89," my contribution to *Law and Society in Later Medieval England and Ireland: Essays in Honour of Paul Brand,* edited by Travis R. Baker. Chapter 5 also advances my work in "Competing Institutions and Dispute Settlement in Medieval England," which was included in *Law and Disputing in the Middle Ages: Proceedings of the Ninth Carlsberg Academy Conference on Medieval Legal History 2012,* edited by Per Andersen, Kirsi Salonen, Helle Moller Sigh, and Helle Vogt. The book also builds on my individual contributions to two Festschrift volumes: *Texts and Context in Legal History: Essays in Honor of Charles Donahue,* edited by Sara McDougall, Anna di Robilant, and John Witte Jr.; and *Studies in Canon Law and Common Law in Honor of R. H. Helmholz,* edited by Troy L. Harris. I am grateful to the editors of these volumes for advancing my research.

I acknowledge with great appreciation the support of the Héctor Mairal Faculty Research Fund at SMU Dedman School of Law, the SMU University Research Fellowship, and the Lloyd M. Robbins Senior Research Fellowship at the University of California, Berkeley. I owe a debt of gratitude to TaLibra Ferguson, John Lowe, Becca Henley, Laurent Mayali, and others for helping me secure those opportunities. Bill Frucht, Karen Olson, and Ann-Marie Imbornoni at Yale University Press have been extremely helpful and patient as I have slowly worked toward completion, and I am also grateful to Mike O'Malley (formerly of the press) for showing initial interest. Dr. Johann Tomaschek of the Stiftsbibliothek Admont kindly allowed me to obtain a reproduction of the Admont manuscript of Huguccio's *Summa decretorum* from the Hill Museum and Manuscript Library; the British Library furnished a digital copy of the Hänel edition of *Ulpianus de edendo;* and the Lincolnshire Archives sent images of the register of Hugh of Wells. Those images, and one from the Norfolk Record Office, are used by permission. I am grateful to Bill Henry for his excellent copyediting and to Kate Mertes for her careful work preparing the index. Finally, I would like to thank my children Charles and Ellen—and my wife, Lisa, to whom this book is dedicated—for giving me good reasons to finish it.

ABBREVIATIONS

English Sources

AALT   The Anglo-American Legal Tradition: Documents from
Medieval and Early Modern England from the National
Archives in London (digital archive curated by Robert C.
Palmer et al., http://aalt.law.uh.edu)

BNB   *Bracton's Note Book*

Bracton   "Bracton," *On the Laws and Customs of England*

CRR   *Curia Regis Rolls*

Glanvill   "Glanvill," *Treatise on the Laws and Customs of the Realm of England*

Lincs.   *The Earliest Lincolnshire Assize Rolls, 1202–1209*

PKJ   *Pleas before the King or His Justices, 1198–1202*

PRS   *Publications of the Pipe Roll Society*

RCR   *Rotuli Curiae Regis*

RHW   *Rotuli Hugonis de Welles*

Staffs.   *Staffordshire Suits Extracted from the Plea Rolls*

TNA   The National Archives (U.K.)

VCH   *Victoria History of the Counties of England*

Terms of Court

Hil.	Hilary Term
Pas.	Easter Term
Trin.	Trinity Term
Mich.	Michaelmas Term

Canon Law

C.	*Causa*
c.	*canon* or *capitulum*
COD	*Conciliorum Oecumenicorum Decreta*
Comp.	*Compilatio*
Conc. Lat.	Lateran Council
D.	*Distinctio*
PL	*Patrologiae cursus completus, series latina*
q.	*questio*
WH	Walther-Holtzmann-Katalog
X.	*Liber Extra* (*Gregorian Decretals*)

Roman Law

CJ	*Code* of Justinian
Dig.	*Digest* of Justinian
Inst.	*Institutes* of Justinian
Lectura	Medieval English commentary to Justinian's *Institutes*, in *The Teaching of Roman Law in England around 1200*
LP	*The Liber Pauperum* of Vacarius

CHAPTER ONE

INTRODUCTION

The rise of the English common law is richly documented, but one who looks only at the names, dates, and legal formulas in the surviving records of the royal courts will miss a great deal of the story. This is true of a suit brought in 1225 by the abbot of Saint Benet's, Holme, against William de Warenne, fifth Earl of Surrey, and Maud his wife.[1] The royal clerk tells us that the abbot sought to claim the advowson (right of patronage) of a one-third part of the church of Felmingham. The case was resolved, without objection from the defendants, by following a standard procedure called the assize of darrein presentment (about which more later). The abbot won his case, and the earl was fined for making a false claim. And so this bit of history was preserved forever on parchment as part of the long series of records that we know as the plea rolls.[2]

But what was the case really about? The facts presented in the plea rolls concealed a more complex dispute. Earl William was related to King Henry III by descent from William's father, a bastard son of Geoffrey Plantagenet and half brother of King Henry II. William was also kin to Hubert de Burgh, justiciar of England, through Hugh's marriage to

Beatrice de Warenne, the daughter of William's cousin. Having switched sides multiple times during the war between King John and the rebel barons, William accumulated a debt of one thousand marks to other barons by the war's end and spent the following decade trying to obtain money for repayment. He supported Hubert de Burgh in a dispute during the winter of 1223–24 and was rewarded with two royal castles (one of which he was later forced to surrender to its rightful heir).[3]

The abbey of Saint Benet of Holme (sometimes spelled Hulme or Holm) was not a particularly distinguished religious house.[4] However, the abbey did have friends in high places, particularly the bishop of Ely, who had been presented by the abbot as the last parson of Felmingham.[5] That bishop was Geoffrey de Burgh, the justiciar's brother.[6] At the time Geoffrey was presented as the parson of Felmingham, he was serving as archdeacon of Norwich. Perhaps grateful that the abbey did this favor for the archdeacon, the bishop of Norwich later approved a deal ensuring that the abbey could rely on revenues from the church of Ludham.[7] That bishop, Pandulf, was a papal legate who had retired to Italy by the time the abbey brought its lawsuit concerning Felmingham, and would die in 1226.[8] Pandulf would be replaced in 1226 as bishop of Norwich by Thomas de Blundeville (d. 1236), nephew of Geoffrey de Burgh.[9]

Had the justiciar been forced to pick a side in the dispute between Earl William and the abbey, the choice would have been a difficult one. Ruling against William would mean alienating a political ally who also happened to be Hubert's relative. On the other hand, ruling in favor of the abbey could present difficulties for Hubert's family, given the past favors the abbey had granted and the promises that had been made (or implied) in return. How could the justiciar resolve this case without making an enemy or losing a friend?

Fortunately for Hubert, he did not have to make this choice. A mechanism already existed for resolving this type of case, one that we will easily recognize today as a jury. Twelve jurors were summoned and asked who presented the last parson to the church, to which they responded that the abbot last presented the archdeacon of Norwich, who is now bishop: that is, Geoffrey de Burgh.[10] What might have been a difficult political decision for the king's chief minister was instead a routine matter, thanks to the institution of the jury.

FIG. 1. Gatehouse, Saint Benet's Abbey, Norfolk. Photo by Joshua Tate.

FIG. 2. Confirmation by William, prior of Norwich, of the impropriation by Bishop Pandulf to Saint Benet's Abbey of the church of Ludham. Photo by Joshua Tate, published with permission of Norfolk Record Office.

In modern times, at least in the United States, we tend to take the common-law jury for granted. It has seemingly always been there, ready to perform its service when needed. And yet things could easily have been otherwise. Taking into account the ever-present human desire to obtain and accumulate power, it is quite remarkable that the English kings were willing to give way to ordinary men to decide disputes in which the king might have preferred a specific outcome.

As Daniel Lord Smail has noted in a different context, the medieval practice of law takes on different aspects when seen through the perspective of the litigants rather than kings and royal officials.[11] My principal argument in this book is that the common law developed procedures that were effective and resilient not by accident but because they faced competition in the form of other courts, particularly the ecclesiastical courts. The jury proved to be a popular and lasting institution with advantages for both the king and his subjects.[12] Nevertheless, its success was not initially ensured. Like a modern business introducing a new product into the market, the English royal courts in the late twelfth century had to offer something that was superior to the existing alternatives, at least from the perspective of one group of customers. Moreover, the continued existence of alternative forums meant that the common law had to develop procedures and rules that were seen as fair and reasonable by all parties, at least most of the time. The development and entrenchment of fair and efficient procedures made it difficult for any king or royal official to put his thumb on the scales of justice, even if some temporary advantage might be gained from doing so.

The ecclesiastical court system was not only a source of competition for the common law but also a possible inspiration. Did ideas from Roman and canon law inspire common-law institutions? For centuries, legal scholars and jurists have given much attention to the question of whether law can be transplanted from one system to another. Many have shared the view that the law of a particular society changes at least partly in response to forces originating within that society, but external to law.[13] According to this view, it is not necessarily easy for a legal rule to be transplanted from one society to another, because the conditions of each society are unique, and rules that are acceptable or desirable for one society may not be suitable for another.[14] Even if two societies share similar social conditions, moreover, the absence of a fertile and welcoming legal culture might prevent the successful transplantation of doctrinal concepts or rules.

The notion of law as *Volksrecht* was challenged by the legal historian and comparative lawyer Alan Watson. Watson viewed law as not only intellectually autonomous but also readily transplantable from one society to another. According to Watson, "Usually legal rules are not peculiarly devised for the particular society in which they now operate."[15] Although Watson did not claim that the relationship between law and society is nonexistent, he certainly downplayed its significance.[16]

More recently, Gunther Teubner offered a novel take on cross-border legal influences. Viewing the concept of legal transplantation as an unhelpful metaphor, Teubner has proposed instead that influences be viewed as "legal irritants."[17] Unlike a transplanted biological organ or machine, a legal institution does not remain the same in its new environment. Instead the institution will "unleash an evolutionary dynamic in which the external rule's meaning will be reconstructed and the internal context will undergo fundamental change."[18]

The theories of Watson and Teubner are relevant to modern comparative law, but most of their examples come from legal history, particularly the history of Roman and European law. These scholars thus contribute to a narrower debate about the reach of Roman law (and also canon law) in medieval Europe, including England, a country that eventually produced Roman law's greatest rival on the world stage. Because the systematic revival of Roman and canon law in medieval Europe overlapped in time with the birth of the English common law in the twelfth century, historians have debated the extent to which the English legal pioneers borrowed from Romano-canonical learning. Some remedies, doctrines, and rules of the early English common law bear a resemblance to certain features of Roman or canon law, thus prompting the question of whether the resemblance reflects conscious or unconscious borrowing or simply coincidence.

Even if we could answer that question—and we almost certainly cannot, at least conclusively—the answer would lead only to further questions. If the resemblance between certain English and Romano-canonical doctrines is not coincidental, does the fact of influence support the general notion of universality of legal principles, or does it instead reflect some more specific commonality in the problems faced by English society and the societies on the Continent? Conversely, to the extent that the English common law followed a different path than that suggested by Roman or canon law, one might ask why this occurred. Given the cultural and political connections between medieval England and its neighbors across the Channel, why would England diverge from the rest of Europe in rejecting significant aspects of the Romano-canonical tradition? Is it because legal transplants must be accompanied by a receptive legal culture, and the legal culture in England was somehow unreceptive to the Romano-canonical tradition? Or were social or political conditions in England too different from those on the Continent for Romano-canonical ideas or institutions to take root?

Over the centuries, legal scholars have offered various opinions about the extent to which Romano-canonical learning (which eventually evolved into the *ius commune* of Europe) has played a role in the development of the English common law. At one extreme, the sixteenth-century professor Sir Thomas Smith drew a sharp distinction between "the forme and manner of the government of Englande, and the policy thereof," on the one hand, and "the policie or government at this time used in Fraunce, Italie, Spaine, Germanie and all other countries, which doe follow the civill lawe of the Romanes compiled by *Justinian* into his pandects and code," on the other.[19] At the other extreme, Charles P. Sherman, a Yale Law School instructor writing in the early twentieth century, discerned Roman law influence in a multitude of common-law doctrines, asserting that "a summary of specific contributions from Roman to English law reveals the great indebtedness of our law to the law of Rome."[20] It is difficult to believe that these two men were writing about the same legal system, and yet they were.

More recent scholarship has tended to take an intermediate position on the question of influence, acknowledging that the *ius commune* had an impact on the development of the English common law while being careful not to overemphasize that impact.[21] The argument that influence did occur seems to be strongest when applied to the late twelfth century and the early thirteenth, when the common law was still in its infancy. Even for that period, however, the best case for influence amounts to "a balance of probabilities," as Richard Helmholz demonstrated in his study of the relationship between Magna Carta and the *ius commune*.[22] Some scholars would agree with John Barton, who found clear evidence that the early common lawyers were aware of Roman and canon law, but less evidence that their knowledge had a substantial impact on what actually happened in the courts, at least after the thirteenth century.[23] Nevertheless, some today continue to assert the independence of English law from Europe as heartily as Sir Thomas Smith once did,[24] while others continue to voice the opposite theory—that English law had a strong European orientation—as well.[25]

Historians generally point to the second half of the twelfth century as the time when the English common law was born.[26] Beginning in the reign of Henry II (1154–89), the English royal courts dramatically expanded their jurisdiction, creating a national legal system that would eventually supplant the preexisting framework of local and seigneurial courts. The rules and procedures developed by the royal courts during and after the reign of Henry II have left a permanent imprint on the law of England and the lands it colonized or conquered. While a modern American or English lawyer would recognize few of the substantive rules, and none of the writs, used by Englishmen in the late twelfth century, an unbroken chain of descent exists between the law of 1189 and the law of the present day. It is not surprising that Parliament once selected the year 1189 as the theoretical limit of legal memory for proving certain rights under the common law.[27] If we are to find evidence of legal transplants—or, alternatively, explain why English law diverged from the Romano-canonical legal tradition—our search must begin in the second half of the twelfth century.

FIG. 3. Memorial to King Henry II, Chinon, France. Photo by Joshua Tate.

FIG. 4. Effigies of Henry II and Eleanor of Aquitaine, Fontevraud Abbey, France. Photo by Joshua Tate.

The reforms of Henry II have been the subject of much discussion. Historians have debated whether legal remedies such as the assize of novel disseisin, the assize of mort d'ancestor, and the writ of right were meant to upset or strengthen the existing feudal framework.[28] Historians have also disputed whether the assize of novel disseisin was inspired in some sense by canon law or Roman law, either by specific actions available in those other legal systems or by the general tenor of their laws regarding possession.[29] Scholarly discussion of these questions has involved some of the leading English historians of the modern era, including F. W. Maitland and S. F. C Milsom. At times, the discussion has seemed to ignore or downplay the emergence in the latter part of the twelfth century of Romano-canonical texts in England, as well as the contemporaneous use of Romano-canonical procedures in the English ecclesiastical courts. While preconceived notions about common-law exceptionalism may have led some to ignore this evidence, however, a contrary belief in the universal appeal of the Roman tradition has encouraged others to find supposed doctrinal parallels that may reflect little more than coincidence.

To date, the debates over the property reforms of Henry II have concentrated almost exclusively on writs dealing with land. There is no doubt that land was of considerable importance in the late twelfth century; most of the cases in the royal court records have something to do with land. Nevertheless, Henry II was also responsible for legal reform concerning another kind of property: advowsons of churches. Henry decreed that advowson litigation was to be held in the royal courts, and created a special assize—the assize of darrein presentment—to recognize the claim of the last person who had presented before the living became vacant. Legal historians have generally paid little attention to the law of advowsons in examining the early growth of the common law. This is unfortunate, for the law of advowsons not only highlights the problem of Romano-canonical influence or its absence but also underscores the connection between the development of the common law and the complex political interactions between the king, his barons, and the church.

An advowson, in English law, is "the right to present a clerk [cleric] to the bishop for institution as parson of some vacant church; the bishop is bound to institute this presented clerk or else must show one of some few good causes for a refusal."[30] Advowsons were property and, like land, could be inherited or transferred from one person to another. Unlike land, however, advowsons were incorporeal and had the special characteristic that they could be exercised only when the church in question became vacant, for example, by the death or resignation of the parson.[31] An advowson could lie dormant for many years before the time came to exercise it, and in the meantime there was no visible manifestation of the right of presentation.[32] This characteristic of advowsons engendered a great deal of litigation, much of it in the central royal courts. That litigation, and the law that lay behind it, is the focus of this book.

The common law of advowsons does not have a definite beginning. It might be possible to start in 1164, when Henry II asserted royal jurisdiction in advowson disputes in clause 1 of the Constitutions of Clarendon.[33] That proclamation, however, was not the first instance of royal involvement in advowson disputes, and a truly comprehensive story might go back to the Norman Conquest in 1066 or even earlier.[34] Alternatively, one might start with the death of Henry II in 1189 and focus on the rules that the royal justices developed to untangle the scheme of advowson writs set in motion during Henry's reign. I do not aim to cover the entire history of the common law of advowsons. I take as my starting point the year 1154, the beginning of the reign of Henry II, although the paucity of evidence makes it difficult to say much about the development of the law until the very end of Henry's reign. The study ends at the adoption of the Provisions of Westminster in 1259,[35] near the completion of the great treatise known as *Bracton*.[36] This is the crucial first phase in the history of the common law of advowsons and must be studied first before we can understand later developments.

Under the classic theory of Everett Rogers, those who first use an innovation are termed the "innovators," followed soon by the "early adopters."[37] Without such people, an innovation cannot find broader acceptance among the public. As a new way of resolving disputes, the English common law in the age of the Angevins was certainly an innovation. Litigants who sought recourse to the royal courts to resolve their advowson disputes in the late twelfth and early thirteenth centuries were among the first to use the common law and its procedures—thus they were the common law's innovators and early adopters. In this book, I consider what made the common law attractive for its earliest customers, and why its popularity continued to spread thereafter.

Harold Berman famously argued that the Western legal tradition emerged as a consequence of the "papal revolution," in which the universal church controversially asserted its primacy over secular rule.[38] As is well known, the birth of the English common law also coincided with a famous clash between the church and secular authority, this time taking the form of the dispute between Henry II and Archbishop Thomas Becket concerning the privileges of clergy accused of crimes.[39] Less well known is that jurisdiction over advowson disputes was also a point of contention between King Henry and the church, and one in which the crown ultimately got the upper hand, although not without some compromise.[40] Churchmen, who were the most likely individuals in England to have some training in the Romano-canonical legal tradition, had a strong interest in shaping the king's law of advowsons. Thus we can analyze the common law of advowsons not only as a neglected branch of legal doctrine and a part of intellectual history but also as a locus of political and social conflict. Moreover, these two modes of analysis are interrelated.

I begin chapter 2 by discussing advowsons as a social phenomenon: how they came about, how they were exercised, and who could own them. Advowsons lay at the heart of a broader conflict between the church and the laity, exemplified by the famous dispute between King Henry II and Archbishop Thomas Becket, and the first part of the chapter tells this story. The remainder is devoted to the development of the three principal royal advowson writs. After laying out the bifurcated writ system in *Glanvill*, I explain how the third writ, *quare impedit*, was designed to provide a remedy for parties claiming an advowson on the basis of a gift, and what implications this had for the balance of power in England.

Papal decrees, and in particular canon 17 of the Third Lateran Council, were an important driving force behind the development of the early common law of advowsons. Canon 17 allowed the bishop to fill a benefice within a certain period of time, which created the need for a mechanism to resolve advowson disputes more swiftly in the royal courts. The custom and practice of the ecclesiastical courts may also have offered some inspiration for the development of this mechanism, namely, the assize of darrein presentment. Moreover, the religious houses of England played a significant role in developing the royal scheme of advowson writs, although their impact was delayed until relatively late in the process. I conclude that the writ of *quare impedit* was created at the behest of the religious houses, which often claimed by virtue of a donation and were (at least originally) unable to bring either of the alternative advowson writs. By any reckoning, the conflict between church and king did much to shape the scheme of advowson remedies developed during and immediately after the reign of Henry II.

In chapter 3, I address the question of influence from Romano-canonical learning. The chapter provides a brief summary of the rules of Roman and canon law relating to ownership and possession, drawing on sources that would have been known in England in the period under discussion, especially by churchmen. After some discussion of the existing literature regarding Romano-canonical influence on the early common law and the development of the rules regarding land, I consider whether the different English advowson writs and related rules might have been shaped by Roman or canon law ideas. I conclude that although the English common law of advowsons has some points of commonality with

Roman law, no wholesale adoption of Romano-canonical learning occurred, and the writ of *quare impedit* in particular was distinctly English.

The basic distinction between ownership and possession was a part of Romano-canonical learning, both in theory and in practice, as it was known in England in the latter half of the twelfth century. This distinction can arguably be seen in the first two advowson writs, and it cannot be explained there, as it has been in the land context, by reference to the feudal relationship between lord and tenant. English right and seisin were not the same as Roman ownership and possession, but those who created the assize of darrein presentment might have been inspired in part by Roman and canon law ideas.[41]

The writ of *quare impedit*, on the other hand, does not fit easily into this framework. Although it generally had the quality of a Romano-canonical possessory action and could be a preliminary to a subsequent action of right, *quare impedit* also had some characteristics of a proprietary action, in that it could be brought by a donee who did not have "possession" of the advowson in what we might imagine to be a Roman or canon law sense. Thus, while the first two advowson writs show how developments in the common law might have been foreshadowed by the scheme of Roman and canon law, the writ of *quare impedit* illustrates how the common law remained independent of that scheme well into the thirteenth century, if not later. In this way, *quare impedit* is similar to the writs of entry, which are also difficult to categorize in Romano-canonical terms.

By the time of the earliest surviving plea rolls, the three main advowson writs had already been created. It was up to the justices to decide what rules of substantive law would apply to those writs and to preside over the pleading in court. In chapter 4, I examine the development of the law of advowsons, including procedural law, in the twelfth and thirteenth centuries. I focus on three aspects of that development: (1) how pleading worked in advowson cases; (2) how advowson donees, especially religious houses, protected their gifts; and (3) how courts evaluated troublesome written evidence offered by the religious houses.

I begin by explaining some of the basic pleading moves made by defendants in advowson cases, including the exception of plenarty (valid in all suits except those begun by writ of right) and the exception of gift. I then discuss typical rejoinders made by plaintiffs, including two important rules that might be called the rule of subsequent presentation and the rule of subsequent transfer. These rules made it more difficult for a donee to prevail on the basis of a gift. Although the creation of the writ of *quare impedit* protected the interests of the religious houses, the royal justices eventually crafted rules regarding the admissibility of charter evidence, and the legal status of advowson gifts, that tended to undermine those interests and favor the lay lords. Thus the picture that emerges is one of judicial compromise in the broader dispute between the laity and the monasteries over the control of parish churches.

Chapter 5 deals with the rules of canon law applicable to advowsons and the interplay between the royal and ecclesiastical courts. When a parish church became vacant, both the local lay lord and the bishop of the diocese had an interest in selecting the next parson. Either would have been more than happy to make the decision alone. Instead the lay lord and the bishop both had input into the choice. When a dispute arose, however, either party could turn to two different systems of courts: those of the church and those of the king. Over the course of the period under discussion, these two sources of central authority worked out a rough arrangement concerning the division of jurisdiction, and each made some concessions to the other.

Among the rules discussed are those that governed how advowsons could be transferred. Gifts of advowsons to religious houses posed problems not only under the common law but also under canon law, which had to grapple with the same conflict between the church and secular authority. I conclude the chapter by discussing the overlap between royal and ecclesiastical jurisdiction, noting how the ecclesiastical courts continued to play a role in advowson disputes even after Henry II declared that such disputes belonged in the royal courts. I also present quantitative research on the impact that the ecclesiastical courts were likely to have had on the development of litigation in the royal courts. Chapter 6 offers some concluding observations.

CHAPTER TWO
THE ADVOWSON WRITS

When a parish church became vacant, the bishop, other ecclesiastical officials, and any laymen with ties to the church all had an interest in selecting the next parson. Any of the potential claimants would have been more than happy to make the decision alone. Advowsons represented a compromise, through which both the laity and the church were given a say. In cases where the parties could not agree, they could choose to take their case to the royal court or to the ecclesiastical court, depending on how the parties chose to characterize the dispute. In this chapter, I discuss the early development of advowson litigation in the king's courts; ecclesiastical jurisdiction over advowsons will be examined in chapter 5.

Advowsons in English Society

Advowsons have their origins in how churches came into being in early medieval Europe. Private persons, intending or claiming to serve the spiritual needs of their feudal tenants and others who lived on their land, founded many churches before the tenth century.[1] Because they furnished the materials and labor for these churches, the founders quite reasonably expected they would be the ones to select the priests and oversee the churches' finances.[2] In many cases, the patrons appointed priests and personally invested them without even seeking the local bishop's consent.[3] Such churches are often referred to as proprietary churches, or *Eigenkirchen*. The exact origins of this tradition are much debated.[4]

In the eleventh century, shortly before the Norman Conquest, local thegns in Anglo-Saxon England began to build proprietary churches, and this practice would shape the parochial system of medieval England.[5] Because it was not uncommon at the time for a priest's son to assume his father's benefice, however, the right of presentation had only limited value after the initial priest had been selected.[6] Bishops were generally unhappy with the proprietary church system, as the power exercised by the lay founders threatened the bishops' control over the clergy in their dioceses. In the eleventh and twelfth centuries, the popes began to assert greater control over the Western church, and a great controversy emerged concerning the power of kings to invest bishops with the symbols of their authority.[7] The church held a series of ecumenical councils, which ruled that priests should not receive churches from lay patrons without episcopal consent.[8] These councils aimed to make the bishop, rather than the lay patron, the ultimate source of the priest's authority.[9] Moreover, the church campaigned to stop the custom of hereditary benefices and met with considerable success, which added additional significance to the right to select the priest.[10]

With the right of presentation becoming increasingly valuable, the church could not expect laymen to give up their long-standing prerogatives without a fight. A compromise practice emerged, whereby the lay patron presented the clerk to the bishop, who examined the candidate and, if he was deemed acceptable, instituted him in the church. Presentation could, in theory, occur at a formal ceremony with both the lay patron and the bishop being present.[11] In an English case from 1220, a party claiming the advowson alleged that he had personally appeared before the bishop to present his clerk.[12] But it became settled practice over the course of the thirteenth century for the lay patron to make his presentation by means of a letter, which the priest or a third party brought to the bishop.[13] When the bishop received the letter of presentation, he generally ordered the archdeacon of the district where the church was located to hold an inquest, the purpose of which was to examine thoroughly all aspects of the presentation.[14] Upon receiving a report that the church was indeed vacant and there was no litigation concerning the vacancy, the bishop was supposed to examine the priest presented to determine if he was canonically ordained and suitable for the appointment. To receive a cure of souls without a dispensation, a priest had to be at least twenty-five years of age and of sufficient learning and character.[15] We do not know how scrupulous the English bishops generally were in enforcing these requirements, but we do read in one royal case that a bishop refused to institute a clerk because he was insufficiently literate (*minus literatum*).[16]

If the bishop decided to accept the priest presented by the patron, he gave the priest a letter of institution, stating that at the presentation of A, the patron, he instituted B, the priest, as parson of the church.[17] The bishop also issued a mandate to the archdeacon or another diocesan official to induct the priest into corporeal possession of the church.[18] Induction was the formal ceremony by which the new priest took possession of the church, and unlike presentation and institution, induction always took place at the church to which the priest had been instituted. At the induction, the archdeacon or his delegate read the letters of the bishop and delivered to the priest the ring of the door,[19] books, and vestments; and the new parson rang the church bell.[20] The ceremony of induction might be recorded in a charter, which could be kept by the priest or given to the patron.

Induction is the only part of the process that we know for certain to have been a theatrical ceremony laden with symbolism. We have no indication that the patron or the bishop played any role at the typical induction; the primary actors were the archdeacon (or his delegate, often the rural dean) and the new parson. However, the mere fact that presentation and institution were formally done in writing does not mean that these acts were accomplished without any ceremony.

In an English ecclesiastical case from 1271 regarding the presentation of a parson,[21] witnesses were asked how they knew the identity of the true patron. Two of the witnesses, one being illiterate and the other "slightly lettered," said that they were present when the patron gave the sealed letter to the priest, naming the date and the place where this occurred.[22] One witness explained that he "saw and heard this," implying that the patron told those present what he was doing.[23] Two other witnesses, who were literate, responded that the presentation was "common knowledge in the neighborhood."[24] The testimony of these witnesses suggests that the patron read (or summarized) his letter of presentation and gave it to the priest in the presence of others, who understood the significance of the act and were likely to remember it. Thus, even though the patron did not formally appear before the bishop to present his candidate, presentation was a public or quasi-public act that left an impression on those who witnessed it.

For the most part, the priest who was presented and instituted in this way was called the parson (*persona*),[25] and his endowment was known as a benefice (*beneficium*); the parson received the tithes of the church and was the spiritual leader of the parish. But the parson of the church was not always able to tend to the cure of souls in person. When the parson was a religious house,[26] held multiple benefices, or was otherwise unable personally to tend to the cure of souls, it was necessary to hire another priest to do this. Such a priest was called a vicar (*vicarius*), meaning substitute. Advowson litigation in the royal courts usually concerned the right to present a parson, not a vicar, since the proper forum for litigation over vicarages during this period was normally the ecclesiastical court.[27] Vicars are frequently mentioned, however, in the context of determining who the last parson was. This is unsurprising, because the job of vicar generally involved the actual work of serving the church, while the position of parson could provide a steady stream of income without much in the way of day-to-day responsibilities.

Some churches were divided into moieties or other fractions, and each fraction might have a different parson.[28] Because each fraction could also have its own patron, this might lead to confusion when a dispute arose concerning the advowson. When a lawsuit was brought concerning moiety A, the defendant might respond that his claim applied not to moiety A but rather to moiety B.[29] This problem, however, came up relatively infrequently, suggesting that local communities were generally able to keep track of which moiety was vacant at any particular time.

An advowson was understood to be a property right independent of the church itself, although the advowson might be appurtenant to land in the vicinity of the church. For this reason, a clerk might record a party in a lawsuit as stating that an advowson "belonged to him" (pertinebat ad se).[30] Although an advowson was intimately connected with the church to which the right of presentation applied, the law was careful to distinguish the advowson as a property right from the physical church itself.[31]

Advowsons could be held by all sorts of people, both lay and religious, provided that they were Christians and not part of the small Jewish minority.[32] Most of the laymen who held advowsons were part of the upper orders of English society—knights and noblemen—but any freeman could legally hold an advowson. The king himself held many advowsons, and when an advowson dispute arose between the king and one of his subjects, the king would sue in his own court through an attorney, although he could not be sued by others.[33] Because women were allowed to own property under certain conditions, they could also own advowsons. A daughter could inherit an advowson if her father died without leaving a male heir, although if she was married and a dispute arose concerning the advowson, she had to sue with her husband.[34] She could even inherit an advowson from her mother.[35] In some circumstances, a woman could also hold an advowson as part of her dower after her husband's death, though again, if she had remarried, she would have to sue with her husband.[36] The patron was not required to be a resident, or even an occasional visitor, of the parish or diocese where the church was situated; the abbot of Mont-Saint-Michel in Normandy claimed an advowson in Wiltshire,[37] and the archbishop of Rouen claimed one in Nottinghamshire.[38] A parson of one church could claim the advowson of another church, either in its own right or as a chapel pertaining to his own church,[39] in which case the appointee would be a chaplain (*capellanus*), not a parson.[40]

Religious houses, as legal corporations, could acquire advowsons from laymen and might choose to confer the church on a particular priest,[41] either as a reward for past service to the monastery or with the expectation of some future service. But when a lay donor conferred an advowson on a religious house, it was more common for the religious house to be instituted as parson as part of the arrangement. The religious house would then choose a vicar, or if the church already had a parson, that priest might be pressured into resigning as parson and becoming the vicar.[42]

When a religious house became parson of a church, financial arrangements between the vicar and the religious house varied: the vicar might pay a pension to the religious house, or the religious house might keep the tithes (or a portion of them) for itself and pay the vicar wages, depending in part on how close the religious house was to the church in question.[43] In any case, because religious houses were immortal, the advowson became irrelevant once a monastery or priory became its parson. Although new vicars would be appointed from time to time, the religious house became the perpetual parson, unless and until some rival claimant was able to recover the advowson by a lawsuit. Religious houses therefore had a powerful financial incentive to acquire advowsons and augment their income, either through the vicar's pension or directly through the appropriation of some portion of the tithes. When the interest of religious houses came into conflict with that of powerful laymen who claimed advowsons by right of inheritance, however, litigation was the likely result.

The Birth of the Common Law

Because no plea rolls or registers of writs survive from before 1194, it is impossible to say precisely how many royal advowson writs were available in the decades before the completion of the late twelfth-century treatise known as *Glanvill* and what purposes they might have served. Describing a case from circa 1157, the cartulary of Darley Abbey records that twenty-four recognitors, summoned by royal order, swore that the church of Saint Peter of Derby was in the donation of Hugh of Derby.[44] The nature of the royal order that produced this inquest is not specified, but the fact that the case involved twenty-four recognitors rather than a jury of twelve suggests that this particular order established an ad hoc commission and was not a regular writ of the sort that would become common later in the century. It is possible that the inquest concerned the king's own rights in the advowson and not any claim by a third party, in which case the use of sworn recognitors would not carry great historical significance.[45]

We find further evidence of royal involvement in advowson disputes from early in the reign of Henry II in a writ from the cartulary of Saint Benet's, Holme, dating to the period 1155–58.[46] In this writ, one of several surviving documents concerning the church of Ranworth, King Henry orders the bishop of Norwich to cause the abbot of Holme to have the advowson of the church "as he justly ought to have it and as it was recognized by the oath of lawful men" (sicut eam juste habere debet et sicut recognitum erat per sacramentum legalium hominum). The *nisi feceris* clause says that if the

FIG. 5. Norwich Cathedral. Photo by Joshua Tate.

bishop does not follow the command, the archbishop of Canterbury will do it "so that he does not lose his right for lack of right or full justice" (ne pro penuria recti vel plene justicie jus suum amittat).[47]

While the language "recognitum erat per sacramentum legalium hominum" in the Saint Benet's advowson writ might seem to indicate a royal proceeding involving a jury of some kind, the reference to *jus suum* would suggest that the issue was right rather than seisin, if that distinction had any meaning at the time. However, the cartulary of Saint Benet's also includes a letter from Archbishop Theobald to the bishop of Norwich detailing an ecclesiastical hearing concerning the precise location of the church, as well as a separate royal writ directed to the same question.[48] The dispute over Ranworth therefore apparently focused on the church as an appurtenance to the estate, and not necessarily on the right to present the parson. Thus the use of a *sacramentum legalium hominum* regarding this particular church does not necessarily mean that jury proceedings were common in advowson disputes at the beginning of the reign of Henry II. Moreover, the evidence does not suggest that any of the proceedings were to be held in a royal court as opposed to an ecclesiastical court.

The record of the litigation between Battle Abbey and Hamo Peche concerning the church of Thurlow, discussed in more detail in chapter 5,[49] raises the possibility that there might have been a writ that referred to the aggressive action of the defendant in seizing the advowson. According to the chronicler, the abbey commenced suit in both the royal and the ecclesiastical court, the royal action based on *militis violentia,* the ecclesiastical on *clerici intrusione.*[50] The reference to *violentia* might be read as suggesting that the royal writ was somehow delictual in nature, but the chronicler may not have been thinking in a technical legal sense. Only from the time of *Glanvill* do we have a clear picture of what advowson remedies were available in the royal courts.

Between November 29, 1187, and the death of Henry II on July 6, 1189, the treatise traditionally known as *Glanvill* was completed.[51] Although historians have proposed various distinguished authors (including the traditional choice, royal justiciar Ranulf Glanvill) for the text, it is more likely that the treatise was written by a young man who had an excellent understanding of the procedures employed in the royal courts, but had not yet reached the peak of his career.[52] From the treatise, it is evident that the author had some understanding of Romano-canonical learning, and particularly of Justinian's *Institutes.*[53] The treatise begins with a nearly verbatim quote from the *Institutes,*[54] and the author uses a number of terms drawn from Roman law, especially in his discussion of pleas concerning debts.[55] The prologue reads like an apology for the disorganized and unwritten nature of English law, seemingly addressed to an audience who viewed systematization and writing as essential components of an advanced legal system.[56] An audience of men with a Romano-canonical background and previous practical experience in the ecclesiastical courts would fit this description.[57] Along these lines, Paul Brand has suggested that the treatise was meant to be "a kind of 'conversion kit'" for men with some Romano-canonical training "that would allow them to operate in the rather different world of the royal courts in addition to (or perhaps even in place of) the ecclesiastical courts."[58]

When describing the law of the royal courts, *Glanvill* follows a method that Maitland characterized as "dilemmatic."[59] As he begins a new topic, the *Glanvill* author suggests two or more alternative possibilities of what might occur: for example, either the defendant appears in response to a summons, or he does not appear. The author first describes what happens in one situation, then moves to the alternative. We see the first bifurcation of this kind in book 1, in which *Glanvill* divides all pleas into the categories of "criminal" and "civil."[60] Having delineated the criminal pleas, *Glanvill* next divides civil pleas into two categories: those that "are discussed and determined in the king's court only," and those that "fall within the jurisdiction of the sheriffs of counties."[61] Focusing next on pleas that belong in the king's court, *Glanvill* further distinguishes between pleas that "relate to the [ownership] of the thing only" (placita solummodo super proprietate rei) and those "which refer to the possession, and which are discussed and decided by recognition" (illis autem quae super possessione loquuntur et per recognitiones placitantur et terminantur). The *Glanvill* author considers the former pleas first and defers discussion of the latter until later in the text.[62]

After his classification of pleas, *Glanvill* continues by examining the *precipe* writ of right for land.[63] This writ, later to be invalidated by clause 34 of Magna Carta,[64] commanded the defendant to render a certain tract of land to the plaintiff. Should the defendant fail to do so, he would be summoned by good summoners to appear before the king or his justices at a specific day and place, at which point the defendant could explain why he had failed to follow the order in the first clause of the writ.[65] Over the next three books, *Glanvill* describes the cumbersome procedure associated with this writ. Because that procedure also applies to the equivalent writ for advowsons, I will examine it here.

Once the sheriff had summoned the defendant, he was entitled to essoin himself on three successive return days, and various essoins were allowed, such as those for falling ill at home or on the way to court, for being abroad, and for having undertaken a pilgrimage.[66] If the defendant failed to appear and did not send an essoiner or representative, he would be summoned three times, after which the land would be taken into the king's hand.[67] If the land were taken into the king's hand, the defendant would have a fortnight to redeem (replevy) the land by offering sureties.[68] Once the defendant did appear, the plaintiff would state his claim—that the land was his right and inheritance, and he or one of his ancestors was seised of it in the reign of Henry I or since the first coronation of Henry II—and offer to prove it by one or more of his men, one of whom would be selected as his champion. The defendant would then choose between battle and the grand assize.[69]

This last element of the procedure accompanying the *precipe* writ of right, the election between battle and the grand assize, was a fairly recent innovation, the grand assize having been introduced by the assize of Windsor in 1179.[70] Before that date, writs of right were generally decided by battle, which, as *Glanvill* describes it, involved six possible essoins, three for the defendant and three for his champion.[71] The grand assize involved fewer essoins, but its procedure was scarcely expeditious: four local knights were summoned to elect twelve knights from the same neighborhood, and those knights were then summoned to decide the matter.[72] At any stage, one or more of the knights might fail to show up, which would further slow things down. By the time *Glanvill* was written, however, the cumbersome nature of the writ of right for land was less significant, because an alternative existed in the form of the assize of novel disseisin.[73]

Having finished his discussion of the *precipe* writ of right for land, *Glanvill* next moves on to pleas concerning advowsons. *Glanvill* first notes that advowson pleas "are accustomed to be [brought], as well when the church is vacant, as when it is not vacant" (moveri solet tum ecclesiis ipsis vacantibus tum non vacantibus).[74] For this reason, "It must be distinguished, whether the dispute be concerning the advowson itself, in other words, the right itself of presenting a parson, or whether it merely relates to the last presentation, that is, the seisin of the right of presenting a parson" (distinguo utrum fiat contencio super ipsa advocatione, id est super iure ipso praesentandi personam, vel super ultima praesentatione, id est super saisina iuris praesentandi personam).[75]

In the event that the plaintiff either claimed the last presentation to a vacant church or asserted that some third party last presented to a vacant church, while the defendant claimed the last presentation for himself, the issue would be decided by an assize (recognition) concerning the last presentation and not by the writ of right.[76] Whichever party prevailed at that assize "shall thereby recover seisin of the presentation of the vacant church, concerning which the dispute is; so that he shall lawfully present a parson to the church, saving the right and claim of the demandant with respect to the right of advowson" (eo ipso saisinam praesentationis ecclesie vacantis super qua contentio est dirationabit, ita quod personam ad eandem ecclesiam licite praesentabit, salvo iure et clamio [alterius] super iure advocationis). On the other hand, if the plaintiff claimed only "the right of advowson" (ius advocationis tantum), then he would "subjoin to his claim" (adiciet) either that he or one of his ancestors presented the last parson, that the defendant or one of his ancestors did, that a third party did, or that he does not know who did. If the plaintiff conceded that the defendant or his ancestors made the last presentation, "without having recourse to a recognition, he shall present one [parson] at least" (sine recognitione unam personam praesentabit ad minus).[77] In all other cases, the dispute would be resolved by the recognition.[78] Thus, according to Glanvill, only two outcomes are possible if the church is vacant: either the dispute will be resolved by the recognition, or else the defendant will be permitted to present the next parson without a recognition.[79]

For the modern reader, Glanvill's introduction to the law of advowsons raises more questions than it answers. When the church is vacant, the party successfully claiming the last presentation will be the one to present the next parson. Why, therefore, does Glanvill not simply state that the appropriate way to resolve a dispute over a vacant church is by recognition? In addition, what kind of procedure is envisaged in this discussion? It is necessary to continue with Glanvill's account before we can answer these questions—if indeed they can be answered.

Glanvill tells us that once the issue of the last presentation has been decided, either by recognition or otherwise, and the church is no longer vacant, the party claiming the right of advowson would have "the writ for making a summons concerning advowsons of churches":

> The King to the sheriff, [greeting]. Command N. that, justly and without delay, he [relinquish] to R. the advowson of the church, in such a vill, which he claims to belong to him, and of which he complains that he unjustly deforced him; and, unless he do so, summon him by good summoners, that he be on such a day before us, or our justices, to shew why he has failed; and have there the summoners and this writ &c.[80]

Although it replaces the words regarding land with references to the advowson, the wording of this writ is otherwise very close to the precipe writ for land.[81] Glanvill explains that the procedure associated with the advowson writ is identical with that applicable to its counterpart for land, except that it requires a unique procedure to take the right of presentation into the king's hand in the event that the summoned party fails to appear.[82] In this unique procedure, the sheriff would go in the presence of trustworthy men (*coram probis hominibus*)[83] to the church and announce that he was seizing (*se saisiasse*) the presentation of the church into the king's hand, which gave seisin (*saisina*) to the king.[84] Thus, through this fiction, the common law overcame the problem that the intangible advowson could not be physically controlled.

Once the defendant had exhausted his essoins (if applicable) and both parties were present in court, the plaintiff would appear and state his claim as follows:

> I demand the advowson of this church, as my right, and appertaining to my inheritance, and of which advowson I was seised, or one of my ancestors was seised, in the time of King Henry the First, the grandfather of our Lord King Henry, or after the coronation of our Lord the King; and being so seised, I presented a parson to the same church when vacant, at one of the beforementioned periods; and I so presented him, that upon my presentation he was instituted parson into that church; and if any one would deny this, I have some credible men who both saw and heard the fact, and are ready to prove it as the court shall award, and particularly [the following named] persons.[85]

This claim would be followed either by battle or by the grand assize, at the election of the defendant.[86]

At this stage, we can reach three conclusions about the *precipe* writ of right of advowson as described in *Glanvill*.[87] First, like the *precipe* writ for land, the writ does not use the word *ius*. The only indication that the writ concerns right rather than seisin appears in *Glanvill*'s discussion. Second, the count made by the plaintiff uses both terms. The plaintiff refers to the advowson as *ius meum* but also states that the plaintiff or his ancestor was seised (*saisatus*) of the advowson in the reign of the specified king, and this seisin was on account of having presented a parson. The language of the writ and of the count may have been considerably older than the treatise itself. While the distinction between *ius* and *saisina* with regard to advowsons may have been interpreted or understood differently by *Glanvill*'s day, the concept of seisin of an advowson was already established by the time the treatise was written. This is also shown by the statement of the sheriff, in taking the advowson into the king's hand, that he is "seizing" (*se saisiasse*) the presentation of the church, a relatively advanced concept when applied to an intangible.[88]

Finally, nothing in either the writ or the count indicates that the plaintiff claims (or does not claim) the last presentation. The procedure *Glanvill* describes as taking place before the issuance of the *precipe* writ, in which the plaintiff makes his claim concerning the last presentation, does not seem to be part of the actual pleading under the writ. Instead it appears to be a preliminary hearing of some sort to determine whether the writ will be issued in the first place. However, the earliest plea rolls give no indication that such preliminary hearings took place, although preliminary hearings may conceivably lurk behind some entries that appear to record assizes of darrein presentment. Perhaps *Glanvill* described this imagined hearing merely in an effort to help the reader understand the difference between disputes over right and disputes over seisin. If indeed it was ever used, the actual procedure may have been rare in *Glanvill*'s day.[89]

In the remainder of book 4, *Glanvill* examines three other advowson writs: the writ of *quo advocato*, by which a clerk is summoned to explain by which of two patrons he claims to hold the church; and two writs of prohibition to prevent advowson disputes from being held in the ecclesiastical courts.[90] I consider the two writs of prohibition in chapter 5.[91] As for the other writ, of *quo advocato*, *Glanvill* describes it as a way of initiating an advowson dispute when the church is not vacant.[92] Through this writ, the king summons the clerk holding the benefice to explain by what patron (*quo advocato*) he claims to be parson.[93] If the clerk responds by naming the plaintiff as his patron, or if the defendant concedes that he claims no right in the advowson, then the lawsuit in the king's court terminates, at which point the plaintiff may institute a proceeding in the ecclesiastical court against the clerk if he so chooses.[94] On the other hand, if the clerk names the defendant as his patron, and the defendant contests the plaintiff's claim, *Glanvill* says that the case will proceed as under the *precipe* writ of right.[95]

Next *Glanvill* discusses what to do with the current occupant of the benefice if he claims that the defendant presented him but the plaintiff prevails in the royal action. *Glanvill* explains that "in the king's court, indeed, nothing farther is to be done in the matter, unless as it concerns the advowson between the two patrons. But the patron, who has recently recovered the right of advowson, shall proceed against the clerk in the ecclesiastical court before the bishop or his official. . . . If, at the time of presentation, the person presenting such clerk was considered to be the patron, then, the church shall continue to be held by the clerk, during the remainder of his life."[96] *Glanvill* goes on to state that "in the reign of the present king, concerning those clerks who have obtained livings upon the presentation of such patrons as have, in time of war, violently intruded themselves into ecclesiastical advowsons; and by such [settlement] it is provided, that clerks thus presented shall not lose their churches during their lives."[97] Mulling over the possibility that a decision on the right might be followed by an action concerning the last presentation, the treatise author ultimately proposes that the judgment in the action of right, to the extent it can be proved, will constitute a good defense to any subsequent assize.[98]

Later in the treatise, the author discusses the several "recognitions" devised during the reign of Henry II, all of which summoned a jury-like body called an "assize" composed of freemen from a particular area to resolve a question or questions specified in the writ.[99] The question put to the assize jurors in the recognition pertaining to advowsons was "what patron [in time of peace] presented the last parson who died, to the church of such a vill, which is, as it is said, vacant, and of which N. claims the advowson" (quis advocatus praesentavit ultimam personam quae obiit ad ecclesiam de illa villa, quae vacans est ut dicitur, et unde N. clamat advocationem).[100] The assize thus concerned the last presentation, that is, the *ultima presentatio*, or, in the French of *Glanvill*'s day, the "darrein presentment."

The assize of darrein presentment, like the assize of mort d'ancestor and the assize of novel disseisin, summoned an assize of twelve.[101] The defendant could claim two essoins, but on the third day, the assize would be taken whether the defendant appeared or not.[102] When he appeared, the defendant might offer an exception to the assize, such as that the plaintiff's ancestor gave him the fee to which the advowson is appurtenant by some good title, or that the plaintiff or his ancestor made the last presentation as of wardship and not of fee.[103] The parties might join issue on the exception of a gift if the defendant claimed one had been made; or if the defendant claimed that the last presentation was by reason of wardship, a separate recognition on that point would be summoned by writ.[104] Otherwise the assize would proceed. The person or persons found to have presented the last parson (or whose ancestor or predecessor was found to have presented the last parson) recovered seisin of the advowson and were entitled to present the next parson.[105]

The assize of darrein presentment may trace its origins to a development in canon law. In 1179, the same year that Henry II introduced the grand assize, the Third Lateran Council created a complication for parties involved in an advowson dispute during the vacancy of a church. As discussed hereafter, the council was interpreted to give the bishop the authority to fill a benefice when a dispute over the patronage lasted longer than six months.[106] The royal courts needed a procedure that could quickly decide an advowson dispute before the passage of time triggered the conciliar canon and gave the bishop the prerogative to choose whatever clerk he deemed suitable for the benefice. English bishops and clerks at the council were in a position to act on its provisions as soon as they returned home.[107] One such bishop, Reginald fitz Jocelin, was significantly involved in the king's affairs, appearing at the king's Easter court in 1176 and attesting a royal charter at Rouen the following year.[108] John of Oxford, another attendee, was an important royal justice who attested about sixty royal charters between 1176 and 1189 and was involved in several diplomatic missions on the king's behalf.[109] These men would certainly have immediately reported what happened at the Third Lateran Council to the king upon their return to England.

The earliest surviving reference to the assize of darrein presentment dates to 1180. In that year, a final concord was entered into between Ralph Murdac and Hugh of Bourton concerning a "recognitio summonita . . . in curia domini regis de presentatione persone que ultimo . . . obiit" in the church of Black Bourton.[110] Some scholars have accordingly assumed that the assize was created in response to the Third Lateran Council one year before.[111] On the basis of the papal decretal *Consultationibus*, however, Peter Landau has argued that the assize must have been created before 1176.[112] At some point between 1173 and 1176, Alexander III ordered in *Consultationibus* that a clerk instituted in a church at the presentation of one who believed himself patron ought not to lose his benefice when another recovers the advowson in court, provided that the one who presented him "*possessed* the right of patronage of the church" and was not merely "believed to be patron without possessing the right."[113] This rule, or perhaps the possession it describes, is attributed to an "English custom."[114] Landau reasons that the distinction drawn by the decretal makes sense only if an action was available in English law to recover "possession" of an advowson, because otherwise no way existed to distinguish the mere putative patron from the possessor.[115] Landau concludes that the assize of darrein presentment was that action.

It is therefore possible the assize was created before the Third Lateran Council. Still, the procedure of the assize seems tailored to solve the problem the council created.[116] One may doubt whether the earlier decretal of Alexander was in fact referring to the assize, which is otherwise unknown before 1180. Another possibility, which Landau does not consider, is that the pope could have been referring to a local custom originally applied not in the English royal courts but in the English ecclesiastical courts.[117]

The problem addressed by *Consultationibus* arose when a patron who successfully had his clerk instituted subsequently lost in a secular action of right. An English ecclesiastical court deciding whether the parson could keep his benefice might have looked to whether the parson's predecessor was also presented by the losing party in the secular action (or by the losing party's ancestor). Did the defeated patron already have possession of the advowson when he presented the current parson? If so, the parson would keep his benefice; if not, the parson would be forced to step aside. Such a determination could have been made independently by the ecclesiastical court when the benefice was claimed, without reference to a secular judgment. In other words, the English custom referenced by the pope might have been a custom of the English ecclesiastical courts in cases where a layman had recovered the advowson by writ of right.

Alexander III, in *Consultationibus,* was addressing a lawsuit in an ecclesiastical court between rival clerks, not the corresponding lawsuit in the secular court between the rival patrons. We have no compelling reason to conclude that the "English custom" in question was a custom of the royal courts or even dependent on a judgment in the royal courts. Medieval canonists and popes generally took the position that patronage disputes belonged in ecclesiastical courts, subject to certain pragmatic exceptions.[118] In light of the church's desire to maintain control over patronage disputes, why would Pope Alexander III, in this particular decretal, have made the outcome of a dispute between clerks depend on a superseded ruling in a secular court? One could read the decretal just as easily to suggest that the English ecclesiastical courts were making an independent determination of possession based on the penultimate presentation. It would have been logical for the ecclesiastical courts to make such a determination before 1180 if the royal courts were not yet doing so.

English ecclesiastical courts in the second half of the twelfth century were familiar with the legal concept of possession,[119] and they applied it in lawsuits concerning benefices as early as 1161.[120] The English ecclesiastical courts thus had several years to develop a customary rule for dealing with the problem in *Consultationibus* before it came to the pope's attention. Custom was a legitimate source of law in canonist theory, although it yielded to natural law and enacted laws.[121] In his reference to the *consuetudinem Anglicanam*, Alexander III might have alluded to a custom followed in the courts of his English bishops. Indeed, another decretal of Alexander III, addressed to the bishop of Exeter, specifically refers to a "custom of the English church."[122] Such language could be used to refer to local ecclesiastical customs, although a "custom of the English church" is not necessarily the same as an "English custom."

Arguing that the assize of darrein presentment was not a response to the Third Lateran Council, Landau makes the point that the conclusion of the assize did not necessarily end the advowson dispute, because it might continue in the form of an action of right.[123] The assize, in Landau's view, was not a solution to the problem posed by the Third Lateran Council. Nevertheless, this argument does not address the fact that, at the conclusion of an assize of darrein presentment, the prevailing party would be adjudged seisin of the advowson and would be entitled to present a clerk to the bishop. Were the assize followed by an action of right, it would take place after the institution of this clerk, when the church was no longer vacant. Filling the vacancy in the church was the purpose of the conciliar canon. After the vacancy had been filled, the bishop would no longer be able to institute a parson by virtue of the council, and the king's prerogative to decide advowson disputes would not be challenged. Actions of darrein presentment were not necessarily followed by an action of right, and the assize itself could put an end to the litigation. In short, we have no compelling reason to doubt that the assize was created in response to the council, because the earlier decretal of Alexander could have referred to the custom of the English ecclesiastical courts in disputes between clerks.

If the English ecclesiastical courts were already awarding benefices on the basis of possession, was the assize of darrein presentment in fact modeled on the existing practice of the ecclesiastical courts? It is at least possible that the king's advisers were not the first to think in possessory terms, and canon law presented them with a solution to the problem posed by the council.[124] The "English custom" referred to in Alexander's decretal is explained differently by *Glanvill*, who says in book 4 that the incumbent whose patron "at the time of presentation . . . was considered to be the patron" (tempore praesentationis credebatur . . . patronus) would be protected, not mentioning possession.[125] *Glanvill*'s explanation does not suggest that the ecclesiastical courts inspired the possessory aspect of the royal assize. Nevertheless, the procedure in those courts was tangential to *Glanvill*'s treatise, and he may simply have been alluding in general terms to a rule that he knew to be more complex.[126] Moreover, the creation of the assize of darrein presentment made it difficult for a mere putative patron, lacking possession or right, to have his clerk instituted in a vacant church. Thus the distinction in *Consultationibus* may have diminished in practical significance after 1180 in England.

If *Consultationibus* did indeed refer to a *possessio* recognized in the royal courts, it need not have been determined by an assize of darrein presentment. Before the creation of the assize, it is possible that the king's court occasionally held ad hoc proceedings to decide the issue of the last presentation in a dispute over a vacant church, or that Chancery once offered a different writ for a vacant church that ceased to be available after 1180. This may help to explain the ambiguity in the first chapter of book 4 of *Glanvill*.

As discussed earlier, *Glanvill*'s account of the procedure followed by the royal courts in a dispute over the right of presentation to a vacant church may not have reflected any actual practice at the time the author wrote the treatise. In fact, it is possible that *Glanvill* may have been summarizing what happened before the assize of darrein presentment was created in 1180, making necessary (albeit clumsy) amendments to address the assize and leaving out key details.[127] Before the creation of the assize, it might have been useful for the court to hold a kind of preliminary hearing to address the issue of the last presentation whenever the process was initiated by the *precipe* writ set out in *Glanvill* 4.2. Moreover, if the assize had not yet been invented, the king's court might have had the authority to deal on an ad hoc basis with the issue of the last presentation before proceeding under the *precipe* writ, if it deemed the vacancy sufficiently important (and the matter sufficiently urgent) to warrant such special treatment.

Even before the Third Lateran Council, the king might not have wanted an important benefice to remain vacant for a long period of time, and the cumbersome process initiated by the *precipe* writ might prevent the king's judges from hearing the dispute until much time had passed. By forcing the plaintiff to specify his claim with regard to the last presentation at the outset, a preliminary hearing of the sort alluded to in *Glanvill* would give the royal justices the chance to decide whether some extraordinary intervention was needed to fill the vacancy pending the dispute. By the time the *Glanvill* author wrote his treatise, however, the details of the older procedure might have been forgotten or misremembered.[128]

No direct evidence survives that the royal courts intervened on an ad hoc basis to determine possession in advowson disputes before 1180. However, two early records concerning the churches of Shinfield and Swallowfield (Berks), quoted in the cartulary of Carisbrooke, ought to be considered. In the first of the writs, dated by Raoul van Caenegem to between March 1164 and March 15, 1166,[129] King Henry orders Osbert of Bray to "seise without delay the monks of Lire of the church of Swallowfield and its appurtenances, as was recognized at Wallingford by the oath of jurors before my justice and adjudicated to them" (Precipio tibi quod sine dilatione saisas monachos de Lira de ecclesia de Swalewefeld et de pertenentiis suis sicut recognitum fuit apud Walengeford sacramento juratorum coram justicia mea et adjudicatum eis). The king goes on to command that if Osbert will not do it, the sheriff of Berkshire is to do it ("Et nisi feceris, vic[ecomes] de Berchesira faciat").[130] Although the writ does not state that the dispute involved an advowson, a royal notification issued about a decade later referring to the same church does use that word. Dating to either 1173 or 1177,[131] this notification is directed by the king "to his archbishops, bishops, earls, barons, and justices, and ministers of England." Henry II proclaims that "it was recognized and deraigned in my court before my barons that the

churches of Shinfield and Swallowfield belong to the advowson and donation of the abbot and monks of Lire" (in curia mea coram baronibus meis
recognitum et dirationatum fuit quod ecclesie de Sinigefeld et Swalewefeld
sunt de advocatione et donatione abbatis et monachorum de Lira).[132]

The wording of both the notification and the writ calls to mind later
writs used to enforce an assize judgment.[133] For example, *Glanvill*'s writ for
restoring seisin to a plaintiff who prevails after the grand assize reads as
follows:

> The king to the sheriff, [greeting]. I command you that, without delay, you
> [seise M.] [Praecipio tibi quod sine dilatione saisas M.] of one [hide] of
> land, in such a vill, which he claims against R. of which the said R. put
> himself upon my assise [posuit se in assisam meam], because the said R.
> has recovered that land in my court by a recognition [dirationavit terram
> illam in curia mea per recognitionem].[134]

Moreover, although *Glanvill* does not reproduce the writ of *quod admittas*,
by which the bishop is directed to institute a parson after an assize of darrein presentment, the early thirteenth-century register "Hib" gives it as
follows:

> The king to such-and-such a bishop, greeting. Know that A has deraigned
> in our court, by a recognition of last presentation [disracionauit in curia
> nostra per recognicionem ultime presentacionis], his seisin [seisinam] of
> the presentation to the church of N. And therefore we command you that
> on his presentation you admit a fit parson to that church. Witness etc.[135]

The language of these writs bears obvious similarities to that of the royal
writ and notification in the Carisbrooke cartulary.[136] While the notification
uses the phrase "in curia mea . . . dirationatum" to indicate a final judgment
in the king's court, *Glanvill*'s writ says that M. "dirationavit terram illam in
curia mea," and "Hib" says that A "disracionauit (seisinam) in curia nostra."
Both of the Carisbrooke records use the word *recognitum* in connection with
the earlier royal proceedings, while the writs in *Glanvill* and "Hib" refer to a
recognitionem. Both Carisbrooke records clearly refer to prior proceedings in
the royal courts, proceedings that did not involve trial by battle.[137]

Neither of the Carisbrooke records specifically refers to *ius* or suggests
that the royal proceedings concerned the abbey's right, even though the
1164–66 writ has a *nisi feceris* clause where such a reference could have

been inserted. Rather, the 1164–66 writ orders the addressee to seise (*saisas*) the monks, although the object of the *saisas* command is the church (*de ecclesia de Swalewefeld*) rather than the advowson. In contrast, the earlier 1155–58 writ concerning the abbey of Saint Benet's, Holme, discussed earlier, refers to the *ius* of the abbot in the *nisi feceris* clause but makes no reference to seisin.[138] Perhaps the 1155–58 writ did not use the term *ius* in a technical sense. Nevertheless, its omission from the Carisbrooke records should be noted.

On the other hand, we can also identify important differences between the Carisbrooke records and the later writs in *Glanvill* and "Hib."[139] Stating that a decision *recognitum fuit* in the royal court, as Henry II did in the Carisbrooke records, is not quite the same as referring to a *recognitionem*. The bishop of the diocese would be the most likely addressee of a writ after an assize of darrein presentment, as shown in "Hib," but the Carisbrooke writ is not specifically addressed to the bishop. Finally, neither Carisbrooke record refers to "my assize" (assisam meam), as does the writ in *Glanvill*, or to a "recognition of last presentation" (recognicionem ultime presentacionis), as does the *quod admittas* writ in "Hib." The proceedings with regard to Shinfield and Swallowfield could have been ad hoc in nature and not associated with a formal assize of darrein presentment. That, of course, is precisely what one would expect if the assize of darrein presentment was invented in 1180.

Other plausible explanations could exist for the Carisbrooke evidence. In his discussion of the 1164–66 writ, Van Caenegem suggests that it was issued in connection with the campaign that followed the king's famous royal assize (ordinance) on disseisin, from which others have traced the later writ of novel disseisin.[140] Van Caenegem finds evidence for this in a pipe roll entry recording a forty-shilling fine assessed on Osbert of Bray in connection with a plea in Berkshire.[141] Although the entry does not mention that the fine was for a disseisin, Van Caenegem explains that the amount of the fine "was very common for disseisins and the eyre was concerned with disseisins."[142] Furthermore, the fact that the 1164–66 Swallowfield writ refers not only to the church but also to its *pertinentiis* could be said to imply that the plea was not simply about an advowson but also involved some land. Nonetheless it is clear from the subsequent notification that some dispute later arose over the advowson to the church, whether or not it involved Osbert of Bray. Furthermore, if the dispute over Swallowfield involved the king's assize on disseisin, one would expect to see some reference to the assize in the writ itself.[143]

Whatever the context for the Carisbrooke writ may be, the later notification clearly concerns an advowson, and the fact that the king addressed it "to his archbishops, bishops, earls, barons, and justices, and ministers of England" might suggest that the judicial proceeding in question was extraordinary in nature, although we should not read too much into such formulaic language. At minimum, the notification is consistent with the theory that ad hoc proceedings were used to resolve advowson disputes before 1180. The preliminary hearing suggested by *Glanvill* might have served to identify disputes that were sufficiently important to be decided through ad hoc proceedings rather than by the regular action of right. Some of the ad hoc proceedings could have focused on the last presentation, although neither Carisbrooke record indicates as much. On the other hand, once the assize became available, a preliminary hearing would have been unnecessary. A plaintiff who claimed the last presentation to a vacant church would simply begin with the assize.

Glanvill's procedure would have been useful after 1180 only when a plaintiff claimed the advowson of a vacant church but was willing to concede that the defendant made the last presentation. However, in such a case, the plaintiff could allow the defendant to present the next parson, but subsequently challenge the defendant's right by bringing a writ of *quo advocato* during the plenarty of the church. In any event, most plaintiffs would not have conceded the last presentation if they had any chance of recovering by the assize, because the rule of *Consultationibus* protected the clerk whose patron made the last presentation.[144] Any plaintiff who conceded the last presentation might not have another chance to present for a generation. The preliminary procedure described by *Glanvill* may already have been obsolete by *Glanvill*'s day, which would account for the absence of references to that procedure in the early plea rolls. But perhaps the treatise author still recalled the outlines of the earlier procedure (or had talked to someone with such a recollection) and used it to introduce the concepts of right and seisin as applied to advowsons.[145]

If this theory is plausible, it offers another possible explanation for the reference to "English custom" in *Consultationibus*. The assize of darrein presentment might trace its origins to earlier ad hoc hearings in the royal court regarding the last presentation, in cases where the king or his court wished, for whatever reason, to circumvent the usual process by the *precipe* writ. This, in turn, would mean that the royal courts protected the concept of *saisina iuris praesentandi* mentioned in *Glanvill* before 1180, and Alexander III might indeed have had a royal custom regarding *possessio* in mind when he issued his decretal. The primary innovation of the assize could have been the procedure by which the dispute was decided, and not the substantive equation of seisin with the last presentation.

Whatever its origins, the assize of darrein presentment offered plaintiffs in advowson cases the possibility of a swifter judgment in comparison with the writ of right. In addition, it provided a fixed mode of dispute resolution in the form of a jury drawn from the locality, which undoubtedly attracted plaintiffs who did not wish to face the possibility of a battle and thought that representatives drawn from the community would decide in their favor.[146] In light of these advantages, it comes as no surprise that the assize of darrein presentment is the most common type of advowson action in the early plea rolls. Even so, the assize did not provide a final answer about who had the superior right to the advowson. Only the writ of right could offer a successful plaintiff some assurance that the matter would not be taken up again in the king's court.

When judgment was given against the defendant in the assize, the defendant could subsequently bring a writ of right.[147] Could a party who lost by writ of right subsequently bring the assize? That was a closer question, or at least the author of *Glanvill* pretended it was for the sake of argument. *Glanvill* ends the discussion of the writ of *quo advocato*, as mentioned earlier, by addressing the question of whether a judgment in an action of right precludes any later assize of darrein presentment. On the one hand, the treatise author suggests that, in principle, a plaintiff should be able to bring the assize on the basis of his ancestor's seisin "notwithstanding anything that may have been done, concerning the right itself of presentation" (non obstante aliquo quod factum sit super iure ipso praesentandi).[148] On the other hand, allowing the assize to be brought by the party who lost the advowson by writ of right would mean that "it should seem, that the judgments of the king's court are not of perpetual obligation" (non videtur quod perpetuo firma sint ea quae in curia domini regis per iudicium semel sunt terminata negotia), and judgment in the action on the right ought to conclude the matter.[149]

The Origins of *Quare Impedit*

The writ of right of advowson, the assize of darrein presentment, and the writ of *quo advocato* are the only actions discussed in *Glanvill* by which a putative patron could claim an advowson.[150] In the earliest plea rolls, however, we find reference to an action not mentioned by *Glanvill:* the writ of *quare impedit*. The first three unambiguous references to *quare impedit* appear in the rolls from Hilary Term 1196.[151] A version of the writ, however, may have been available earlier, perhaps before *Glanvill* was completed. A final concord from 1186 records an advowson action involving a vacant church that is not an assize of darrein presentment.[152] Although the wording differs somewhat from the finished form of *quare impedit*—it states that the defendants were summoned *ostensuri quare impediebant,* rather than using the present tense as in the developed form of the writ—it is sufficiently close to be identifiable as an early forerunner. The absence of the writ in *Glanvill* may mean that the portions of the treatise dealing with advowsons were written before 1186, although they were completed after that date. Alternatively, this might be an early, experimental form of the writ, not yet formalized as a writ *de cursu*. The *Glanvill* author states at the outset that he intends only to record some "more frequently used" rules that "generally occur in court" (quaedam in curia generalia et frequentius usitata),[153] not every writ that could conceivably be issued. If the writ of *quare impedit* predated the assize of darrein presentment and was used regularly at the time the treatise was written, *Glanvill* would almost certainly have discussed *quare impedit* along with the assize. Since the treatise writer did not discuss *quare impedit*, it is safe to assume that *quare impedit* was the last of the three principal advowson writs to develop.

What the writ of *quare impedit* was, and what purpose it was originally meant to serve, are not questions for which the surviving sources provide easy answers. The earliest examples of the *quare impedit* writ are contained in *Bracton* and the pre-Mertonian register "CA." CA, made some time in the 1220s, gives the writ as follows:[154]

The writ called *quare impedit.*

> To the sheriff, greeting. Command B. that, justly and without delay, he permit A. to present a suitable parson to such a church which is vacant, as it is said, and as to which he complains that B. impedes him unjustly [quod . . . eum iniuste impedit]; and if he does not do this and the aforesaid A. shall have given you security for prosecuting his claim, then summon, by good summoners, the aforesaid B. that he be before our justices at Westminster on such a day to show why he has not done this, and have there the summoners and this writ.

This form makes clear that *quare impedit* was a *precipe* writ, taking the form *precipe . . . quod . . . permittat.* The defendant is to allow the plaintiff to present a suitable parson or else appear before the justices to explain why he has not done so. The writ explains why the defendant is being summoned—because he unjustly impedes the plaintiff. In the plea rolls, this becomes a question, *quare impedit,* thus giving the writ its familiar name. Like the writ of darrein presentment, the writ of *quare impedit* includes the claim that the church is vacant, which was a requirement of both writs (in contradistinction to the writ of right of advowson). Unlike darrein presentment, however, *quare impedit* has a "trespassory aspect": the plaintiff alleges that the defendant interferes with his exercise of the advowson.[155]

Bracton includes a version of the *quare impedit* writ virtually identical to that preserved in CA. Some of the *Bracton* manuscripts, however, substitute *non permittit* for *impedit,* and the treatise authors explain that there are actually two writs, *quare impedit* and *quare non permittit.*[156] The writ called *quare impedit* in CA is referred to by the treatise authors as *quare non permittit.*[157] The writ *Bracton* calls *quare impedit* is to be brought by a plaintiff who has already recovered an advowson by judgment. Samuel Thorne translated the Latin as follows:[158]

> The king to the sheriff, greeting. Since A. has made us secure with respect to his claim etc., put B. by gage and safe pledges that he be etc., to answer the same A. as to why he impedes the same A. from presenting a suitable parson to the church of N., the advowson of which church A. recently recovered in our court . . . against the same B. (or "against another, such a one") by an assize of darrein presentment there taken between them (or "by the judgment of our court," or in some other way) as to which the same A. complains that the aforesaid B. wrongfully and against our crown (or "in contempt of our court") impedes him.

38

The treatise writer offers some thoughts on the difference between the two writs: *quare non permittit* is to be brought when the plaintiff "has no seisin at all, or *quasi*-seisin," for example, by gift, dower, curtesy, or lease, while *quare impedit* is reserved for cases where the plaintiff has seisin by the prior judgment of a royal court.[159] The distinction is explained by the etymology of *impedire*, which means "to place his foot (*pedem*) in another's right,"[160] which, unlike many medieval etymologies, is correct.[161]

The discussion in *Bracton* would suggest that there were in fact two writs, *quare impedit* and *quare non permittit*. At first glance, the early plea rolls seem to bear this out; we find references to pleas of *quare impedit* and pleas of *quare non permittit*. Closer inspection, however, suggests that these terms could have been interchangeable, at least in the plea rolls. In 1198, for example, the prior of an abbey claimed an advowson by gift in a *placito quare impedit;* no prior judgment was at issue.[162] In Easter Term 1229, a plea concerning the church of Walcot (Lincs) was referred to alternatively as *placito quare impedit* and *placito quare non permittit*.[163] The plaintiff, Thomas prior of Sempringham, was claiming on the basis of a gift and not because of a prior judgment.[164] In Hilary Term 1233, Peter of Goldington offered himself in a plea concerning the advowson of the church of Stoke Goldington (Bucks),[165] which he allegedly had recently recovered by the grand assize; the plea was called *placito quare non permittit*, even though the facts would be covered by *Bracton*'s writ of *quare impedit*.[166] In Easter Term 1244, Margaret de Burgh, Countess of Kent, claimed the advowson of the church of Eastwood (Essex) on the grounds that the king presented the last parson, Geoffrey, while her late husband Hubert de Burgh was in prison and his lands were in the king's hand.[167] The plea was referred to as *quare impedit* even though it did not mention a former judgment.[168]

These examples from the plea rolls could be taken as evidence that the terms *quare impedit* and *quare non permittit* did not denote two distinct writs in the manner suggested by *Bracton*. It is not unreasonable to conclude that the writ referred to in CA as *breue quod dicitur impedit* was in fact called the writ of *quare impedit* from the outset, even if it could also be referred to as the writ of *quare non permittit*. The treatise authors apparently needed to explain that a separate writ existed for claiming an advowson recovered by prior judgment, and they did so by rechristening the writ we find in CA as the writ of *quare non permittit*.[169] But it was the writ in CA, called *quare non permittit* by *Bracton,* that would be known for the next six centuries as the writ of *quare impedit* and would eventually become the sole means of recovering an advowson in the royal courts.

Unlike the assize of darrein presentment, the writ of *quare impedit* did not specify how the dispute was to be resolved, nor did it give any indication of the precise issue (that is, right or seisin) to be determined in the proceedings. Instead the writ simply stated that the defendant had to permit the plaintiff to present or else appear before the justices to explain why he impeded him. Parties to *quare impedit* actions appear to have been uncertain about precisely how they were to be resolved. In Hilary Term 1199, Henry de Colombières appeared in a *quare impedit* suit he brought against Adam of Port concerning the advowson of Cholderton (Hants).[170] Henry asserted that the church was founded in his fee, all his ancestors had presented to it since the time of the Conquest, and his father had presented the last parson. Henry then put himself on a jury of the neighborhood. Adam denied this claim and asserted that Cholderton was a chapel pertaining to the mother church of Amport, which was of Adam's donation, and Adam's ancestors had presented the last parson both to the mother church and to the chapel. Adam put himself on a jury of the neighborhood concerning the last presentation or, alternatively, on the grand assize concerning who had the greater right in the church.[171] Adam seems to have been uncertain whether Henry's claim was based on the last presentation by Henry's father or the presentations by Henry's ancestors since the Conquest, which might determine the proper mechanism for resolving the dispute. The dispute was eventually settled by a final concord.[172]

Adam's doubt about the proper mode of resolution for a *quare impedit* suit was not resolved in the first few decades of the writ's history. In 1229, Hugh of Saint Philbert brought a writ of *quare impedit* against Gilbert III de Clare, Earl of Gloucester, concerning the advowsons of Caldecote and Shingham (both in Norfolk). Hugh's claim was that Gilbert's father (Richard III de Clare),[173] after presenting a parson to both churches, assigned the advowsons, along with some land, to Hugh's uncle.[174] Gilbert argued, inter alia, that Hugh offered no evidence that the advowsons were given to his uncle along with the land and that Gilbert's father presented the last parson, Robert de Clare, to Caldecote before the assignment and to Shingham after the assignment.[175] Hugh offered to prove by a champion his claim that the advowsons had been given to his uncle; offered the king half a mark for an inquisition into whether Gilbert's ancestor had presented a clerk before the assignment; or, as a third alternative, put himself on the country (that is, a jury).[176] Gilbert offered a champion of his own to do battle with Hugh's champion but refused to put himself on the country "because he was summoned to explain why he impeded and he has sufficiently shown why."[177] The court gave judgment for Gilbert on the grounds that Hugh offered no evidence that the advowsons were given to his uncle.[178] It is significant that both parties were ready to see the dispute decided by battle, a procedure normally associated with the writ of right. Cases like these suggest that, at least during the early thirteenth century, no set method existed for resolving suits brought by writ of *quare impedit.*

Another way in which the writ of *quare impedit* differs from the writ of right of advowson and the assize of darrein presentment is that we can find no obvious explanation for its origin: it was neither the first writ for the recovery of an advowson, nor, as far as can be ascertained, was it occasioned by a change in canon law. Chancery would not have needed to create a new writ unless the writ of right and the assize of darrein presentment were inadequate for some plaintiffs. It is therefore worth noting that *Glanvill* mentions no writ that would be available for a plaintiff who claimed an advowson by virtue of a gift.

Discussing the assize of darrein presentment, *Glanvill* explains that the defendant may raise the exception that an ancestor of the plaintiff, after presenting the last parson, conveyed the fee to which the advowson is appurtenant to the defendant or his ancestors.[179] A donee, however, could not successfully bring the assize of darrein presentment as a plaintiff. When the assize proceeds in the presence of one or both parties, *Glanvill* explains, "the person, to whom, on his own, or his ancestor's seisin, the last presentation shall be adjudged, is understood thereby to have recovered seisin of the advowson itself."[180] The plaintiff had no opportunity to explain that although the defendant's ancestor had presented the last parson, he subsequently gave the advowson to the plaintiff. If neither the plaintiff nor his ancestors had ever presented a candidate, the jury would answer the question *quis advocatus presentavit ultimam personam* in favor of the defendant, and that would end the matter. Thus the donee's ability to plead successfully in a darrein presentment action depended on the other party bringing the writ first.

A donee who sought to bring a writ of right faced two difficulties according to the rules set forth in *Glanvill*. First, as discussed earlier, *Glanvill* tells us that a plaintiff who claims the advowson of a vacant church must first state whether or not he or his ancestor last presented. If the plaintiff conceded that the defendant or one of the defendant's ancestors made the last presentation, "without having recourse to a recognition, he shall present one [parson] at least."[181] Second, according to *Glanvill*, a plaintiff who brought a writ of right had to state in court that he or one of his ancestors was seised of the advowson in the time of Henry I or since the time of Henry II's coronation (1154). To sustain such a claim, the plaintiff must further assert that he or his ancestor presented a parson at one of those times and that parson was instituted by the bishop.[182] A donee could not make such a claim. In the time of *Glanvill*, therefore, a donee's ability to prevail in the royal courts depended on the other party's willingness to act as the plaintiff and obtain a royal writ. If the other party preferred to rely on self-help, the donee would have difficulty seeking intervention from the royal courts.

The writ of *quare impedit*, created within a decade after the completion of *Glanvill*, offered the donee of an advowson a new remedy in the royal courts when the church became vacant. One of the earliest *quare impedit* suits in the rolls, a dispute concerning the advowson of Stokenham, in Devon, was brought by a monastery claiming the advowson by gift; the first surviving entry from the case dates to Easter Term 1198.[183] The plea is designated in that entry as *placito quare impedit presentationem*.[184] Another *quare impedit* plea from 1200 also involves a donee as plaintiff. The prior and monks of Lenton claimed the advowson of Nuthall, in Nottinghamshire, from William of Saint Patrick on the grounds that William's grandfather, Geoffrey of Saint Patrick,[185] had given them the advowson by his charter, which they offered.[186] The roll states that William was summoned to show "quare non permittit . . . presentare."[187] It is evident that, at least by the end of the twelfth century, a donee could use the writ of *quare impedit*. It does not necessarily follow, however, that the writ was specifically created to offer a remedy for donees, and the picture of advowson litigation that emerges from the early plea rolls is not as clear as that painted by *Glanvill*. Donees in the late twelfth century and the early thirteenth can be seen as plaintiffs both in actions of darrein presentment and in actions of right.

As discussed earlier, the procedure described in *Glanvill* for the assize of darrein presentment does not give a donee plaintiff an opportunity to refer to the gift in his initial claim. Absent consideration of this fact, the jury would normally have no basis to render a verdict in favor of a donee plaintiff. Under some circumstances, however, this would not be a bar to recovery. If the defendant was neither the person who last presented nor his heir, the defendant might not allow the assize to proceed, pleading an exception instead. At that point, the plaintiff could raise the issue of his gift, bringing it to the attention of the jurors and the court.

The early plea rolls offer examples of this scenario. For example, in 1214, an assize of darrein presentment was taken between Robert de Muscegros, plaintiff, and the prior of Bruton concerning the advowson of Charlton Musgrave, in Somerset. The prior said that the assize should not proceed because John de la Rivere, who presented the last parson, gave the advowson to the priory by his charter.[188] Robert, asked by whom he claimed right in the church, responded that he claimed it by Walter de la Rivere, son and heir of John, who gave Robert the land in which the church is situated. The parties were given a day in the quindene of Easter; no judgment is recorded.[189] In 1217 we find the prioress of Langley bringing the assize against William Pantolf concerning the church of Dalby (Leics). Both parties claimed the advowson by gift, the prioress from William Pantolf the elder and the defendant from yet another William Pantolf, the heir of the prioress's donee.[190] The assize was postponed when William the defendant vouched the daughter of his donee, Isolda Pantolf, to warrant. When Isolda appeared, she warranted the prioress's charter instead; the defendant withdrew his claim, and the prioress recovered her presentation.[191]

A more complicated example of this phenomenon dates to 1222, when Geoffrey de Lucy brought the assize against the prior of Southwick to recover the church of Wellsworth (Hants). The plaintiff claimed by gift from Geoffrey de Mandeville, fifth Earl of Essex. The prior initially argued that the church was not vacant, but the plaintiff responded that the current parson was presented by reason of the Third Lateran Council, suggesting that the occupation of a church by a clerk presented without a patron did not constitute plenarty for purposes of the assize.[192] The prior then argued that the advowson had been given to his house by Maud of Buckland, aunt of the fifth earl, and Robert fitz Peter, the earl's uncle.[193] The plaintiff responded that Maud only had dower through her husband, and Robert never had seisin. At that point, an attorney appeared for the prior and contended that the prior had presented the penultimate parson, which the plaintiff denied. At the conclusion of the pleading, the prior conceded the assize, but it was postponed for default of recognitors. No judgment survives.[194] While the defendant in this case did claim to have presented one or more parsons, the plaintiff seems to have been confident that the jury would return a verdict that Geoffrey de Mandeville had last presented, in which case the plaintiff could rely on his gift.

While *Glanvill* tells us that the person who (or whose ancestor) presented the last parson was automatically awarded seisin of the advowson,[195] things were not always so straightforward in practice, particularly when only one of multiple defendants could claim descent from the last presenter. In 1206, for example, an assize was taken between the prior of Saint Neot's, plaintiff, and Thurstan of Mundford and the abbot of Thorney, defendants, concerning the church of Wing, in Rutland. The jurors said that Thurstan of Mundford, grandfather of Thurstan the defendant, presented the last parson, Nicholas Clerk. The prior, having heard this, said that Thurstan the elder gave his right in the advowson to the priory of Saint Neot's by a charter. The abbot responded that Thurstan had given a moiety of the advowson to the abbey, to which the prior replied that Thurstan had presented a parson subsequent to the gift to the abbey but before the gift to the priory.[196] The abbot then vouched the younger Thurstan to warrant. Thurstan's attorney conceded the assize but said he was not made attorney concerning the warranty and could not respond in that regard. The lawsuit was postponed several times, but no judgment is recorded.[197] Rather than award seisin to Thurstan alone on the grounds that his ancestor presented the last parson, as the rule stated in *Glanvill* would seem to require, the royal justices gave both the prior and the abbot the opportunity to make their respective claims of gift.

Another situation in which a donee might bring darrein presentment arose when the defendant did not claim to have made the last presentation to the living concerned, and the dispute instead turned on whether the last clerk in the church was a parson or a vicar. In the 1229 rolls, we find Ralph Nowers bringing the assize against Gilbert Marshall, parson of Oakham, claiming the advowson of the church of Knossington (Leics). Ralph asserted that William Pantolf, grandfather of Robert of Tateshalle (by whose gift Ralph claimed the church), presented a certain William Chaplain to the church, who was admitted at William Pantolf's presentation. William, Ralph claimed, died thirty years ago, and the bishop then gave the church to another parson (the one who last died) by reason of a dispute between rival patrons. Gilbert responded that Knossington was not a church but rather a chapel pertaining to his church of Oakham, and William Chaplain and the parson who last died were not parsons but vicars, paying one mark to Oakham as pension.[198] Ralph responded that William was parson of the church and put himself on the assize. The assize proceeded, and the jury determined that William Pantolf presented William as parson, and Ralph received that manor, including the advowson, by gift from Robert of Tateshalle, heir of William Pantolf.[199] Ralph recovered his seisin.[200]

In short, situations occurred in which a donee could bring the assize of darrein presentment and prevail in the royal courts. No absolute bar prevented donees from bringing the assize, despite the strong language in *Bracton* to the contrary.[201] Nevertheless, when the donee's grievance lay against the person who presented the last parson or the heir of the last presenter, the assize of darrein presentment might be of little use, because it seemingly did not afford the plaintiff an opportunity to mention the gift if the defendant allowed the assize to proceed. While the dispute over the church of Wing offers an apparent counterexample, the unusual facts of that case may have encouraged greater flexibility on the part of the royal justices.[202] In general, the assize of darrein presentment did not offer an effective remedy for the donee who sought to sue the last presenter or his heir. The question, then, is whether such plaintiffs could ever bring the writ of right. *Bracton* clearly thought that they could not,[203] but the plea rolls from the early thirteenth century seem less consistent.

The early plea rolls offer some examples of cases where a donee brought the writ of right of advowson and the royal justices did not immediately dismiss the suit. In Easter Term 1201, for example, the abbot of Warden claimed the advowson of a moiety of the church of Warden

(Beds) as the right of his church (*sicut ius ecclesie sue*) by gift of William II de Bussy, against William of Coleville and Beatrice his wife. William and Beatrice responded that they claimed nothing except dower by gift of Bartholomew de Bussy, son of William de Bussy, vouching Bartholomew's heirs to warrant. William and Beatrice were given a day in Trinity Term to have the warrantors in court,[204] but no entries survive from that term, so we do not know what happened to the suit.

In Easter Term 1206, the prior of Merton claimed the advowson of the church of Malden from Brian fitz Ralph and Gunnora his wife by writ of right. The prior asserted that Eudes of Malden gave the church to the priory upon entering the priory as a canon,[205] and the former parson withdrew from the church at Eudes's request, paying half a mark to the priory as pension. The prior offered to prove this by two champions. The defendants put themselves on the grand assize, at which point the prior offered a charter from Eudes, which the defendants objected to on the grounds that it was made after Eudes had become a canon.[206] The parties were subsequently given a day to hear judgment, which is unfortunately not recorded.[207] In Michaelmas Term 1219, a donee who had previously been sued (and lost) in an assize of darrein presentment brought a writ of right; the donee eventually recovered by default when the other party repeatedly failed to appear.[208]

Entries such as these show that the justices might not immediately dismiss a writ of right of advowson even when it became evident that the plaintiff was a donee. In other cases, however, the rule that a donee could not bring the writ of right was forcefully applied. In Hilary Term 1203, an action of right brought by the prior of Sempringham against the Knights Templar concerning the advowson of the church of Donington (Lincs) was dismissed by the justices "because the prior seeks another's right given to him by charter and not his own right."[209] In Hilary Term 1223, Alan of Bassingbourn brought an action of right against Robert Lisle to recover the advowson of the church of Wimpole (Cambs). Alan asserted that Berenger de Beray was seised of the advowson on the day of the death of Henry I and gave the church to a certain Robert his chaplain, who was admitted at his presentation. From Berenger, Alan argued, the right descended to Gerard his son. Gerard gave the advowson with half a knight's fee to Alexander of Bassingbourn, and from Alexander, Alan alleged, the right

descended to Alan the plaintiff. Robert Lisle put himself on the grand assize, but the court held the assize to be null and amerced Alan because he
"speaks concerning another's right and another's seisin than that of his
own ancestors."[210] Finally, in Hilary Term 1231, Peter of Danesy brought an
action of right against the prioress of Nuneaton to recover the advowson
of the chapel of Saint Peter, Alsthorpe (Rutland).[211] Peter asserted that
Hugh Wake was seised of the advowson in the time of Henry II and presented the last parson; subsequently Hugh gave the fee with the advowson
to Thomas of Danesy, and from Thomas the right descended to Peter as
his son and heir. The prioress sought judgment on the grounds that neither
Thomas nor any of his ancestors were seised of the advowson by virtue of
a presentation: Peter sought the advowson from the seisin of Hugh, from
whom nothing descended to Peter by hereditary right, but only by gift.
Because Peter could not contradict this, the prioress went without day, and
Peter was amerced.[212]

These plea roll entries demonstrate that a donee who attempted to sue by
writ of right might find that judgment would summarily be awarded to the
defendant on the grounds that the plaintiff sought not his own right but the
right of another given to him by charter. It is not clear why this rule was
enforced in some cases but not in others, but it is possible that not every defendant specifically raised the issue, and the justices did not always dismiss
the case *sua sponte*. The fact that a plea roll does not record an objection by
the defendant does not necessarily mean that no objection was made in
court. When the defendant did not object to the charter, however, or failed
to appear and defend his claim, the thirteenth-century justices might occasionally have let the case proceed, knowing that a writ of *quare impedit* would
be available to the donee in the event that they dismissed his action of
right. It is also possible, however, that the cases simply reflect inconsistency
or lack of knowledge on the part of some of the royal justices.

As discussed earlier, the donee might bring the assize of darrein presentment if he knew that the defendant would not be able to claim the
last presentation. Nevertheless, if the donee wanted to sue the person
who last presented or his heir, the writ of *quare impedit* was the only fail-
safe remedy.[213] It is tempting to conclude that the original purpose of the
writ of *quare impedit* was to close this gap and offer a clear remedy for the
donee. One alternative explanation, however, must be considered. Under

certain circumstances, a widow could claim the right of presentation to a church for life after the death of her husband. Until she had presented a candidate herself, she could not assert that she had seisin of the advowson or that her ancestors had such seisin. The same was true of a widower who claimed an advowson by curtesy. It would seem, therefore, that widows and widowers ought not to have been able to bring the writ of right or the assize of darrein presentment, and that the writ of *quare impedit* was designed to provide a remedy for them rather than (or in addition to) donees.

The possibility that *quare impedit* was designed in part to provide a remedy for widows and widowers, however, is belied by the fact that we see widows at the beginning of the thirteenth century bringing both the writ of right and the assize of darrein presentment. In Easter Term 1203, Isabel of Clinton claimed the advowson of Cassington (Oxon) as pertaining to her dower, bringing a writ of right against the abbot of Eynsham. Isabel argued that Jordan, father of her late husband William, presented a certain Roger to the church "as of the right of his advowson" (sicut de iure advocationis sue), and Roger held the church all his life in the time of Henry II. Isabel offered to prove this by a champion. The abbot did not object that Isabel sought *alterius ius,* arguing instead that William's son, who ought to warrant Isabel, was underage, and offering a charter of gift from Jordan's alleged ancestor Geoffrey of Clinton. Isabel responded that Geoffrey had no right to give the church to a religious house, because he had only wardship on account of Jordan, who was Geoffrey's nephew. The case was postponed,[214] and it was eventually put before the king.[215]

In Michaelmas Term 1207, Ralph de Trubleville and Alice his wife appeared in an assize of darrein presentment they brought against John of Brancaster, archdeacon of Worcester, and Master Michael of Ringfield, concerning the advowson of the chapel of Saint Giles, Topcroft (Norfolk).[216] The plaintiffs asserted that Robert son of Henry presented the last parson, Benedict of Bedingham, and that Robert's son Philip was the late husband of Alice and gave her in dower the manor of Topcroft to which the advowson of the chapel pertained. The court summarily awarded seisin to the plaintiffs.[217]

These cases show that a widow who claimed an advowson by reason of dower might be allowed to step into the shoes of her late husband and bring the writ of right or the assize of darrein presentment. The same might be true of a widower who held by curtesy. In Hilary Term 1229, Richard of Desborough successfully recovered the advowson of the church of Hargrave (Northants) by assize of darrein presentment from the prior of the hospital of Saint John, after the jurors reported that Richard's wife Amice was the heir of the person who last presented and the court determined that Richard had his wife's inheritance and the wardship of her heir according to the custom of the realm.[218] Despite the insistence in *Bracton* to the contrary,[219] *quare impedit* was not the only remedy available in the early thirteenth century for a widower who claimed by curtesy.

Given that widows and widowers were allowed to bring other actions even after the writ of *quare impedit* was created, it is difficult to surmise that *quare impedit* was originally designed principally to assist widows and widowers. Only donees were expressly forbidden from relying on another's seisin in the royal courts, at least with respect to the writ of right, and the darrein presentment cases where a donee was able to act as plaintiff are arguably exceptional. It is not unreasonable to conclude that the original purpose of the writ of *quare impedit* was to offer a remedy for a donee who claimed an advowson from the person who last presented or his heir. Indeed, Maitland suggested this conclusion more than a century ago, before the date of the creation of the writ had been ascertained.[220]

Religious houses benefited significantly from the creation of the writ of *quare impedit*.[221] Of the six cases from the reign of Richard I that we can positively identify as *quare impedit*, four involve religious houses, and in three of the four, the religious house is the plaintiff.[222] The three earliest cases involving a religious house, from Hilary Term 1196, record only a failure to appear, and thus we cannot divine the basis for the lawsuit from the evidence. The fourth case, however, may give some indication about what fact pattern might lurk behind the other entries.

In Easter Term 1198, the abbot of Stanley appeared in a plea of *quare impedit* that the abbey brought against Matthew fitz Herbert concerning the church of Stokenham, in Devon.[223] The abbot claimed that the advowson belonged to the abbey by gift from Matthew's mother-in-law, Mabel Patric. While the litigation between Matthew and the abbey was pending, Mabel— or, more likely, someone writing in Mabel's name—sent a letter to the royal justiciar, Geoffrey fitz Peter, confirming the abbey's side of the story.[224] The letter explained that Mabel had given the advowson to the abbey, emphasizing that the gift was made before Mabel's daughter was married or even betrothed. As the lawsuit progressed, the case spawned a separate plea between the abbey and Mabel, with the abbot seeking to have Mabel warrant her alleged charter in court.[225] Mabel claimed that she could not appear on account of bed sickness, and knights were sent to determine if Mabel wanted to warrant her gift.[226] When the knights returned, they informed the court that, according to Mabel, she had made the gift to the abbey at the queen's request and after Matthew had married her daughter, at which point the tenement to which the advowson was appurtenant was no longer in her hand.[227] For this reason, the knights explained, Mabel did not wish to appear before the court or name anyone to act as attorney in her place.[228] No judgment is recorded.[229]

Considering this case, and other similar cases from the reign of John,[230] we may suspect that, in many early *quare impedit* suits, a religious house was claiming the advowson by gift as attested in a charter, and the dispute turned on the timing, validity, or effect of the gift.[231] This is not to say, of course, that the only plaintiffs who benefited from the writ were religious houses.[232] Nevertheless, in light of the involvement of religious houses in the early actions of *quare impedit*, it is not unreasonable to conclude that the writ was created, at least in part, in response to pressure from the monasteries, which were appropriating churches at a rapid pace during this period.[233] During the twelfth century, many laymen gave their advowsons to religious houses with the church's approval.[234] A religious house therefore usually traced its right in an advowson back to some gift by a layman, and in many cases that layman, and not the religious house, had made the last presentation. Religious houses frequently found themselves in this position, and they probably used whatever influence they had at the royal court to create a remedy that would cater to donees.

After *quare impedit* was created, a plaintiff in an advowson case could choose between three different primary writs according to the facts of his dispute and his preference regarding the mode of resolution. If the plaintiff claimed the last presentation to a vacant church, he could use the writ of darrein presentment. If he could not claim the last presentation, and the church was not vacant, he could use the writ of right of advowson. Finally, if the church was vacant, but he could not claim the last presentation, he could use the writ of *quare impedit*. Religious houses often found themselves in the third of these situations, but they were not the only plaintiffs who benefited from *quare impedit*'s broader scope.

This tripartite scheme remained in place throughout the period under discussion in this book, and all three writs appear with some regularity in the plea rolls. In the next chapter, I situate this scheme in the context of Romano-canonical learning in the late twelfth century and explore whether Roman or canon law ideas regarding ownership and possession had some influence on the development of the early common law of advowsons.

CHAPTER THREE
OWNERSHIP AND POSSESSION

In this chapter, I provide a brief summary of the rules of Roman and canon law relating to ownership and possession, drawing on sources that would have been known in England, especially by churchmen, during the period examined in this book. The distinction between ownership and possession is one of the characteristic features of Roman law.[1] Speaking simply, ownership is title, and possession is actual enjoyment.[2] Classical Roman jurists were careful to distinguish between the two. According to Justinian's *Digest*, Ulpian wrote that "ownership has nothing in common with possession" (nihil commune habet proprietas cum possessione).[3] In the Latin of the Roman jurists, possession is *possessio;* ownership could be denoted by the words *proprietas* or *dominium*. Medieval English writers did use these terms, and they are particularly prominent in *Bracton*.[4] On occasion, the term *possessio* appears in the actual plea rolls, usually in quotations of letters from prelates discussing benefices.[5] However, two other terms more commonly appear in the early records of the English royal courts: *ius*, or right, and *seisina*, or seisin.[6] I will consider the extent to which these English concepts might correspond to *proprietas* and *possessio* in Roman law, and what this might tell us about the influence of Romano-canonical learning on the nascent common law.

Frederic William Maitland, the great English legal historian, thought that *ius* and *seisina* were roughly equivalent to *proprietas* and *possessio* respectively.[7] Maitland described two important royal remedies for the recovery of real property as protecting either ownership or possession. Right was seen as protected by "the proprietary action," the writ of right.[8] In contrast, by the late twelfth century, seisin of land was protected through the assize of novel disseisin, which Maitland called "a distinctly possessory action."[9] Maitland thus denoted the early actions of the common law by words derived from the Latin *proprietas* and *possessio*, suggesting that English law, like Roman law, clearly distinguished between the two concepts.

S. F. C. Milsom strongly challenged Maitland's assumption that seisin and right were merely the English equivalents of possession and ownership. Milsom does not see seisin and right as synonymous with Roman ownership and possession. For Milsom, we must view seisin and right through the prism of the lord-vassal relationship. A lord "seised" his tenant of his land; thus "seisin" originally denoted the tenant's condition of having been seised by a lord.[10] Right, on the other hand, "was not a sort of ownership, but just the right to hold of the lord."[11] According to this view, the concepts of seisin and right were not mutually exclusive, for both reflected the feudal bond between lord and tenant. Milsom finds implausible the notion that Roman law had some influence on the early English law of property, other than supplying it with Latin words.[12]

Milsom's interpretation of English law and its relationship with Romano-canonical learning has not found universal acceptance. Other modern scholars have detected modes of influence between the two systems. For example, Mary Cheney suggested that the assize of novel disseisin emerged in the context of an effort by the church (specifically Archbishop Thomas Becket) to recover property that had been illegally alienated according to canon law.[13] Donald Sutherland, writing before Milsom's main work but after Milsom's initial explication of his ideas,[14] held the view that the assize may have been partly inspired by the Roman interdict *unde vi*, which protected the possessor of property from being put out by force.[15] While Sutherland recognized differences between *unde vi* and novel disseisin, he would not have challenged Maitland's characterization of novel disseisin as a distinctly possessory action. Sutherland had enough confidence in the similarity between the Roman and English actions to state that the "influence of Roman law thus seems to be clear."[16] However, Sutherland also acknowledged that the parallel between Roman *proprietas/possessio* and English *ius/seisina* was not complete. The latter were more like points along a spectrum, whereas the former were completely distinct.[17]

Before asking whether the early common law was influenced by concepts of ownership and possession in Romano-canonical learning, one must first establish that these ideas were important not only to ancient Roman law but to Roman law as it was understood in the twelfth century, and to canon law. In a persuasive essay, Mary Cheney demonstrated that the concepts of *proprietas* and *possessio* were invoked in ecclesiastical courts in England by the mid-twelfth century.[18] Less attention, however, has been given to the academic development of these ideas in England, chiefly in the *Liber Pauperum* of Vacarius, or in the early *ordines* devoted to matters of procedure. Nevertheless, such works constitute an important piece of the puzzle and must be considered as part of Romano-canonical learning of the late twelfth century.[19]

Much of the scholarly discussion about ownership and possession in the early common law has also been limited in another respect. In general, those who have explored the subject have tended to focus on what today we would call corporeal interests in land. Scholars have given less consideration to whether Roman or canon law had any influence on the advowson writs, or whether the early common law of advowsons distinguished between ownership and possession.

I have argued that the basic distinction between ownership and possession was a part of Romano-canonical learning, both in theory and in practice, as it was known in England in the latter half of the twelfth century.[20] We can arguably see that distinction in the first two advowson writs, and it cannot be explained there, as it has been in the land context, by reference to the feudal relationship between lord and tenant. English right and seisin were admittedly not the same as Roman ownership and possession, but the men who created the assize of darrein presentment might have been inspired in part by Roman and canon law ideas.

The writ of *quare impedit*, on the other hand, does not fit easily into this framework. Although it generally had the quality of a possessory action and could be a preliminary to a subsequent action of right, *quare impedit* also had some characteristics of a proprietary action, in that it could be brought by a donee who did not have "possession" of the advowson in what we might imagine to be a Roman or canon law sense. Thus, while the first two advowson writs show how developments in the common law might have been partly inspired by the scheme of Roman and canon law, the writ of *quare impedit* illustrates how the common law remained independent of that scheme well into the thirteenth century, if not later. In this way, *quare impedit* is similar to the writs of entry, which are also difficult to categorize in Romano-canonical terms.

Ownership and Possession in Romano-canonical Learning

To understand how ownership and possession were distinguished in Romano-canonical learning around the time of Henry II, it is best to start with the texts of Roman law that were known in England during that period. Key to this analysis are two introductory texts that are known to have been studied in England in the late twelfth century: Justinian's *Institutes*, which were the subject of an English commentary circa 1200,[21] and the *Liber Pauperum* of Vacarius, a twelfth-century English collection of extracts from the *Digest* and *Code*.[22] According to the scholarly consensus, the *Liber Pauperum* probably originated in Oxford, Northampton, or Lincoln in the 1170s or 1180s,[23] and the *Institutes* were most likely used as a companion to the *Liber Pauperum*.[24] Some versions of these texts may have been used early enough to have had an impact on the creation of the assize of darrein presentment, even if they emerged too late to have an impact on earlier reforms of Henry II. In addition, the teachings contained in the *Liber Pauperum* may predate the text that is preserved in the surviving manuscripts.[25] Furthermore, while the English commentary on the *Institutes* probably dates to the beginning of the thirteenth century, the ideas contained therein may have been taught in England for several years before the text was written.

Southern Britain was a part of the Roman Empire, but little trace of Roman law survived the Saxon invasions.[26] The Norman Conquest in 1066 did not bring about a revival of Roman law in England.[27] Nevertheless, interest in Roman law began to revive among Englishmen in the mid-twelfth century. The future archbishop of Canterbury and martyr Thomas Becket spent a year in Bologna in the 1140s.[28] Vacarius had studied in Bologna at the time of the Four Doctors, arrived in England sometime in the mid-1140s, and supposedly began teaching Roman law soon thereafter, although John of Salisbury claimed that Vacarius's teaching career was cut short when King Stephen banned the study of Roman law in 1152.[29] However, it is possible that Vacarius's teaching career may have begun later in the twelfth century.[30]

By the time of Henry II, an increasing number of Englishmen were studying law in Bologna, if not in English schools.[31] During his conflict with Archbishop Becket in the 1160s, King Henry "had advice from counselors skilled in both civil and canon law" and relied on Gratian's *Decretum* and the primacy of temporal rule under the civil law to bolster his case before the pope.[32] Before the end of the twelfth century, the abbey of Peterborough owned a two-volume set of the entire *Corpus Iuris Civilis*, together with a copy of the *Summa* of Placentinus.[33] Most of the royal justices in the twelfth century may not have had Roman law training,[34] but there were men in England with such experience to whom the justices could have turned, had they cared to learn how Roman law dealt with issues of property.[35]

If King Henry's advisers did indeed consult men learned in Roman law, such men would have known about the difference between ownership and possession. Any English student of Roman law in the late twelfth century would almost certainly have been taught the distinction between *proprietas* and *possessio*. The *Liber Pauperum* included Ulpian's statement in the *Digest* that "ownership has nothing in common with possession."[36] *Proprietas* and *possessio* were acquired and retained in different ways and were protected by different remedies.

Course books of Roman law used in twelfth-century England do not provide a formal definition of ownership. They do, however, give considerable attention to how it was acquired. In the *Institutes*, one finds a list of several different "natural" modes of acquiring ownership that are discussed in the English *Lectura*. These include the taking of wild animals (*occupatio*),[37] the finding of gemstones (*inventio*),[38] and the making of a new thing from someone else's materials (*specificatio*).[39] Delivery (*traditio*) was also considered a "natural" mode of acquiring ownership,[40] but for ownership to be transferred by delivery, there had to be a sufficient *causa*, such as gift, dowry, or sale.[41] Regarding sale, the *Institutes* say that the buyer had to pay the price or otherwise satisfy the seller for ownership to pass, unless the sale was made on credit.[42] Inheritance was not considered a means of acquiring ownership but was a separate category, treated in a different book of the *Institutes*.[43]

In addition to "natural" modes of acquiring ownership, the sources also describe the "civil" modes of usucapion (*usucapio*) and long-term possession (*longi temporis possessio*). Property could be acquired by these "civil" modes when it was possessed in good faith for a fixed period of time, three years for movables under *usucapio* and ten or twenty years for immovables under *longi temporis possessio* (ten years *inter praesentes*, twenty years *inter absentes*).[44] The possession, according to the English commentary on the *Institutes*, had to be just at the outset and for an acceptable cause, "one as a result of which ownership is normally transferred, such as sale, barter and the like."[45] However, things possessed in bad faith could be acquired in "not less than thirty years," according to the commentary.[46]

The ancient action of *rei vindicatio*, an action that applied to all movable property as well as land, protected ownership.[47] *Rei vindicatio* was an *in rem* action, which meant that the defendant did not need to be obliged to the plaintiff as in an *in personam* action.[48] The action focused on the plaintiff's right rather than the defendant's wrong, and the plaintiff did not have to show that the defendant was bound under the law of contract or delict to hand over the property. Furthermore, the action could be brought against a defendant who possessed the thing or had fraudulently ceased to possess it.[49] So long as the defendant had the necessary relationship with the thing, nothing required him to have some relationship with the plaintiff. "In an action *in rem* we seek what is ours," the English commentary on the *Institutes* explained, "and one's own thing is owed to no one."[50]

Possession, like ownership, is left undefined in the sources of Roman law that I consider in this chapter, but the jurist Paul does offer an etymology in a passage excerpted in those sources. Paul says that the origin is from *sedibus*, seat, and *positio*, position, because there is a natural holding by the one who stands on a thing.[51] This suggests that physical control was understood to be an essential type of possession. Possession was acquired both physically and mentally: *corpore et animo*.[52] So long as the requisite intent was present, one could possess by physically holding the thing, although that holding was not always necessary.

Only a corporeal thing could be possessed in the full sense. Roman sources do, however, acknowledge a kind of possession of incorporeal rights: hence the concept of *quasi possessio*, a state that could be achieved by the exercise of a right such as a servitude.[53] Two key *Digest* texts on quasi possession appear in the *Liber Pauperum*. In the first passage, Paul explains that it is possible to have quasi possession of a servitude that is attached to the ground.[54] In the second, Ulpian explains that someone may obtain the right to channel water by long use and quasi possession and is in that case exempted from the requirement to establish legal title.[55] The term *quasi possessiones* also appears in the English commentary on the *Institutes* in a passage about possessory remedies, explaining that "actions and defenses apply more to the assertion or acquiring of ownership in things or to the enforcement of debts than to claiming or keeping possession or quasi possession" (tam actionibus quam exceptionibus ad rerum dominia uendicanda uel optinenda uel debita adipiscenda magis utuntur quam ad possessiones uel quasi possessiones sequendas . . . uel retinendas).[56]

These references suggest that students of Roman law in England knew that there could be such a thing as quasi possession of incorporeal rights, which would presumably include not only servitudes but also advowsons. This was certainly the position of the French school of canonists around the year 1200. The French apparatus *Materia auctoris*, interpreting the reference to "possession" of an advowson in Alexander III's decretal *Consultationibus* (1 Comp. 3.33.23 = X 3.38.19), explains that the pope meant to say "quasi possession," because "incorporeal things cannot be possessed."[57] This explanation was incorporated into the ordinary gloss to X 3.38.19 by Bernhard of Parma.[58] The decretal itself, however, dates from much earlier (1173–76) and specifically refers to "possession" of a right of presentation as recognized by an "English custom," as contrasted with the mere assertion of such a right.[59] The concept of possession (or quasi possession) of incorporeal rights, therefore, may have been familiar in England by at least the mid-1170s, if not earlier in the reign of Henry II, even if it had not been fully developed in Justinian's *Digest*.

Possession in Roman law was protected by interdicts, which were originally forms or sets of words used by the praetor to order or prohibit.[60] In a passage included in the *Liber Pauperum,* Gaius wrote that one who sought restitution of some property would be better off suing first by some interdict rather than bringing the *rei vindicatio,* because it is far better to be in possession oneself and put the burden of being plaintiff on one's opponent.[61] The *Institutes* note that, for this reason, "there is often, in fact almost always, a hot dispute as to possession itself."[62]

According to the *Institutes,* possessory interdicts fall into three categories: those for obtaining (*adipiscendae*), retaining (*retinendae*), and recovering (*recuperandae*) possession.[63] Less important for present purposes, the first category involved the situation where someone else was in possession of property that belonged to a person with a right of inheritance; this category awarded possession to someone who never had it.[64] The latter two categories, on the other hand, protected a possessor of property against disturbance or dispossession and were of critical importance in the Roman law of property as presented in the *Institutes* and *Liber Pauperum.* The interdicts for retaining possession were the interdict *uti possidetis* and the interdict *utrubi.* Applicable to land and movables respectively, these interdicts served to decide which of two parties possessed the property in dispute and thereby determined which would be the plaintiff and which the defendant in a *rei vindicatio,* for "without first identifying the possessor, it is impossible to begin the vindication."[65] In classical Roman law, the winner in *uti possidetis* was

> the party in possession at the date of the interdict itself, as long as his possession had not been obtained from his opponent by force, stealth or license. It was irrelevant that the possessor had forcibly driven out a third party, had secretly usurped a third party's possession, or had obtained a third party's license to possess. With *utrubi* the winner was the one who had possessed for the greater part of the year, not counting possession obtained from the opponent by force, stealth or license.[66]

Justinian later harmonized the working of the two interdicts, so that the winner, for both land and movables, was the party who possessed when issue was joined, "still discounting possession obtained from the opponent by force, stealth or license."[67] It made no difference whether the possession was just or unjust, for every possessor had a greater right than one who did not possess.[68]

Utrubi and *uti possidetis* were both formulated as actions preventing the use of force.[69] In the more important of the two actions, *uti possidetis,* the praetor issued the following order to the parties: "I forbid force to be used to prevent him of you two who is at present in faultless possession of the disputed building from possessing it as he at present does."[70] The purpose was to protect the possession of the one who the praetor decided was the preferred possessor of the land.[71] The interdict's formulation, however, allowed for two possibilities: it could be a double action in which both parties claimed possession, or it could be a simple action brought against a disturber who did not claim to possess.[72] Early continental glossators understood the interdict primarily as a double action but also held that the dispute over possession could be only implicit and follow from the behavior of the disturber. Azo, writing around the early thirteenth century, envisaged two kinds of interdict *uti possidetis:* one intended to settle a dispute over possession, and the other to sanction a simple disturbance.[73]

When one examines texts of Roman law from England in the late twelfth and early thirteenth centuries, it is evident that while *uti possidetis* was understood as a double action, it was also seen as a way to prevent the use of force. The English commentary gives an explanation very similar to that in the *Institutes:*

> In [the interdict *uti possidetis*] the winner is the one who was in possession at the time of the interdict, and it applies to the land. . . . Since the question of the legal right of possession is of the utmost importance, it is necessary, in proceedings of this kind, for it to be clear which party should be called plaintiff and which defendant. But since usually the party in possession is in the better position, in interdicts of this kind there is usually the greatest dispute between the parties. For each of them claims that he is in possession, and since each of them appears to be both plaintiff and defendant, interdicts of this kind are, as described later, called double, since the parties seem to litigate in two ways.[74]

On the other hand, a gloss on the relevant rubric in the *Liber Pauperum* states that the interdict was "for retaining possession lost secretly" but was also "a prohibition by which the possessor prevented his adversary from using force to possess."[75] The interdict was "offered on account of force," but on account of "force of repulsion," whereas the interdict *unde vi* (discussed hereafter) was on account of "force of revenge."[76] Both the idea of *uti possidetis* as a double action and the notion of the interdict as a remedy against force, therefore, were part of the English understanding of Roman law in the late twelfth century.

In the law of Justinian and the *Liber Pauperum*, the remedy for recovering possession was the interdict *unde vi*, by which the person who was forcibly ejected could recover possession from the ejector.[77] The ejector, the *Institutes* make clear, was compelled to restore possession to the dispossessed plaintiff "even if he himself acquired possession from the violent ejector by force, stealth or license."[78] The interdict did not apply to the loss of movables; it applied only to eviction by force from land and buildings.[79] One who had not acquired possession *corpore et animo* could not bring the interdict, for the interdict protected only those who had possession and lost it, not those who were simply not admitted to possession.[80] The action would have been known to Englishmen who studied Roman law in the late twelfth century; the *Liber Pauperum* contains several extracts relating to *unde vi*.

All the Roman possessory interdicts share a common assumption: that a plaintiff seeking to recover property should claim possession first before any further proceedings take place.[81] A plaintiff who lost a suit brought under one of the interdicts could subsequently bring a *rei vindicatio*. Meant to be heard first, the possessory action was not necessarily the final word.

Canon law eventually developed counterparts to the Roman possessory interdicts. By the end of the twelfth century, the canonists would create an action similar to the Roman interdict *unde vi*, allowing a clerk who was violently ejected from his benefice to find a remedy.[82] In time, this canon law action would evolve into something later referred to as the *actio spolii*, which was eventually available to laymen as well as clerks.[83] In Maitland's view, the *actio spolii* was the inspiration for the English assize of novel disseisin, because both actions protected the possessor of property against despoliation regardless of whether he had a claim to ownership.[84] Maitland also attached some significance in the assize of novel disseisin to the phrase *iniuste et sine iudicio*, which he claimed pointed to canon law origins.[85] W. S. Holdsworth, in his multivolume history of English law, adopted Maitland's view.[86] Maitland had been careful to point out that although the assize of novel disseisin was influenced by the canon law, it was not identical to the canon law action.[87] Even so, the link Maitland drew between the two institutions was strong.

Maitland's theory went unchallenged for decades, until H. G. Richardson and G. O. Sayles argued that the assize of novel disseisin cannot have been based directly on the *actio spolii*. The canon law *actio spolii* had not evolved in time to influence the assize in 1166; in fact, the term *actio spolii* was not even known in the Middle Ages.[88] Instead the medieval term, referring to the first word of two canons in Gratian's *Decretum*, was *condictio ex canone Redintegranda*.[89] The canonists' *condictio ex canone Redintegranda*, as far as has been determined, was first mentioned by Sicard of Cremona in his *Summa* written around 1179–82,[90] several years after the development of the assize of novel disseisin. Even at that stage, it is not clear exactly what the *condictio* protected or who could avail themselves of it.[91] Only after 1215, when canon 39 of the Fourth Lateran Council gave the dispossessed plaintiff a cause of action against third parties, did the canonists begin to elaborate on the significance of the *condictio ex canone Redintegranda*.[92] The conciliar canon, which expressly contradicted the "rigor of the civil law," forced the commentators to explain the difference between *redintegranda* and the new action apparently created by the council.[93]

That the *actio spolii* did not exist in the mid-twelfth century, however, does not mean that the basic idea behind it was unknown to canon law at that time. Since the days of the False Decretals attributed to Pseudo-Isidore, which were composed in the ninth century by an unknown author or authors, the canon law had recognized two relevant principles regarding bishops. Any bishop who had been despoiled must be restored, and a bishop who has been despoiled must have his property restored before answering charges.[94] The (forged) papal letters stating these principles were collected in Gratian's *Decretum*,[95] copies of which would have been available in England by 1166.[96] Raoul van Caenegem links these principles with the old Germanic idea of *gewere*, or "peaceful and actual enjoyment of any right," and argues that the *condictio ex canone Redintegranda* drew on this older concept, expanding it in canon law to cover all persons.[97] However, the notion that possession must be protected against despoliation also has an obvious parallel in Roman law.

During the mid-twelfth century, scholars in the Roman law tradition began to compile procedural treatises known as *ordines iudiciorum*. One of the earliest of these, which was written in England by an unknown author sometime between 1140 and 1170, is known as *Ulpianus de edendo*.[98] Organized according to the titles of Justinian's *Code,* this early *ordo* contains some discussion of ownership and possession and the procedural advantage of the latter. Discussing the procedure to be followed in property disputes, for example, the author quotes without attribution CJ 4.19.2, a rescript of Emperor Caracalla from the *Code* title *De probationibus.* This text explains that the possessor is not charged with the burden of proving that the property belongs to him, for if the other party defaults, the possessor will retain the ownership ("nec enim possessori incumbit necessitas probandi, eas ad se pertinere, cum te cessante in probatione dominium apud eum remaneat").[99] That the author of *Ulpianus de edendo* was familiar with this passage indicates that he understood the basic concepts of ownership and possession, even if he avoided a detailed description of the relevant actions in Roman law.[100] If the *ordo* dates to the mid-twelfth century, moreover, the teaching contained in Vacarius's *Liber Pauperum* may have been current in England long before he completed his own treatise.

The distinction between proprietary and possessory actions appears more regularly and in greater detail in procedural *ordines* by the 1180s. The *Summa Quicumque vult* of Johannes Bassianus, dating to around 1185, describes separate forms for actions *in rem* and possessory actions.[101] Johannes explicitly compares his *in rem* formula to the Roman *rei vindicatio* and, as in Roman law, gives separate forms for actions for recovering and retaining possession. The same may be said of the *Summa* of Ricardus Anglicus, and according to Wahrmund's edition, the passage in question appears in a version of the text that scholars now believe to have been composed in England before 1190.[102] An Anglo-Norman school of canonists was producing a number of works devoted to Roman and canonical procedure in the late twelfth century,[103] and Ricardus's work should be assigned to this category. European canonists of that period were beginning to internalize property concepts from Roman law, and the use of those concepts in English *ordines* could have had a particularly strong impact on canonists in England.

Although canon law texts from the twelfth century drew a sharp distinction, as in Roman law, between ownership and possession, canonists would eventually develop a concept that complicated matters somewhat: namely, the *ius ad rem.* This doctrine gave a clerk initially presented to a benefice (or elected to an office) a right to claim that benefice or office if another clerk was subsequently instituted or confirmed in his place. The extent to which the *ius ad rem* departed from Roman law ideas concerning ownership and possession, however, is controversial.

The concept *ius ad rem* first appears in canon law sources in the apparatus *Animal est substantia,* dating from between 1206 and 1210.[104] Discussing the effects of the election of a bishop, the author reports that the bishop-elect has no *ius in re* (right in the thing) by virtue of the election until he is confirmed, but he has a *ius ad rem petendam* (right to seek the thing).[105] The anonymous author seems to have drawn this conclusion on the basis of the 1204 decretal *Pastoralis,* in which Innocent III expressed a similar idea, although not the actual term *ius ad rem,* in the advowson context.[106] Dealing with a situation where a lay patron presented two successive priests to the bishop for a single benefice, and only the second was confirmed, Pope Innocent determined that the second candidate would retain possession, but the bishop was required to offer an equivalent but different benefice to the first clerk.[107] The following year, in the decretal *Cum Bertholdus,* the pope went further and allowed a clerk presented by the true patron to reclaim a benefice from a clerk presented by a false patron, even though the latter clerk was in possession.[108]

Because later canonists maintained that the *ius ad rem petendam* was a right to seek institution or confirmation to an office, they had difficulty reconciling *Cum Bertholdus* with *Pastoralis* and could not easily explain why the clerk in *Cum Bertholdus* was able to unseat the possessor, while the clerk in *Pastoralis* was not. In his apparatus on the *Compilatio Tertia,* completed around 1216, Johannes Teutonicus offered the view that either the possessor in *Cum Bertholdus* had failed to raise the defense, or the other clerk in that case had brought an action merely as a *procurator in rem suam:* that is, as the assignee of someone else's claim, presumably that of the bishop.[109] Johannes's explanation, which would be adopted by Tancred around the year 1220,[110] suggests that canonists writing in the early thirteenth century were not certain that the *ius ad rem* gave a direct right against third parties in possession of the thing claimed, the feature that has led some to characterize *ius ad rem* as a concept midway between a personal and a real right.[111] In any event, if such an intermediary concept did develop, it did not emerge until the pontificate of Innocent III, after all three of the principal English advowson writs had been created.

In the late twelfth century, therefore, the Roman concepts of ownership and possession were emphasized in texts known in England and were not yet muddled by any canonistic theories that would later develop concerning the *ius ad rem*. Moreover, the distinction between possession and ownership is evident not only in Roman and canon law academic writings from the second half of the twelfth century but also in court cases from the same period.[112] The evidence has been discussed by Mary Cheney and others,[113] but it is worth reviewing. Court cases and papal decretals show that ideas being discussed among scholars were also playing out in practice, especially the notion that a possessory suit should be brought first before claiming ownership.

A priest who claimed a benefice before an ecclesiastical tribunal was likely to sue first for possession before claiming ownership. A certain Alan, in a lawsuit held in the court of Archbishop Theobald of Canterbury (who died in 1161), sought a benefice of which he had allegedly been despoiled. John of Salisbury wrote a letter to the pope on behalf of Archbishop Theobald, noting that Alan initially sued by a possessory (*possessorio*) action, but when this claim appeared to be barred by prior judgment, he dropped his possessory suit and brought a proprietary claim (*petitorium*), arguing that he had been the rector in the time of an earlier bishop and had proved this in court.[114] The discussion of the case clearly distinguishes between possessory and proprietary claims and shows that a plaintiff was likely to start with a possessory claim.

Another case, heard between 1154 and 1161, shows that the disposition of a possessory action was understood not to preclude a subsequent proprietary action. A certain Peter claimed possession of lands pertaining to the archbishop's manor of Wimbledon and Barnes. Although the case did not involve a benefice, King Henry ordered that the dispute was to be decided before the archbishop. Without mentioning inheritance or fee, Peter claimed seisin on the basis that his father had possessed the land on the day Henry I died ("dictus Petrus seisinam prefate terre quia eam pater suus ut dicebat die qua rex H. primus obiit possederat . . . postularet, nulla tamen habita mentione hereditatis uel feodi"). Since Peter offered no proof that the land was held heritably, he was denied seisin, but the question of right was reserved.[115] Peter was told that he could bring a subsequent action concerning the right, suggesting that the possessory suit was considered to be preliminary in nature.

The canon law rule that an individual despoiled of a benefice had to be restored to possession before further proceedings took place would become the basis for the *condictio ex canone Redintegranda* and was known in England in the second half of the twelfth century. A decretal of Pope Eugenius dated February 5, 1152, for example, orders the bishop of Hereford to restore certain property to a certain Henry, reserving the cause concerning the ownership (*causa proprietatis*) for the monks.[116] Likewise, a decretal of Alexander III addressed to the bishop of Worcester and dating to the period from 1164 to 1179 orders the restoration of a certain clerk to the possession of a benefice from which he had been despoiled. Once possession has been restored, the rival clerk would be allowed to institute an action concerning the ownership.[117]

The notion that the question of possession should be decided first had been a working assumption of the papal court since the 1140s, if not earlier. For example, a decretal of Pope Eugenius III dated January 16, 1146, orders the bishops of Angoulême and Limoges to put certain clerks back into possession (*in possessione*) of a church and allows them to bring an action concerning the ownership (*causam de proprietate*).[118] A similar order was given in September 1146 to the bishop of Perigord.[119] These decretals use technical Roman law terms, now part of Romano-canonical learning.

Notions of *proprietas* and *possessio* affected not only churchmen but also powerful laymen who became involved in ecclesiastical litigation. Reginald Earl of Cornwall became involved in a dispute in the mid-twelfth century over the church of Hinton, of which the earl claimed the advowson. As recorded in a letter of Theobald to the pope drafted by John of Salisbury, a clerk named Ernald claimed the church by presentation of a certain knight. The earl had apparently dispossessed the clerk but was persuaded to grant restitution on condition that he might be able to bring a proprietary claim (*petitorium*).[120] Laymen who sued in the church courts would have understood that possession must first be restored before any dispute concerning ownership could proceed. If they did not understand this in the beginning, the ecclesiastical court would teach them the lesson.

King Henry II was the nephew of Reginald. As Cheney explains, the king was expected to understand the distinction between proprietary and possessory suits.[121] This is clear from a report sent by a panel of ecclesiastical judges convened at Henry's command to resolve a dispute between the abbot of Saint Vincent and the bishop of Llandaff over the church of Saint Cadoc of Caerleon. In the report, which probably dates to between 1155 and 1157, John, bishop of Worcester, explains that he and his fellow judges decided, notwithstanding pending appeals to the pope and the king, to receive the abbot's proof, "both because it was only concerned with possession [super sola possessione fiebat] and because it was produced for the third time at great expense and trouble."[122] As seen by the reference to *sola possessione*, possessory actions were considered to be distinct and preliminary; they could be followed by a proprietary action. The bishop expected the king, to whom the report was addressed, to understand that.

Such references in cases and papal decretals to proprietary and possessory actions suggest that Richardson and Sayles were too quick to dismiss the possibility of canon law influence on the assize of novel disseisin. Even if the *condictio ex canone Redintegranda* was not created until the 1180s, canon law possessory actions were evidently available in England, by the 1150s if not earlier, to restore dispossessed persons to their property. Whether these actions inspired the assize of novel disseisin is another question, but the fact that the *condictio* was created after the assize should not be taken to rule out the possibility of influence.[123]

Cheney, in her article on possessory and proprietary concepts in twelfth-century English ecclesiastical litigation, concludes that it was the "example and pressure of the papal court" that spread notions of *proprietas* and *possessio* among the English prelates.[124] But that conclusion prompts the question of how the distinction became part of the parlance of the papal court. One suspects that the writings of academic jurists had some effect on the development of this distinction in practice. Some of the pope's advisers might have had training in Roman law. At the least, the development in practice of possessory and proprietary concepts was consistent with the contemporary theoretical development of the same ideas. As Cheney notes, "There seems to be no doubt that the concept of possession was revived as a result of the academic study of Roman Law in the early twelfth century in Italy."[125]

It is clear that the revived study of the *Corpus Iuris Civilis* had an impact on what was happening in ecclesiastical courts. This leads back to the question of whether the revival of Roman law influenced the formation of the English common law, either directly or (more likely) indirectly through the example of the ecclesiastical actions. To this question I shall now turn.

The Land Writs

In his groundbreaking work on the early history of the common law, Maitland identified the writ of right for land and the assize of novel disseisin as, respectively, the proprietary action and the possessory action, using terms expressed in *Bracton* and implied by *Glanvill*.[126] Later scholarship has focused on these two writs as possible evidence for—or against— a Roman or canon law influence on the early English law of property. To evaluate whether the early common law distinguished between ownership and possession, therefore, it is best to start with these two writs.

By the time *Glanvill* was written, the English common law in fact contained two principal writs of right for land. The first, the writ *precipe*, was discussed in chapter 2. The second, the writ of right patent, was directed to a particular lord and commanded that lord to "without delay . . . hold full right" with respect to a certain parcel of land that A claimed to hold of the lord and of which B was deforcing A.[127] Should the lord fail to do right to the plaintiff, the plaintiff could have the case removed to the county court by a procedure known as tolt.[128] From there, the plaintiff could have the case transferred to the royal court by a writ of *pone*.[129] The essential concept was that when a lord failed to do justice to one of his tenants, the king could be asked to intervene.[130]

As discussed earlier, the *precipe* writ for land, like its counterpart for advowsons, could involve a slow and cumbersome procedure, with multiple summonses and essoins.[131] If a writ of right patent was transferred to the royal courts, the defendant would have the same opportunities for delay. The dilatory nature of these writs, together with the unseemliness of trial by battle, may have prompted the invention of the assize of novel disseisin, the most important legal innovation of Henry II's reign.[132] This conclusion, however, must be qualified by the fact that our knowledge of the procedure followed in the action of right comes from the end of the reign of Henry II, and the assize is likely to have developed earlier.

Glanvill provides the earliest evidence for the form of the writ of novel disseisin, in which the king informs the sheriff of A's complaint that B "unjustly and without a judgment, disseised him of his free tenement, in such a vill, since my last voyage into Normandy." After a restoration of the chattels, the tenement would be viewed by "twelve free and lawful men of the neighbourhood," called the recognitors. Either B or his bailiff would also be attached to hear the recognition.[133] No essoins were allowed, and the assize could proceed even if the defendant failed to appear.[134]

Maitland believed that the assize was created by a royal ordinance around 1166, possibly at the council held in Clarendon early that year.[135] From 1166 onward, the pipe rolls record amercements "for disseisin" against "the king's assize" or "the king's writ."[136] It is nonetheless possible that the ordinance was made before 1166, possibly as early as 1155.[137] It could be that the initial ordinance established only a "criminal" offense, and the regular "civil" remedy developed later, perhaps soon before the writ appears in *Glanvill*.[138] Even the basic notion that the assize was created by a formal act of legislation is not universally accepted.[139] Nevertheless, the assize as it appears in *Glanvill* looks like a "deliberately co-ordinated design," and since no evidence exists of a later enactment, the most likely inference is that *Glanvill* preserves the original form of the assize from 1155 to 1166.[140]

Raoul van Caenegem, in his study of the history of English writs from the Norman Conquest to *Glanvill*, stressed the continuity between early writs issued by all the Norman kings before 1166 and the eventual development of the assize of novel disseisin.[141] The Norman kings, through these writs, ordered individuals to restore disseised property to other individuals or religious houses who had complained to the king about the disseisin. However, Doris Stenton has pointed out that none of the writs reprinted by Van Caenegem was returnable: the king did not appoint a day for the hearing of the action, indicate how it should be dealt with, or instruct the recipient to "send men to view the land at issue and appear when the case is heard with the summoners and the writ."[142] These were all key features of the fully developed writ of novel disseisin.

Whether the assize of novel disseisin was simply a logical extension of a century-old royal tradition of interfering in disputes over seisin, or the result of brilliant thinking throughout "many night watches," as stated in *Bracton*,[143] the dispute resolution mechanism that it created would have a powerful effect on subsequent English legal history. The development of the assize of novel disseisin in the mid-twelfth century was an eventful step forward for English law.

Maitland, as discussed earlier, believed that the assize of novel disseisin was inspired by canon law and thus indirectly by the Roman interdict *unde vi*. He suggested that the assize originated as a preliminary action to decide who would be the defendant in a subsequent action of right. Maitland envisioned a contest over a particular tenement between independent claimants, one of whom "turns out" the other to secure the advantages of being the defendant in the proprietary suit.[144] The claimants in Maitland's account need not have had anything in common other than a desire to occupy the same property. Maitland did not envision that the assize had any tenurial dimension.

Milsom's work, particularly his *Legal Framework of English Feudalism*, offered a very different view of the origins of the assize of novel disseisin. Acknowledging that the assize later came to be used to protect landowners against ordinary wrongdoers, Milsom argued that its original purpose was to safeguard against abuses of seigneurial power.[145] Rather than view the plaintiff and the defendant as random parties or neighbors involved in a dispute as social equals, Milsom thought that the defendant was likely to be the plaintiff's lord, called to task for disseising him without following the proper procedures.[146] According to Milsom, the assize must be viewed within a feudal framework.

Milsom found support for his understanding of the assize of novel disseisin partly in the wording of the assize and partly in the early plea rolls. First, Milsom contends that the phrasing of the assize shows its tenurial context. Under English law and custom, the lord could lawfully distrain a tenant for failure to do the services due to his tenement, provided that the lord obtained a judgment against the tenant in the seigneurial court: hence the requirement that the disseisin be done without a judgment was not mere surplusage when applied to the lord.[147] From Milsom's perspective, the reference to chattels also makes perfect sense: since the lord would have taken them away in distraining the plaintiff, the sheriff could reasonably be told to have them put back.[148] Milsom also attaches some significance to the reference to the defendant's bailiff, since a lord was likely to have such a local agent.[149]

Milsom also had a novel explanation for the writ of right patent. Milsom saw the writ of right as growing out of the settlement in 1153 between King Stephen and the future Henry II. Chronicle evidence suggests, according to Milsom, that this settlement contained a general provision that those who were disinherited during the Anarchy should be restored to the rights that they held under Henry I.[150] Milsom did not think that the writ reflected a general royal policy of enforcing the customs of inheritance.[151] However, as an accidental consequence of the writ, issues that were formerly the sole province of the seigneurial courts were taken to a new, abstract level. Before the writ of right was created, Milsom explained, a decision by the lord to accept A's homage rather than B's was final; there was no appeal. By giving the descendants of B the power to undo the original decision by invoking the authority of the king's court, the writ of right changed everything.[152]

Robert Palmer has offered a somewhat different account of the writ of right, although he also connects the writ to the 1153 settlement. In Palmer's view, the compromise protected any person who took land away from a tenant during the Anarchy, but when that person died, the tenant who had been dispossessed during the Anarchy had the right to be accepted by the lord. The dispossessed tenant needed the writ of right to make his claim.[153] Accepting that the assize of novel disseisin did not become a private right of action until shortly before *Glanvill*, Palmer concurs with Milsom that the early common-law remedies cannot be characterized as proprietary or possessory in nature.[154]

As Milsom showed, the earliest plea rolls provide some examples of cases where an assize of novel disseisin was brought by a tenant against his lord. In some cases, we may find a defendant pleading that the assize ought not to proceed because he lawfully distrained the plaintiffs by judgment in his court for failure to render services.[155] In other cases, we see A bringing a writ of novel disseisin against B concerning certain land and a writ *de homagio capiendo* (for taking homage) against B concerning land in the same place. In Hilary Term 1199, for example, Absalom son of Absalom brought a writ *de homagio capiendo* concerning land in Cambridge against Bernard Grim, thus signaling that Absalom claimed Bernard as his lord.[156] Later that year, Absalom sued the same defendant concerning land in the same county by an assize of novel disseisin.[157] In 1198 we find Robert son of Osbert bringing an assize of novel disseisin against Walter of Hereford concerning a free tenement in Kingswood; five years later, Robert of Kingswood, probably the same Robert, is bringing a writ *de homagio capiendo* against the same Walter concerning land in the same vill.[158] In Michaelmas Term 1201, Robert de Heriet can be seen bringing both the assize and a writ *de homagio capiendo* against Henry de Braibof.[159] In all these cases, the plaintiff is likely to have been the defendant's tenant.

Other scholars have challenged the inferences Milsom drew from the wording of the assize.[160] Even Milsom conceded that the assize of novel disseisin was not brought exclusively by tenants against their lords, at least by the time of *Glanvill*.[161] In his treatment of purprestures, or encroachments, the *Glanvill* author discusses the possibility that the assize could be brought against one's lord or one's neighbor.[162] The existence of a few cases in which the plaintiff's lord is clearly the defendant does not necessarily prove that the lord was the usual defendant.

In an essay published in the mid-1980s, Mary Cheney argued that litigation between Archbishop Thomas Becket and the royal courtier John Marshal in 1164 may help to explain the development of the assize of novel disseisin.[163] Canon law obliged bishops and abbots to recover lost ecclesiastical possessions, and both Theobald and Thomas Becket worked vigorously in the mid-twelfth century to recover properties they claimed on behalf of Canterbury that been lost during the civil war of Stephen's reign. Around 1164, Becket succeeded in expelling John Marshal from one such estate. In the ensuing litigation, Becket prevailed. One of Becket's biographers noted that Marshal "had no right as the law then stood" (nullo iure munitus, quod tunc lex erat).[164] The comment's phrasing is noteworthy: "as the law then stood" seems to imply that something had changed.

The essence of Cheney's argument is that the 1164 litigation may have been the proximate cause for the assize of novel disseisin. Cheney notes that, during the 1140s, grants of papal privileges often contained a novel clause specifically authorizing English bishops to recover lost church lands, many of which had fallen into lay hands during the chaos of King Stephen's reign.[165] If the church was successfully disseising lay tenants of their land in the mid-twelfth century, that might explain the lack of resistance on the part of English lay magnates to the creation of the assize.

Mike Macnair has offered a somewhat different explanation for the development of the assize of novel disseisin than Cheney, but one that also depends on conflicts between churchmen and laymen over property.[166] As Macnair points out, before the assize, the main tool for deciding property disputes was the writ of right. The church no doubt viewed trial by battle as an unacceptable means of dispute resolution. The church was accustomed to proof by witnesses and documents, but an investigation of that nature would have been unacceptable to the king and to the laymen involved in the disputes (not to mention resource intensive). The assize of novel disseisin, with its trial by recognitors, could reflect a grand compromise between the church and its lay opponents.[167]

If the theories of Cheney and Macnair are on target, then there could be a real possibility of Roman or canon law influence on the assize of novel disseisin. By putting pressure on the king and his advisers to create a new action, church prelates might have drawn on ideas from Romano-canonical learning, which they were applying in their own courts.[168] They might have asked for something similar to the interdict *unde vi* or another possessory remedy being used in the church courts at the time.

Sutherland saw several similarities between the interdict *unde vi* and the assize of novel disseisin.[169] Both embodied the principle that putting the possessor of property out by force, and thus breaching the peace, violated the law.[170] Both applied to land and buildings but not to movables. Both proscribed not merely violence but all force. To prevail at either the assize or the interdict, the plaintiff was required to have been in actual possession. Just as a slave could not bring the interdict, so a villein could not bring the assize. However, a slave's master could bring the interdict if a third party evicted the slave, as the villein's lord could bring the assize if a third party disseised the villein. Under either Roman or English law, the party who failed could bring a countersuit in which he might get the land back. Finally, and most importantly, both the interdict and the assize provided that the prevailing party would get not only the land but the movable property on it together with the income the land had produced during the wrongful occupancy, and both provided that the one dispossessed or disseised could recover possession by suing the original ejector as sole defendant regardless of who currently possessed the land.[171]

Sutherland also noted differences between the assize and the interdict.[172] The heir of a man who had been ejected by force could bring the interdict, but the assize applied only between the original disseisor and his victim.[173] To summon the assize, the disseisin had to have occurred since some fixed event such as the king's last crossing to Normandy, whereas the interdict, at least by the time of Justinian, had no equivalent limitation.[174] Unlike the interdict, the assize protected against nuisances and applied to certain incorporeal property such as rights of common pasture. The interdict did not involve a jury of twelve recognitors like the assize. Most significantly, the assize did not borrow the technical language of Roman law.

These differences notwithstanding, Sutherland reached the conclusion that the interdict "guided the development of the assize."[175] Milsom disagreed completely.[176] Following Milsom's view, if the assize really was directed initially against lords who disseised their tenants without a judgment, then it is hard to draw a parallel with the Roman interdict *unde vi*. The feudal lord-tenant relationship was uniquely medieval; no counterpart existed in Roman law. Milsom's understanding of the assize simply does not admit the possibility of Roman influence.

The Writ of Right and Darrein Presentment

So long as scholarly attention remains focused on the assize of novel disseisin and the writ of right, it is unlikely that we will make much progress in evaluating whether or how the early common law incorporated concepts of ownership and possession from Romano-canonical learning. If the distinction between these two writs can be explained, as Milsom did, in terms of the tenurial direction of the dispute, then it is hard to call one possessory and the other proprietary. However, ideas of ownership and possession derived from Romano-canonical learning were clearly being put into practice in the English ecclesiastical courts by the mid-twelfth century. The key question is whether the common-law property scheme as a whole, not just two writs concerning land, bears a similarity to the scheme of Romano-canonical learning. To address that question, it is necessary to look at the advowson writs, beginning with the writ of right of advowson and the assize of darrein presentment, because those writs by definition applied to churches, not land.

As discussed earlier, the assize of darrein presentment could not provide a final answer about who had the superior right to the advowson.[177] Only the writ of right might offer the successful plaintiff assurance that the matter would not be taken up again in the king's court. Cases from the plea rolls demonstrate that an action of darrein presentment, once concluded, could be followed by a writ of right.[178] For example, in Trinity Term 1200, John Chaplain brought an assize of darrein presentment against the abbot of Saint Augustine and the prior of Leeds concerning the church of Preston, in Kent. The entry is fragmentary, but it appears that John prevailed.[179] Three years later, John brought a writ of right against the abbot concerning the advowson of the same church, and the abbot put himself on the grand assize.[180] John apparently was not satisfied with the judgment awarding him the next presentation and wanted to settle the matter once and for all by writ of right.

The party who prevailed at the assize might subsequently bring an action of right to obtain a permanent judgment. However, it was more common for the party who lost at the assize to bring the subsequent suit, because the losing party had more to gain by continuing to litigate.[181] For example, in Michaelmas Term 1200, John of Langdon brought an assize of darrein presentment against Robert of Sutton and Alberic de Ver. According to the jurors, Payn de Schenefeld presented the last parson. Robert responded that the church was appurtenant to a fee that he held of John son of Payn.[182] Robert recovered his seisin.[183] Two years later, we can see John of Langdon back in court, suing Robert by writ of right.[184] The assize settled the question of the last presentation, but John could pursue the matter further by claiming his right. Other examples may be cited where the parties are reversed in the subsequent action of right.[185] Losing a darrein presentment action did not necessarily end the story, but in most cases the issue of the last presentation was decided first. Indeed, by 1250, it was accepted that a party who brought a writ of right of advowson ipso facto conceded that the defendant had seisin, so that if the plaintiff died while the plea was pending, no one whose claim depended on the presentation of that plaintiff could prevail in a subsequent assize of darrein presentment.[186] This rule, however, may not have been established until the latter part of the thirteenth century, given that, in the reign of King John, a party like John Chaplain who succeeded in the assize might choose to bring a subsequent writ of right.[187]

The double process afforded by the combination of the assize of darrein presentment and the writ of right hearkens back to the Roman law double process by possessory interdicts and *rei vindicatio.* Just as the party who had possession at the time of the lawsuit prevailed at *utrubi* or *uti possidetis,* so the party who had presented the most recent parson would prevail at the assize of darrein presentment. If the defendant conceded that the plaintiff presented the last parson, whether the presentation was unjust was irrelevant,[188] as with the interdicts. Once the issue of seisin was decided, the losing party would have recourse to the writ of right. In the meantime, however, the party who prevailed in the darrein presentment action could have a suitable candidate instituted as parson. It was much better to be in seisin than to be the plaintiff in an action of right.

Advowsons, unlike land, were not held "of" a lord, although they could be appurtenant to land that was so held. The patron did not owe any feudal service with respect to the advowson, which he held in his own right. Lawsuits over advowsons had a horizontal dimension: they were not "upward looking" or "downward looking." In the advowson context, double process cannot be explained as reflecting a feudal framework. Milsom's explanation for the development of two separate land writs, therefore, does not account for the parallel development of separate writs for advowsons.

Apart from the basic similarity between the interaction of the English advowson writs and Roman double process, we can also point to ways in which the advowson writs were different.[189] One possible counterargument derives from the fact that a donee was able to block the assize of darrein presentment by asserting his gift, despite not having seisin.[190] This may suggest that darrein presentment was not a wholly possessory action. However, this defense applied only when some connection existed between the donor and the plaintiff. The defense seems to have been designed primarily to remedy the injustice that would result if the plaintiff had been allowed to repudiate an ancestor's charter while at the same time recovering the advowson on the basis of that ancestor's presentation. Granting the donee a defense when the plaintiff was the heir of the donor would simply allow the donee to compel the completion of the gift. Such a defense did not entail the conclusion that the donee had a claim to ownership or that the assize had a proprietary component.

The limited nature of the defense of gift is reinforced by the rule of subsequent presentation.[191] As I discuss in more detail in the next chapter,[192] by the operation of this rule, when a person gives an advowson away but later (before the donee has a chance to present) presents to the bishop another clerk who is then instituted as parson, the gift of the advowson is null and void because of the donor's subsequent presentation. The rule is understandable if one assumes that the donee originally had neither ownership nor possession, but something like an *in personam* claim, which could be invoked against the donor or his heir provided that there had been no revocation of the gift. That does not mean that the assize of darrein presentment was really meant to decide right rather than seisin.

Thus the defense of gift does not meaningfully distinguish the assize of darrein presentment from the Roman interdicts. However, there are other important differences. First, while the main purpose of the interdict *uti possidetis* was to set the stage for a subsequent *rei vindicatio*, the assize of darrein presentment settled an urgent question about the next presentation and would not necessarily be followed by a dispute about the right. The cases cited earlier,[193] where a darrein presentment action was followed by a writ of right, are the exception rather than the rule.[194] A similar argument has been made regarding the assize of novel disseisin, which was not usually followed by an action of right,[195] and that reasoning may apply equally well here. Moreover, if one accepts the theory that the assize of darrein presentment was invented in response to the Third Lateran Council, then the assize might have been intended primarily as a substitute for, and not a complement to, the writ of right. Nevertheless, even if litigants disappointed in darrein presentment actions did not always avail themselves of the writ of right, the fact is that they could do so if they wished.

The assize of darrein presentment differed from the interdict *uti possidetis* in other ways.[196] Unlike the interdict, the assize of darrein presentment did not prevent the use of force, and one party in the assize was clearly plaintiff and the other clearly defendant, in contrast to the interdict. The assize did not include the interdict's requirement that possession be *nec vi nec clam nec precario*, although the assize's requirement that the presentation must be made in time of peace might be seen as analogous.[197] However, perhaps the most telling difference is that the text of the assize does not refer to either seisin or possession and does not borrow the vocabulary from, or follow the phrasing of, the interdict, which uses the verb "to possess" twice.[198] It seems likely that a remedy modeled on Roman law would be framed in a similar way as the Roman remedy that inspired it, at least regarding the basic concept of possession. It is fair to say that if the king's advisers were attempting to replicate the Roman interdict, they knew how to cover their tracks.

The writ of right of advowson, like the assize of darrein presentment, departs significantly from Roman proprietary ideas. In cases brought by the former writ, the justices frequently held that it was not possible to acquire right by transfer without presenting a candidate. Only a presentation that occurred in the past would entitle a plaintiff to bring the writ of right, for one could not sue on the basis of "another's right given to one by charter and not one's own right."[199] Roman law as it was understood in the Middle Ages acknowledged the acquisition of ownership by delivery, provided that a sufficient *causa* existed, such as gift, dowry, or sale.[200] If the writ of right of advowson had been modeled on the Roman *rei vindicatio*, one would expect the justices to have treated delivery of the charter of gift as a transfer of ownership and allowed the donees to bring the writ. In any event, since the writ of right predates the assize of darrein presentment, it was clearly not conceived at the outset as part of a double process.

Being a patron with the right to an advowson meant that one or one's ancestors had successfully presented a candidate at a specified point in the past, possibly many years ago. To have seisin, by contrast, meant having made the last successful presentation. The distinction was a matter of degree. In short, the English concepts of right and seisin cannot be treated as literal equivalents of Roman ownership and possession. Sutherland noted that the Roman terms "were distinct juridical concepts with no middle ground between them, while seisin and right . . . were reference points in a continuum: the more recent and notorious facts, the relatively older and less well-known facts."[201] This statement aptly summarizes the difference between English right and seisin and Roman ownership and possession.

Nevertheless, the fact remains that the assize of darrein presentment introduced the possibility of something close to double process in the advowson context.[202] To say the least, the scheme in *Glanvill* would not have

struck a contemporary canonist or Romanist as peculiar. The twin features of Roman and canon law mentioned earlier—separate remedies for
ownership and possession and the idea that possession should be determined first—can arguably be seen in the English common law of advowsons, even if the form they took there differs from the form they took in
Romano-canonical learning. While it would perhaps be a stretch to assume that the royal advisers consulted books or teachers of Roman law in
designing the English legal system, it is likely that at least some of the
men responsible for the advowson writs knew about the sort of actions
that were being heard in ecclesiastical courts at the time.

The author of *Glanvill* uses the terms *proprietas* and *possessio* in introducing his discussion of the writs, categorizing the writ of right of advowson
as a plea *super proprietate* and darrein presentment as an action *super possessione.*[203] That an English author, at the end of the reign of Henry II,
would use such phrases in a treatise about the law of royal courts speaks
volumes about the ease with which ideas might have passed from
Romano-canonical learning into the early common law, although the extent those ideas trickled down to the courts is harder to prove.[204] Perhaps
more importantly, the count included in *Glanvill* for the writ of right of
advowson has the plaintiff describe himself or his ancestor as having
been "seised" (*saisatus*) of the advowson by virtue of a presentation,[205] using the word to mean something quite different from the acceptance of a
tenant by his lord.[206] We have no particular reason to think that *Glanvill*'s
wording of the plaintiff's count is not the original language, which could
predate the treatise itself by many years. Moreover, as discussed earlier,[207]
it is possible that the assize of darrein presentment evolved from earlier
ad hoc proceedings held to determine the issue of the last presentation.
As early as 1164–66, in the first of two writs concerning the church of
Swallowfield, Henry II could plausibly issue an order to "seise" monks of
a church (*saisas monachos . . . de ecclesia*) in a dispute that may have involved
an advowson rather than (or in addition to) land.[208] This writ could therefore mark a transitional stage in the understanding of seisin, in which a
concrete feudal concept began to acquire a more abstract meaning.

By the time of *Glanvill,* the English notion of seisin had already evolved
into something that could readily be analogized to Roman possession,
whether or not the Roman term was actually used. Seisin had become "a

condition rather than an event," a relationship between property and its owner independent of the feudal hierarchy.[209] The precise time at which this happened is difficult to pinpoint, and the causal connection to Romano-canonical learning is even harder to establish. At the least, however, *Glanvill*'s discussion of the advowson writs shows that Englishmen in the late twelfth century were using Romano-canonical learning to understand and interpret the major changes occurring in their own legal system.

Quare Impedit, Revisited

The basic distinction between *proprietas* and *possessio*, therefore, can arguably be seen in the first two advowson writs, translated into terms understood by Englishmen and brought into harmony with English ideas. The creation of the writ of *quare impedit,* however, dramatically altered the structure of the English common law of advowsons. Before *quare impedit,* two writs existed: one preliminary, the other final. One writ looked to the most recent presentation, while the other compared the right of the plaintiff to that of the defendant. With *quare impedit,* however, a third alternative emerged. The question, then, is how *quare impedit* fit into the picture, and in particular whether it can best be characterized as a possessory or proprietary action.

If we are to understand the assize of darrein presentment as a possessory (or quasi-possessory) action, then it is necessary to define "possession" of an advowson as the state of having presented the most recent parson, as that is the issue resolved by the assize. This "possession" did not necessarily imply "ownership," a concept that was not used or defined in the early common-law sources but could be seen as analogous to the *ius* at issue in the writ of right. It is clear, however, that a donee who had not yet presented a parson could not have the kind of "possession" that a successful party in a darrein presentment action typically had. If the donee had any claim, it would have to be "ownership," based on the superior claim of the donor, which passed to the donee through the gift.

It is true that, in the event both parties claimed by gift, a donee could still prevail as plaintiff in the assize of darrein presentment.[210] This is because the defendant, who was neither the last presenter nor his heir, would be forced to plead an exception to the assize, rather than simply al-

lowing the assize to proceed. The plaintiff would then be allowed a repli-
cation, and he would put the issue of the gift before the jury. By contrast,
in a *quare impedit* suit, the defendant could not simply plead the general issue, even if he or his ancestor had presented the last parson. Rather, he
would be forced to explain why he impeded—*quare impedit*—the plaintiff's
presentation. The plaintiff would then be given an opportunity to respond to the defendant's explanation, at which point the plaintiff could
raise the issue of the gift.

As discussed earlier with regard to the assize of darrein presentment,
the ability to plead a gift against the donor or his heir could merely constitute an *in personam* claim similar to a warranty of charter. In *quare impedit*
cases, however, the gift could be alleged even when no connection existed
between the defendant and the donor, at least by the mid-thirteenth century. This is shown by a 1242 *quare impedit* suit between the prior of the
hospital of Saint John of Jerusalem and Robert of Bingham, bishop of
Salisbury, over the church of Ansty, in Wiltshire. The prior alleged that
he was entitled to present because he received the advowson by gift from
Walter of Thurberville, former chief lord of the manor, who presented
the most recent parson, Roger of Salisbury. In response, the bishop said
that Roger was presented not by Walter but rather by his predecessor,
Herbert bishop of Salisbury, who presented "as the true patron and not
by reason of the [Third Lateran] Council." A jury was summoned to determine who presented Roger, Walter or bishop Herbert.[211]

What is interesting about the dispute over Ansty is that the plaintiff's
claim is wholly independent of the claim of the defendant. The prior is
not suing his donor or his donor's heir. Instead he is suing a third party
whose claim has nothing to do with the prior's. The prior's claim is *in rem;*
he is claiming a right good against all the world. Yet the prior has never
presented a parson, so he cannot have "possession." The prior is essentially asserting that he owns the advowson and should be able to claim his
right against a third party even though he has not presented. In other
words, the dispute is about ownership, not possession.

Had the prior brought an assize of darrein presentment rather than an
action of *quare impedit*, the bishop would have had the option of simply allowing the assize to proceed and leaving the jury to decide the general issue. This would have prevented the prior from being able to tell his story

about Walter of Thurberville and the gift he made to the hospital. If the assize jury determined on its own initiative that Walter of Thurberville presented the last parson, then the prior might have been allowed to make his argument about the gift after the jury's verdict.[212] The court, however, would not have framed the issue for the jury in such a way as to call attention to the possible presentation by Walter and subsequent gift, and the jurors might not discover these facts on their own (particularly if the last presentation was by reason of the council, or if many years had passed since the last presentation). By giving the prior an opportunity to plead the gift, the writ of *quare impedit* made it feasible for him to make what was essentially a claim of ownership.

The dispute over Ansty is somewhat unusual in that there is plainly no connection between the defendant and the donor. More commonly, both the plaintiff and the defendant claimed by gift from the same person or from related persons. In Hilary Term 1208, for example, the prior of Lenton sued the prior of the hospital of Saint John of Jerusalem to claim the advowson of Ossington (Notts). Both parties claimed by gift, the prior of Lenton by gift from Hugh de Burun, and the prior of the hospital by gift of Hugh's son Roger de Burun. The case turned on a claimed subsequent presentation by Roger.[213] Another early example appears in the roll from Michaelmas Term 1214, when the abbot of Saint Augustine's Abbey, Bristol, sued Guimar of Bassingbourne and his wife Alice over the advowson of Chishall (Essex). The abbot claimed by gift from Nicholas son of Robert, while Guimar and his wife claimed by gift from Roger son of Nicholas, whom they vouched to warrant.[214] Both of these cases show that, early on, the writ of *quare impedit* was understood to give a claim to the donee not just against the donor but against other persons who came into possession of the advowson. Although both parties in each case traced their claims to the same family, the rival donees were able to sue each other directly by *quare impedit*.

Nevertheless, although *quare impedit* could be used to make what were essentially proprietary claims, the successful party in a *quare impedit* suit could find his or her title challenged in a subsequent action of right. We see this in an early thirteenth-century lawsuit about the churches of Nocton and Dunston, in Lincolnshire. In 1204 the abbot of York brought a *quare impedit* suit against the prior of Nocton, who defended on the

grounds that he and his canons were parsons by gift of the former patron, Thomas de Aresci. The prior offered several charters in support of
his claim, and the bishop testified on his behalf, after which the abbot was
amerced for a false claim.[215] A year later, however, the abbot was back in
court, this time suing the prior by writ of right. The prior put himself on
the grand assize.[216] We have no indication that it was inappropriate for
the abbot to make the same claim by writ of right that he had already
unsuccessfully made by *quare impedit*. If *quare impedit* was a true proprietary
action, the prior would have had an easy defense against the abbot's second suit. Instead the prior allowed the action to be litigated a second
time, knowing that the earlier *quare impedit* judgment did not definitively
resolve the advowson dispute.

When we juxtapose the lawsuit concerning Nocton and Dunston
against the suit concerning Ansty, the basic paradox of *quare impedit* appears. *Quare impedit* was not like the Roman *rei vindicatio*, which settled the
issue of ownership once and for all. But neither was it like *uti possidetis* or
utrubi, since it could be used by someone who did not have possession, if
one defines possession as having presented the most recent parson. To fit
quare impedit into a Roman or canon law framework, it is necessary to
bend the concepts of ownership and possession to the breaking point. It
is easier to understand *quare impedit* if one envisions ownership and possession not as distinct concepts but as points along a spectrum, which, according to Sutherland, was the perspective of the early common law.[217]

The ambiguous position of the donee who has not presented a candidate did not escape the attention of the authors of *Bracton*, which says
that the donee has *quasi seisinam* or is *quasi in possessione*.[218] As discussed earlier, *quasi possessio* was used by the Roman jurists to denote the exercise of
a servitude by the grantee.[219] The Romans used this phrase, however, only
because in Roman law it was not possible truly to possess incorporeal
property. By contrast, it was possible in English law to have seisin of an
advowson by presenting a candidate. The seisin of a donee was *quasi* not
because the donee *could* not possess but because the donee *did* not possess.
A single act of presentation by the donee would change quasi seisin to
full seisin and right, and the royal courts could award seisin even to a donee who had not presented, which would allow the donee to make the
next presentation.[220] Thus "quasi seisin" in the advowson context appears

to have been something peculiarly English, a way of recognizing the claim of one who had neither possession nor the full right of ownership but could have both by presenting a candidate when the church next became vacant. Quasi seisin in the advowson context was a *tertium quid* between ownership and possession, something traditionally outside the thinking of Roman law.[221]

Although the state of quasi seisin was close to ownership in that it created a right good against the world, it also shared with possession the characteristic that it could be lost by another's act. As I explain in the next chapter,[222] the rule of subsequent presentation applied to *quare impedit* suits, so that a donee who sued by writ of *quare impedit* stood to lose if the defendant could show that the donor had subsequently presented a candidate who was instituted as parson. The act of subsequent presentation might therefore be analogized to a dispossession.

As Milsom has noted, the intermediate position occupied by *quare impedit* was similar to that of another category of actions in the early common law, namely, the writs of entry.[223] An early version of one of these writs, the writ of gage, appears in *Glanvill*, although it does not include a reference to the defendant's entry.[224] In the years after *Glanvill* was written, Chancery began to grant a variety of different writs in which the plaintiff alleged that the defendant had no entry except for some specified cause, such as holding over after a term had ended or entering into land that the plaintiff alienated during his minority.[225] Four of these were created before 1215: the writs of entry *sur disseisin, ad terminum qui preteriit, cui in vita,* and *in custodia*.[226] The writs of entry began with the formula used in writs of right, but they also had some of the qualities of writs of seisin and occupied a middle position between the petty assizes and the writ of right.[227]

Like the writs of entry, the writ of *quare impedit* highlights the differences between the early common law of property and that of Roman law, and to some extent that of contemporary canon law. If, as I have argued, the double process introduced by the assize of darrein presentment suggests possible inspiration from Romano-canonical learning, the development of *quare impedit* soon thereafter shows that the inspiration was limited. When the remedies of Roman or canon law would not serve the needs of medieval English society, the king and his advisers were quick to respond with new ideas that owed little to those older systems. To speak of inspiration is not to imply a wholesale borrowing of a prior system, nor does it imply that the product of that inspiration slavishly followed the earlier example.

If *quare impedit* drew on any contemporary ideas about ownership and possession, they were revolutionary new ideas, and different from those that English students were reading in the *Institutes* and *Liber Pauperum*.[228] *Bracton* may have borrowed Roman terminology to describe what he saw happening in the courts, but the English justices were not always thinking in Roman terms. After the creation of *quare impedit*, the donee had something that looks distinct from either ownership or possession: a right that is good against the world unless and until it is revoked by the act of someone else. Quasi seisin may not fit into Roman categories, but it made sense to the English justices, who seem to have wanted to give the donee a broad claim while allowing the donor to have a change of heart.

This picture suggests that the early common law had a sharper distinction between ownership and possession before the writ of *quare impedit* was invented. Given that the writ of *quare impedit* was probably created at the behest of religious houses, this raises a problem. Would the monasteries really have pushed for the creation of a third category between ownership and possession?

The answer to this question is likely to be no. Religious houses would likely have preferred to have a full right of ownership in their advowsons, so that a subsequent presentation by the donor would be irrelevant. They may have envisioned the writ of *quare impedit* as an expedited alternative to the writ of right, in which the issue would have been who had the right of ownership in the advowson. By making the writ of *quare impedit* semipossessory in nature and extending the rule of subsequent presentation to *quare impedit* suits (and then to actions of right), the royal justices were working out a compromise that was more acceptable to lay donors. In short, politics, not juristic thinking, may have produced the concept of quasi seisin.

To sum up, while the early common law of advowsons shows some similarities with Roman law, it appears in other ways to have been distinctly English. The assize of darrein presentment was very much like the Roman possessory interdicts, and the concept of seisin it protected was not entirely different from Roman possession, except insofar as the idea that one might have possession of a noncorporeal thing was a new development. It is possible that the royal advisers who devised the assize of darrein presentment were partially inspired by Roman ideas. Moreover, there is no uniquely feudal explanation for the development of two separate writs in the advowson context, as there may be with regard to land. At the same time, however, the writ of *quare impedit,* and the concept of quasi seisin it encapsulated, seems to be in conflict with the old Roman maxim that ownership has nothing in common with possession.

John Hudson has called the assize of novel disseisin "an outstandingly successful exercise not of legal transplant but of judicial bricolage."[229] In a similar way, the English law of advowsons may have borrowed from Roman law when Roman ideas served a useful purpose, but there was no wholesale incorporation of traditional Roman conceptions of ownership and possession in the advowson context. The creation of the writ of *quare impedit* is better understood in terms of the specific needs of English society at the time and the conflict between religious houses and laymen over the control of parochial appointments. In the next chapter, I examine in more detail how the royal justices developed a compromise to mediate that conflict in the thirteenth century.

CHAPTER FOUR

PLEADING AND PROOF

By the time of the earliest surviving plea rolls, the three main advowson writs had already been created. It was up to the justices to decide what rules of substantive law would apply to those writs and to preside over the pleading in court. In this chapter, I examine the development of the law of advowsons, including procedural law, in the late twelfth century and the early thirteenth. I focus on three aspects of that development: (1) how pleading worked in advowson cases; (2) how advowson donees, especially religious houses, protected their gifts; and (3) how courts evaluated troublesome charter evidence offered by the religious houses. Although the creation of the writ of *quare impedit* discussed in the previous chapter protected the interests of the religious houses, the royal justices eventually crafted rules regarding the admissibility of charter evidence, and the legal status of advowson gifts, that tended to undermine those interests and favor the lay lords. Thus the picture that emerges is one of judicial compromise in the broader dispute between the laity and the monasteries over the control of parish churches.

Claims and Procedure

Entries in the plea rolls relating to advowson disputes follow different formats depending on the type of writ used, and even entries corresponding to the same type of writ often vary according to the preferences of different clerks and changes in record-keeping practices over time.

In the late twelfth and early thirteenth centuries, plea roll entries relating to assizes of darrein presentment generally begin simply by stating the nature of the assize and naming the parties: nothing is said about the nature of the plaintiff's claim except that he "said it belonged to him" (dicit ad se pertinere). This is followed by the defendant's response, introduced by the stock phrase *qui* [that is, the defendant] *venit et dicit;* the defendant either concedes the assize or states some reason why it should not proceed to a verdict. After stating the defendant's response, the entry proceeds to recount the plaintiff's rejoinder, and so on until the pleading is finished.

Over the course of the thirteenth century, the standard formula for entries relating to darrein presentment changed. Beginning in the early 1230s, and more regularly by the end of that decade, one finds entries that begin by recording the basis for the plaintiff's claim.[1] In place of *qui venit et dicit,* we begin to find *et unde* [name of plaintiff] *dicit;* only after the basis for the plaintiff's claim is set forth does the entry give the defendant's response. This change is important, for entries following the later formula tend to provide more information about the facts of the case regardless of how the defendant chooses to answer.

As one would expect for the assize of darrein presentment, the most common basis offered for the plaintiff's claim is that some ancestor or predecessor presented the last parson, but another, more intricate basis might be offered. One of the most extreme examples of an elaborate claim in darrein presentment dates to Easter Term 1244. In that case, the plaintiff claimed as (1) the heir of (2) the person who purchased the estate and advowson from (3) the heir of (4) the person who purchased the estate and advowson from (5) the heir of (6) the ward of (7) the person who, as guardian, presented the last parson.[2] In other words, the claim involved five different individuals, two separate purchases, two deaths, and a guardianship intervening between the plaintiff and the individual in whose name the last parson was presented. Entries like these, made possible by the new formula in the plea rolls, give us some indication of just how complicated advowson disputes could be in the mid-thirteenth century.

It is possible that the change in formula for assizes of darrein presentment reflects a change in the way these cases were pleaded in court. Before the mid-thirteenth century, plaintiffs may not have been required to set forth the grounds for their case until the defendant had made his answer to the assize, and *Glanvill* does not mention any such requirement. It is also possible, however, that the royal clerks in the mid-thirteenth century simply began to record on the rolls what had long happened in court: that is, the plaintiff set forth the basis for his claim, and then the defendant made his answer.[3] Because no individual law reports survive from before the final years of Henry III, let alone yearbooks, it is difficult to say whether the change in formula reflects a change in how cases were actually being pleaded.[4]

In cases of *quare impedit*, from the time of the earliest surviving plea rolls, it was not unusual to give some indication of the basis for the plaintiff's claim before recording the defendant's response. The most common basis offered was that the advowson had been given to the plaintiff either by some ancestor or relative of the defendant[5] or by a third party.[6] In some cases, the plaintiff would assert that he or an ancestor or predecessor presented the last parson, although this was asserted as an initial claim less frequently in cases of *quare impedit* than in assizes of darrein presentment.[7] Other possible grounds for recovery in *quare impedit* were that the plaintiff purchased the advowson from a relative of the defendant[8] or of the person who presented the last parson;[9] the advowson pertains to the plaintiff's dower;[10] the plaintiff ought to present by reason of wardship;[11] the defendant leased the manor with the advowson to the plaintiff;[12] the plaintiff or his or her ancestor recovered the advowson by judgment;[13] the plaintiff ought to present by reason of an agreement with the defendant;[14] or an ancestor of the plaintiff was seised of the advowson in the time of Henry II.[15]

This last claim—that the plaintiff's ancestor was seised of the advowson during the reign of Henry II—was clearly modeled on the standard claim made by plaintiffs who brought a writ of right of advowson. A standard entry relating to a writ of right of advowson begins by naming the parties and stating that the plaintiff claims the advowson as his right and inheritance (or as his wife's right and inheritance) because a named ancestor or predecessor presented a named parson in the reign of a specified king. The entry further alleges that the presented parson was instituted by the bishop and subsequently received a certain amount of revenue (*expletia*) from the church.[16] If the presentation was made by an ancestor, the entry then traces the descent of the right of advowson from the ancestor down to the plaintiff or the person by whom he claims the advowson, and states that the plaintiff offered to prove his claim by the body of a certain champion.[17] If the plaintiff was the head of a religious house claiming through a predecessor, it was not necessary to recite the chain of office from the predecessor to the plaintiff.[18]

In most early thirteenth-century plea roll entries relating to writs of right, the king within whose reign the ancestor or predecessor is said to have presented a parson is named as Henry I[19] or Henry II.[20] By the third decade of the thirteenth century, a plaintiff might also claim seisin in the reign of Richard,[21] John,[22] or even Henry III,[23] although these later kings were not mentioned frequently until near the end of the reign of Henry III.[24] Occasionally an entry might record that a plaintiff claimed seisin at some point in the past without naming the king within whose reign a parson was allegedly presented.[25] Such entries, however, may simply reflect carelessness on the part of the royal clerk, who neglected to include the name of the king in whose reign the plaintiff claimed seisin.[26]

In some cases, particularly those brought by writ of *quare impedit,* the plaintiff's claim involved a gift from an ancestor of the defendant or from a third party. The plea roll entry might simply state that the plaintiff claimed the advowson as that which a specified donor gave him by a charter,[27] or the entry might record an allegation by the plaintiff that a specified donor was seised in the time of a particular king and the right descended to the plaintiff from the donee[28] or the donee gave the advowson to the plaintiff.[29] As discussed in the previous chapter, however, the justices generally did not allow a plaintiff to bring the writ of right based on the seisin of a donor who was not the ancestor of the plaintiff (or the predecessor in office, in the case of an abbot, prior, or bishop).[30] For the most part, the *ius* that was the subject of the writ of right was demonstrated by a successful presentation of a parson by an ancestor or predecessor at a definite moment in the past, within the reign of a specific king, followed by (if the presentation was by an ancestor) a clear chain of descent from that ancestor to the plaintiff.

Regardless of what type of writ was brought or whether the plea roll entry records the basis for the plaintiff's claim, the entry invariably will give the defendant's response, assuming that the defendant was present in court and did not have some procedural excuse for failing to answer the plaintiff's claim. Sometimes the defendant would simply concede the assize and put himself on the jury (in darrein presentment cases) or seek the grand assize regarding who had the greater right in the advowson (in cases brought by writ of right), and the pleading would conclude without further comment by the defendant. The defendant was not required to make a specific argument in response to the plaintiff's charge, and the royal clerks may not always have recorded those arguments that were made, except in suits brought by writ of *quare impedit,* where it was customary to note the defendant's explanation why he impeded the plaintiff's presentation or his statement that he claimed nothing in the advowson.[31]

Many defendants, however, chose to set forth their case by way of a specific response, or what would later be termed a special traverse. They could do so for a variety of reasons: the defendant's claim might be such that the recognitors might misunderstand the situation without hearing the defendant's side; the defendant might hope that the plaintiff would be forced to concede the matter; or the defendant might expect the justices to decide the case themselves, without involvement from the jury, after the defendant set forth his or her version of the facts. Specific responses by defendants appear in the plea rolls with some frequency, although it is by no means clear that the clerks recorded every such response.

In cases of darrein presentment or *quare impedit,* one of the most common responses offered by the defendant was that the church was not vacant. As discussed earlier,[32] both of these writs contained an assertion that the church was vacant, and it was therefore a valid response to say that the church was not vacant because it was currently occupied by a parson. If this was determined to be the case, the defendant would go without day, and the plaintiff would be amerced by the court. This may be referred to as the response of plenarty: the church is full (*plena*) because a parson currently holds it.

Although a claim of plenarty could be straightforward, it could also be more complex, involving a dispute over whether a priest currently associated with the church was in fact serving as parson or merely as vicar on behalf of some other person or entity. Cases involving a response of plenarty fall into two categories: those in which the defendant claimed that he (or his religious house) was parson, and those in which the defendant claimed that a third party was parson. In the former type of case, the defendant might or might not specify by whose presentation he claimed to be parson. In the latter type of case, the defendant would often assert that he presented the current parson himself. In cases of both kinds, the defendant might claim that the church in dispute was in fact a chapel pertaining to a mother church, and the parson of the mother church was, by virtue of his position, also parson of the chapel. Whether or not a particular church was "vacant," therefore, might turn on the relationship between the church in question and some other church or corporate body.

When the defendant was the prior or abbot of a religious house claiming to be parson of the church, the claim of plenarty sometimes went hand in hand with a claim that an ancestor of the plaintiff or a third party gave the advowson to the defendant. The defendant would generally produce multiple charters in support of such a claim, including, in many cases, the donor's charter of gift transferring the advowson from the donor to the defendant's religious house and a charter of the bishop attesting to the institution of the monks or canons as parson of the church by presentation of the donor. We find a typical example in a dispute from 1231 between Ralph Hamberd and the prior of Saint Fromund concerning the church of Shaw (Berks). Ralph asserted that he held the manor of Shaw with the advowson at farm from Philip III de Colombières,[33] whose grandfather Philip I de Colombières presented the last parson, Gervase. The prior responded that the church was not vacant because he was parson. The prior offered (1) a charter of Philip I attesting that he gave the church of Shaw to the prior of Saint Fromund in free and perpetual alms; (2) a charter of Jocelin de Bohun, bishop of Salisbury,[34] attesting that at the presentation of Philip I he received the monks of Saint Fromund into the parsonage of the church of Shaw and canonically instituted them as parsons; and (3) a charter of Richard of Dover, archbishop of Canterbury,[35] confirming the gift of the church. As to Gervase, the prior asserted that he was not parson but vicar, having been presented as vicar by the prior at Philip's petition and paying forty shillings a year to the prior as pension.[36]

It was not unusual, as in the dispute between Ralph and the prior, for a dispute to arise about whether an occupant of the church was the parson or a vicar. The defendant might allege that a former parson of the church became vicar when the defendant was instituted as parson. In 1214, for example, Robert of Middleton brought an assize of darrein presentment concerning the church of Milton Ernest (Beds), with one of the defendants being the prior of Beaulieu. The prior responded that the assize should not proceed because the church was not vacant; rather, he and his fellow monks were parsons by gift of Cecily of Middleton, grandmother of Robert.[37] The prior offered in court (1) Cecily's charter saying that, with her firstborn son's consent, she gave her right in the church of Milton to the priory; (2) a charter of Nicholas, archdeacon of Bedford, ratifying Cecily's donation, noting that Cecily presented the monks to him, and stating that Nicholas, the see of Lincoln being vacant, by his authority confirmed the monks in the church, and that the monks, at the archdeacon's request, conceded the vicarage to John of Bedford for an annual pension of half a mark; (3) a charter of Hugh of Avalon, bishop of Lincoln,[38] saying that, by consent and will of the patrons of the church of Milton, the bishop conceded the church to the prior and monks of Beaulieu, saving the right of John of Bedford for his life; and (4) letters of a different archdeacon of Bedford ("A."), directed to the bishop, reporting that the archdeacon made an inquisition and determined that John, who last possessed the church, paid half a mark of pension annually to the monks of Beaulieu. Thus the prior contended that John of Bedford, the former occupant of the church, became vicar when the monks were instituted as parsons. Robert responded that Cecily presented John as parson after she made the charter, a claim eventually affirmed by the jury.[39]

In cases where the defendant claimed that an individual clerk was parson, that clerk might appear in court to attest to the fact that he was parson, or the bishop might appear to say that he had admitted that clerk to the church, or both. In 1225, Robert de Anvers brought an assize of darrein presentment against the abbot of Abingdon concerning the church of Winterbourne (Berks). The abbot responded that the church was not vacant because Robert de Annaeus was parson. Robert de Annaeus appeared and said that he was the parson of Chieveley, of which the church of Winterbourne was a chapel,[40] and that he received two shillings a year from Winterbourne in the name of the mother church, with which the bishop had consolidated the chapel. The bishop then appeared himself and said that a year earlier he had admitted Robert to the chapel of Winterbourne as pertaining to the mother church and no one opposed the claim, and Robert brought his writ afterward. Robert acknowledged this; the abbot went without day, and Robert was told he could sue by writ of right if he wanted.[41]

When the bishop did not appear personally, the parson might offer written documents from the bishop attesting to his institution in the benefice. In 1222, for example, John fitz Alan brought an assize of darrein presentment concerning the church of Keevil (Wilts) against the abbess of the convent of Saint Edward, Shaftesbury.[42] The abbess's attorney said that the church was not vacant because William of Stokes was parson. William appeared and said that he was indeed parson, offering (1) letters of the bishop of Salisbury, Richard Poore,[43] saying that it was clear to the bishop that William was parson by presentation of Mary, former abbess of Saint Edward's, and institution by the bishop's predecessor, Herbert Poore;[44] (2) a charter of Bishop Herbert attesting that he instituted William as parson of the church at Mary's presentation and established that William would receive twenty shillings and eight pence a year from Thomas the vicar; (3) a charter of abbess Mary attesting that she conceded the church to William; and (4) a charter of Jocelin de Bohun, former bishop of Salisbury,[45] attesting that he admitted a clerk named Baldwin to the church at the presentation of the abbess. John responded that Thomas died as parson at the presentation of King Henry by reason of John's barony in the king's hand, and if Thomas made any "collusion," that should not harm John so that the assize not proceed. The justices eventually determined that the church was not vacant after the abbess's attorney offered various charters showing that an ancestor of John had given the advowson to the convent.[46]

A defendant who established plenarty did not automatically prevail. One important exception to the vacancy requirement, enforced by the 1220s if not earlier, was when the current parson had been presented by

reason of the Third Lateran Council, which, as discussed earlier, allowed
the bishop to choose the parson himself if a dispute between patrons
dragged on beyond a fixed period of time.[47] In 1222, John Joscelin sued
the prior of Chalcombe to recover the advowson of the church of Aston
le Walls (Northants). The prior responded that the church was not vacant
because a certain Adam of Saint Bridget was parson and had been before the war. John responded that he had formerly been in the wardship
of William of Duston, and William had presented a clerk in John's name;
when the prior also presented a clerk, a dispute arose between William
and the prior, and if the bishop instituted a parson, he did so by authority
of the Lateran Council. The prior acknowledged this and was ordered to
respond; he eventually prevailed on the basis of a charter of gift from
John's uncle Thomas de Boseville to the priory.[48] The fact that the justices
ordered the prior to respond after he acknowledged that the last institution was made by the bishop in accordance with the council while the advowson dispute was pending shows that John's response was a valid one.
The royal courts were reluctant to dismiss a suit when the current parson
had been collated by the bishop without a patron solely because of the
time limit imposed by canon law.

Another response that a plaintiff might make to a claim of plenarty
was to say that the church was vacant on the day the plaintiff brought the
writ, and if the bishop subsequently instituted a parson, then his doing so
should not count against the defendant. This argument was successfully
made by Basilia de Furmanville in an assize of darrein presentment she
brought in 1219 against the prior of Saint Trinity of Ipswich concerning
the church of Sproughton (Suffolk). The prior initially responded by saying that the church was not vacant because John de Florentine was parson, having been instituted by Pandulph Masca, bishop-elect of Norwich
and papal legate to England.[49] Basilia responded that Pandulph instituted
John unjustly and after she had brought her writ. When the prior acknowledged this, the justices ruled that the assize would proceed. The
prior then vouched the elect to warrant, and the case was postponed.[50]
When the case resumed, the elect appeared by his attorney, warranted
the prior, and said that the church was not vacant because the prior was
parson by gift of Robert de Furmanville, late husband of Basilia, whose
charter the attorney offered. The elect's attorney asserted that the prior

had been parson for forty years. Basilia responded that the church was vacant when the prior was summoned, and if the elect subsequently instituted the prior, it should not harm her because she sued immediately after the death of the previous clerk, Geoffrey. Basilia prevailed when the jurors reported that she presented Geoffrey, who was the last parson (and who had died in Jerusalem).[51] So long as a plaintiff was careful to sue as soon as a church became vacant, subsequent action by the bishop would not necessarily work to the plaintiff's detriment.

The Defense of Gift

Basilia de Furmanville's case illustrates another common defense made by defendants in advowson cases: that the advowson was given to the defendant by charter of gift. In addition to alleging that the church was not vacant because the prior was parson, the elect's attorney offered a charter of gift from Basilia's late spouse, Robert de Furmanville. It was not uncommon for a defendant to respond both that the church was not vacant and that the advowson was given to the defendant by gift. But it was not necessary to claim plenarty to argue that the advowson had been given to the defendant. In cases brought by all three principal advowson writs—the assize of darrein presentment, the writ of right of advowson, and the writ of *quare impedit*—it was a valid defense to say that the advowson had been given to the defendant by charter. The scope of the defense, however, apparently depended on the type of writ brought.

The defense of gift in actions of darrein presentment goes back to at least the end of the reign of Henry II, for it appears in *Glanvill*, which explains the defense as follows:

> It may be asked, whether, from the first, anything can be alleged to prevent the assise from going forward. In order to effect such object, the tenant may admit, that the ancestor of the demandant made the last presentation, as the real lord and the eldest heir, but that he afterwards transferred the fee, to which the advowson is appendant, to the tenant or his ancestors, by a good title; and thus upon this allegation the assise shall cease, and a plea may then be had recourse to between the litigating parties, upon this exception. Upon this exception, either of the parties may desire a recognition, and is entitled to have it.[52]

Glanvill's discussion of the exception suggests that the defense was originally limited to situations where the defendant claimed to have received
the gift from an ancestor of the plaintiff (or, one may infer, from the
plaintiff himself). In such a case, the plaintiff was required to warrant his
ancestor's charter. It would do the defendant no good, however, to offer a
charter from a third party not related to the plaintiff: in that case, the
plaintiff could not be compelled to warrant the charter.

The early plea rolls do not directly confirm this reading of *Glanvill*,
but an entry from 1223 has some bearing on the issue. In 1206, Walter
Biset had brought an assize of darrein presentment against the prior of
Llanthony concerning the advowson of the church of Pencombe (Herefs).
The lawsuit was postponed indefinitely because the prior offered charters
purporting to be from Walter's ancestors, and Walter could not respond to
the charter because he was underage.[53] The case resumed in Michaelmas
Term 1223. After some discussion about whether the prior had defaulted
for nonappearance, the prior's attorney said that Walter was the heir
of his uncle William Torel, who had given the advowson to the priory.
The prior offered William's charter and a confirmation of the bishop of
Hereford.[54] Walter responded that he was not bound by the charter of
William Torel, as he had no inheritance from his uncle. Rather, Walter explained, the manor of Pencombe with the advowson had been given to
Walter's father, Walter Biset the elder, and he claimed as his father's heir
and not as William's. Walter further claimed that the prior had no seisin
of the advowson, and sought the seisin that William had and gave to his
father.[55] The prior's attorney acknowledged that Walter was not the heir
of William, but thought that he should be compelled to warrant the charter as the heir of his father. Asked if the prior ever had seisin of the advowson, the attorney responded that he had not. The justices awarded
seisin to Walter on the grounds that the prior never had seisin and Walter
was not the heir of William Torel.[56]

That Walter was able successfully to defend the darrein presentment
suit on the grounds that he was not his uncle's heir offers some insight
into the nature of the assize of darrein presentment. The exception of
gift was designed not to add a proprietary dimension to the assize but
rather to remedy the injustice that would result if the heir was allowed to
repudiate the donor's charter yet recover the advowson on the basis of

the donor's presentation. When the gift came from a third party, allowing the plaintiff to recover solely on the basis of the last presentation created no inequity.

In cases brought by writ of *quare impedit*, it was often the plaintiff who introduced the issue of a gift, but the defendant could also plead a gift in response to whatever claim the plaintiff made.[57] It does not appear to have been necessary or even helpful to allege that the donor was an ancestor of the plaintiff, although this was often the case. In suits of *quare impedit*, the issue was not who presented the last parson but why the defendant impeded the plaintiff's presentation. When one of the parties relied on a gift, the relevant questions were whether the donor, or his or her ancestor, had presented a parson before the gift, and whether the gift was a valid one.[58] The relationship between the donor and the plaintiff was not relevant.

In 1214 the king sued the prior of Saint Peter's, Ipswich, by writ of *quare impedit*, claiming the church of Saint Clement, Ipswich, as of his donation. The prior responded that he impeded the king justly because he had the church by gift of Jonah the Priest, son of Ralph of Ipswich, offering Jonah's charter. The prior further asserted that Jonah presented the last parson, Walter, and put himself "on the assize, if the court orders, or on the grand assize of right."[59] A day was given to hear judgment.[60] Although no further entries survive concerning the case, it is worth noting that the king did not argue that he was not the heir of Jonah the Priest, which he clearly was not. A party did not challenge a gift in a *quare impedit* suit by responding that he was not related to the donor.

As discussed earlier,[61] the royal justices sometimes allowed donees to bring the writ of right, but cases also arose in which the justices refused to let a plaintiff sue on the basis of the seisin of someone to whom the plaintiff was not related, which meant that donees were excluded from bringing the writ. When the donee was the defendant, however, no rule prevented the defendant from asserting the gift in response to the plaintiff's claim. Defendants in cases brought by writ of right frequently asserted that the advowson had been given to them by some ancestor of the plaintiff or of the person by whom the plaintiff claimed the advowson.[62] But it is not clear that it was necessary to allege that the donor was an ancestor of the plaintiff, and defendants did not always do so.

In Trinity Term 1199, Reginald de Argentein sued the abbess of Elstow by writ of right to recover the church of Wymondley (Herts), asserting that the church pertained to his inheritance, which he held in serjeanty of the king, and asserting that the abbess had no entry save by a wrongful taker.[63] The abbess's attorney responded that Countess Judith, niece of William the Conqueror, gave the vill of Hitchin, including the chapel of Wymondley pertaining to the church of Hitchin, to the church of Elstow; he offered Judith's charter and confirmations of William the Conqueror, William Rufus, Henry I, and Henry II, as well as writings from various bishops. Reginald responded that the church of Wymondley was never appurtenant to the church of Hitchin,[64] and King William never held Wymondley in demesne, but a certain Alfred held that land in William's time and presented to the church, and later the king[65] gave Wymondley as his escheat to Reginald grandfather of Reginald in serjeanty, after which Reginald's grandfather presented two parsons to that church, of whom the last was a certain Osbert. Reginald offered to prove this as the court ordered, and put himself on the country as to whether the abbess had entry other than by wrongful takers. The case was postponed several times,[66] and the parties eventually reached an agreement, the details of which are not recorded.[67] What is worth noting about the case is that the abbess's attorney saw no need to allege a connection between Judith and Reginald the plaintiff, and Reginald did not argue that such a connection was lacking. It is possible, of course, that Reginald knew that he was a descendant of Judith, but it would have been easy to challenge so distant a theoretical relationship. That he did not suggests that, as with *quare impedit,* a defendant who asserted a gift in an action of right was not required to allege a connection between the plaintiff and the donor who gave the defendant the advowson.

The number of different charters offered by the abbess's attorney to evidence the gift was not unusual. As we see in the other cases discussed earlier, when charters were offered in court in support of a claim that a gift had occurred, the party alleging the gift often (but not always) offered multiple charters, for example, the original charter of gift, a confirmation by the donor's heir, a charter of institution by the bishop, and confirmations by subsequent bishops. Sometimes, for good measure, confirmatory charters of kings, archbishops, and even the pope were also offered, whether or not these dignitaries had anything to do with the original gift.[68] Religious houses were particularly keen to impress the court with a long list of charters supporting their claim. But the other party did not have to respond with any charters at all and could respond simply that, for some reason, none of the charters were valid.[69] The royal courts viewed charters with considerable skepticism, not without reason, for they could easily be forged. This skepticism about charter evidence led to specific common-law rules, some of them a bit peculiar, about the legal status of a gift of an advowson.

Charters and Proof: Two Rules

A party could raise many defenses or exceptions to a charter of gift.[70] One of the most frequent responses was to say that the charter in question was made when the person in question was ill or on his or her deathbed and thus not of sound mind.[71] Another common objection was that the seal on the charter was not the alleged donor's seal, and thus the charter was not made by the alleged donor.[72] Other responses might be that the alleged donor had died or become a monk or canon when the charter was made;[73] that the alleged donor had only dower,[74] wardship,[75] or other temporary charge of the advowson[76] and thus could not give away the property; or that the charter was made under duress.[77] Parties often used a combination of these objections, particularly when multiple charters were involved.[78] But perhaps the most interesting objections were (1) that the alleged donor, after making the gift, subsequently presented another parson, thereby rendering the gift null and void; and (2) that the first donee, without having presented a candidate, subsequently gave the advowson to a third party, which meant that neither donee had the right of presentation. The first is an example of what one might call the rule of "subsequent presentation"; the second is an example of what one might call the rule of "subsequent transfer."

The rule of subsequent presentation can be stated as follows: when a person gives an advowson away but afterward (before the donee has a chance to present) presents another clerk to the bishop who is instituted as parson, the gift of the advowson is null and void by virtue of the donor's subsequent presentation. The rule was invoked in dozens of cases in the late twelfth and early thirteenth centuries and was one of the most common responses made to a charter of gift. In the typical subsequent presentation case, the defendant contends that the advowson was given to him (or his religious house) by some ancestor of the plaintiff, and the plaintiff responds that after the gift was made, the donor or his heir presented to the bishop another clerk who was instituted as parson. If this subsequent presentation (and institution) was determined to have occurred, the plaintiff would retain seisin of the advowson.

One of the earliest examples of a subsequent presentation argument in the rolls dates to Trinity Term 1200 and involves an assize of darrein presentment. In the case, Robert de Curci sued Roger de Scures concerning the advowson of Farlington (Hants). Roger responded by offering charters showing that Robert's uncle gave separate moieties of the vill of Farlington with appurtenances to Roger's father and Roger's uncle. Claiming to be the heir of both, Roger conceded that the plaintiff's uncle presented the last parson, but asserted that the gifts followed that presentation. Robert's attorney initially responded that he was not summoned concerning the charters offered by Roger and should not have to respond to them. When the court directed Robert's attorney to respond, he said that after the charters were made, William de Curci, father of Robert, presented the last parson, Andrew, and put himself on the jury concerning that presentation. The court decided to call a jury to determine whether William de Curci presented the last parson. The jury's verdict is not recorded.[79]

The case between Robert and Roger is distinctive in that the parties disagreed not only on whether the last presentation occurred before or after the gift but also on who made the last presentation: Robert's uncle or Robert's father. In the paradigmatic subsequent presentation dispute, both parties agreed on who had presented the last parson, and the sole issue was when that presentation occurred. A dispute in 1212 between Agnes de Roche and the abbot of Beaulieu is typical. Agnes brought an assize of darrein presentment against the abbot concerning the church of Fenstanton (Hunts). The abbot's attorney responded that Roland de Dinan presented the last parson, a certain Richard. Agnes acknowledged this and said that the land and advowson descended from him to Derian her late husband. The abbot's attorney then alleged that after Roland made that presentation, he gave the church to the abbey; a charter was offered. Agnes replied that after Roland made that charter, if he ever did, he presented a parson who was admitted at Roland's presentation. The abbot said that Richard was parson for days and years before the charter was made. Both parties put themselves on the jury, and the jurors said that Roland gave the church (that is, presented a parson) after the charter was made. Agnes was awarded her seisin, and the abbot was amerced.[80]

The rule of subsequent presentation was invoked most frequently in assizes of darrein presentment, and it is quite possible that the rule was first developed in that context. By the end of John's reign, however, parties were also invoking the rule in *quare impedit* cases.[81] In Hilary Term 1214, for example, Roger of Mereworth brought a writ of *quare impedit* against the prior of Leeds, claiming the church of Mereworth (Kent). The prior responded that he justly impeded Roger because Roger's father Eustace gave the advowson to the priory by his charter, which the prior offered. Roger responded that the charter was not his father's because his father used a different seal, and in any case, after that charter was made, his father presented the last parson, Roger. Both parties put themselves on the jury, which was summoned.[82] Although no judgment is recorded, nothing suggests that Roger's invocation of the rule of subsequent presentation was inappropriate for a *quare impedit* suit.[83]

Plaintiffs did not often invoke the rule of subsequent presentation in suits brought by writ of right, but it seems that the rule did apply to such cases, at least by the 1230s. In 1234, Robert de Briwes sued the prior of Bermondsey by writ of right to recover the advowson of the church of Staple Fitzpaine (Somt),[84] claiming that his grandfather had presented a clerk, William, in the time of King Richard, and the right descended to Robert's father John and then to Robert himself. The prior responded by (1) introducing a chirograph from the time of Henry II saying that Robert conceded his right in the church to the monks of Bermondsey; (2) offering a chirograph from the time of Henry III in which Richard de Estre conceded his right in the chapel of Bickenhall, a chapel of Staple Fitzpaine,[85] to the monks, and explaining that John de Briwes was present and was even a justice named in the chirograph and did not oppose the claim; (3) alleging that William of Morton, who held the manor of Staple in demesne, gave the advowson to the monks and later gave the land to Robert, grandfather of the plaintiff, and Robert confirmed the gift to the monks by his charter (which the prior offered); and (4) offering another charter of Robert and John de Briwes, the contents of which are not clear from the plea roll.[86] Robert responded simply that after all the charters and chirographs were made, his grandfather presented William. The prior was then asked whether it was William of Morton or Robert de Briwes who gave him the advowson, and he responded that it was Robert.[87] The action was eventually compromised.[88] The question posed to the prior by the justices shows that it was a valid response for Robert the plaintiff to invoke the rule of subsequent presentation. Thus, by the 1230s at the latest, the rule applied in cases brought by all three of the main advowson writs.

As the case between Robert and the prior shows, the rule of subsequent presentation meant that written evidence of an advowson gift was not dispositive, just as a gift of land was not valid unless the charter of feoffment was accompanied by livery of seisin.[89] By making the gift presumptively voidable by subsequent presentation, the law took the attitude that an advowson gift made in a charter is not final, regardless of what the charter says. Rather, the act of giving must be considered in conjunction with the subsequent acts of the donor. If the donor later behaved in such a way as to indicate that he meant to revoke his gift or that the gift was not intended to be final, the charter was a nullity.[90] The issue of whether a subsequent presentation occurred was normally referred to jurors, who decided the issue on the basis of the community's memory: that is, whether the act of giving occurred before or after the last presentation.[91] The royal justices evidently had greater faith in that memory than in the charters offered by the donees.

The rule of subsequent presentation did not mean that no gift of an advowson was complete or enforceable until the donee had presented. By bringing a writ of *quare impedit* at the first available opportunity, a donee could call on the royal courts to enforce a gift that had occurred during the tenure of the last parson. But when the donor had presented after the alleged gift, then any gift must have occurred before the tenure of the last parson, possibly several decades before the lawsuit. The length of time between the alleged gift and the lawsuit was likely to be greater when a parson's tenure had intervened, and fewer people remained in the community who knew whether the alleged gift had actually occurred. In those cases, the law ignored the alleged gift and awarded seisin solely on the basis of who presented the last parson. The rule could be said to reflect an ambivalent attitude toward the written documents introduced into court by parties claiming by gift: as mentioned earlier, such charters could be forged, and ascertaining their reliability was difficult when the events they recorded had occurred in the distant past.[92]

Another interesting defense that a plaintiff could raise against a charter of gift can be stated as follows: when A gives an advowson to B, and B, without having presented a candidate, gives the advowson to C, by virtue of the subsequent transfer B gives up whatever B had, but C acquires nothing. This rule of subsequent transfer is forcefully and repeatedly stated in *Bracton*,[93] and although it was invoked far less often than the rule of subsequent presentation, it appears in the plea rolls by at least the 1220s. In Michaelmas Term 1224, for example, John de Trailly brought an assize of darrein presentment against the prior of Newnham to claim the advowson of a third part of the church of Southill (Beds). The prior responded that the assize should not proceed because Walter de Trailly, John's grandfather, gave his land in Southill with the advowson to Fawkes de Breauté, who gave the advowson of that third part of the church to the house of Newnham by his charter, which the prior offered. Asked who presented the last parson, the prior responded that Walter did but subsequently gave the advowson to Fawkes. John's guardian, who sued on behalf of the underage John, responded that John could not respond to the charters because he was underage, but in any case Fawkes took the land of Southill away from Walter in time of war, and if the charter was ever made, it was made after Fawkes fortified the castle of Bedford against the king. The prior responded that Walter gave the land to Fawkes in time of peace, and Fawkes was at peace with the king when he made the charter. The justices, however, asked the prior if Fawkes was ever in seisin of the advowson, and the prior responded that he was not. The justices then gave judgment to John because the prior acknowledged Walter's presentation and seisin, and Fawkes never had seisin of the advowson.[94]

The rule of subsequent transfer applied in *quare impedit* suits as well as assizes of darrein presentment.[95] It is not clear whether the rule applied in actions of right, but given that the rule was invoked infrequently in cases of any type, its apparent absence in actions of right does not mean that it would not have applied in such cases. Like the rule of subsequent presentation, the rule of subsequent transfer suggests a skeptical attitude toward charters of gift, but it manifests itself differently. The idea behind the rule of subsequent transfer is not that a gift recorded in a charter is revocable by a subsequent contradictory act by the donor. Rather, the rule of subsequent transfer means that, regardless of the later actions of the donor, a gift recorded in a charter does not by itself give the donee a permanent claim to the advowson.

A party who receives an advowson by gift does thereby acquire something: he has the right to present and can sue by *quare impedit* or defend against an assize of darrein presentment. But his claim is incomplete; he does not have seisin. Absent a successful act of presentation or other manifestation of seisin, the first donee's claim to the advowson does not entitle him to give it to a third party. If he tries, not only will the second donee acquire nothing, but the first donee will lose what he had. For the subsequent gift to be legally enforceable, the first donee must present a candidate who is instituted as parson or give other evidence of seisin. The royal courts would not trust a string of charters unless some additional evidence proved transfer of seisin, in the form of either an intervening presentation or the taking of seisin of land to which the advowson was appurtenant.

A darrein presentment case from Trinity Term 1227 suggests that taking seisin of the manor to which the advowson was appurtenant might rebut an attempt to rely on the rule of subsequent transfer, although the facts are somewhat unusual. In the suit, Roger de Mohaut claimed the advowson of Elford (Staffs) against Philip de Oreby, on the grounds that Ralph de Mohaut, Roger's uncle, presented the last parson, William of Haye.[96] While Philip's attorney conceded that Ralph de Mohaut presented the last parson, he claimed that Ralph subsequently gave the manor and its appurtenances to another Roger de Mohaut, brother of Ralph and uncle of the plaintiff. This Roger, the attorney alleged, "held the manor with its appurtenances for his whole life" (manerium illud cum pertinenciis tenuit tota vita sua). After the death of the elder Roger, the manor descended to Roger's daughter Leuca, and from Leuca to her daughter Agnes, whose guardian was Philip. Philip's attorney offered a charter of the elder Roger, asserting that Philip gave Roger one hundred marks of silver for the wardship of Agnes and all the inheritance descending from the elder Roger to Leuca in Elford and Cassingland, together with their appurtenances. Since the charter did not except the advowson, and the church had not been vacant before the suit, Philip's attorney claimed seisin.

Roger's attorney responded that the other Roger to whom his ancestor Ralph gave the land was never in seisin of the advowson, nor was Leuca or Agnes. However, Roger's attorney acknowledged that the charter did not except the advowson, and said he did not know whether Ralph made the gift. Roger sought judgment on the issue of whether the gift could be made when the donor did not have seisin of the presentation, even assuming he had been enfeoffed of the land ("dicit quod Rogerus feoffatus nunquam habuit seisinam de presentacione, et petit iudicium"). The court decided against Roger the plaintiff on that issue and adjudged seisin instead to Philip as guardian of Agnes, on the grounds that Roger the plaintiff "never showed that the advowson was excepted nor offered proof, nor did he show a charter nor anything except his simple voice, and he acknowledges moreover that Roger died seised of that manor with appurtenances, and Leuca in the same way."[97]

An interesting fact about the Elford case is that Philip, who claimed by virtue of a donation from Ralph to the elder Roger, did not introduce a charter of Ralph into evidence; his only proffered charter came from the elder Roger, the ancestor of his ward. He did, however, make another key allegation: that the elder Roger was seised of the land to which the advowson was appurtenant.[98] This was a fact that could be proved by witnesses independently of the missing charter from Ralph, and the plaintiff's attorney made no serious effort to contest it. Thus, although Philip claimed by virtue of a subsequent transfer (in this case, the purchase of a wardship) from an initial transferee, the fact that the initial transferee had seisin of the land to which the advowson was appurtenant seems to have prevented the court from applying the usual rule of subsequent transfer. Because the case turned on the purchase of a wardship rather than two successive donations, however, it may be distinguishable from other subsequent transfer cases, and how broadly the court intended its rule to apply is not clear.

Like the rule of subsequent presentation, the rule of subsequent transfer privileged more recent evidence that could be verified even by the illiterate. A donee who relied exclusively on written records, particularly ancient ones, might face a hostile audience before the royal courts. In the last chapter, we saw how Chancery helped donees, principally religious houses, by creating the writ of *quare impedit*. Here we have seen that there were limits to the willingness of the royal courts to acknowledge the claims of the monasteries. Secular lords may not have been happy to see the creation of a new writ for the benefit of abbots and priors, who had an advantage in literacy that they could deploy to protect their interests. The rules of subsequent presentation and transfer, therefore, may have been devised specifically to mollify the king's unhappy lay subjects. The writ of *quare impedit* was more palatable if the lords were given some opportunity to undo donations that had subsequently proved to be unwise, or to circumvent the introduction of a forged charter evidencing a gift that had never in fact occurred. Any rules that limited the use of charter evidence were more likely to favor the lords, who claimed by inheritance more often than by donation.

In the development of common-law rules regarding the donation of advowsons, it is possible to see a rough compromise being worked out. Donees do have a remedy, but not every gift is actionable. Religious houses had a place in the royal courts, but their superior skill in creating documents had to be considered. Spotting forgeries was particularly hard when they involved long-dead individuals or events in the distant past, as was the case when a claimed gift occurred before the last presentation or before a more recent gift. Events that occurred before the lifetime of the king's jurors were beyond their competence to verify.

If layman A brought an assize of darrein presentment against a monastery, the monks could easily come up with a forged charter from some remote ancestor of A if intervening presentations were deemed to be of no consequence.[99] On the other hand, if the monastery happened to have a verifiable charter executed by B, a layman unrelated to the plaintiff with an ambiguous claim to the advowson, the monks might easily fabricate additional charters showing a direct chain of title to B from that same remote ancestor. The common-law courts accordingly developed safeguards to limit the admissibility of such evidence, focusing the jurors' attention on more recent facts within the community's collective memory. In the case between the abbot of Stanley and Matthew fitz Herbert, discussed in the previous chapter, the royal justiciar wrote to the justices at Westminster, ordering them to treat the monks justly "according to the custom of the realm."[100] Religious houses were indeed treated justly according to the custom of the realm, but that custom had to take into account their natural advantage when it came to written evidence.

The English royal courts of the late twelfth century and the early thirteenth were beginning to develop rules of substantive law particular to advowson cases. Nonetheless, ecclesiastical courts continued to hear disputes over the rights of priests to particular benefices, which were effectively the flip side of disputes over advowsons. If rival claimants to the patronage of a vacant church preferred to have their dispute settled by the bishop, that option was always available to them. In the next chapter, I explore the ecclesiastical court system and attempt to determine why some litigants rejected that alternative and chose to have their disputes resolved in the royal courts.

CHAPTER FIVE

CANON LAW AND JURISDICTIONAL COMPETITION

When multiple courts exist within the same legal system, a court's assertion of jurisdiction does not guarantee that litigants will come. No matter how often the royal courts might insist that advowson cases were rightfully theirs, parties could always opt to take their case to the bishop if he was willing to hear it. If neither party complained, the royal courts might lose their opportunity to decide a case without even knowing that a dispute had existed. For the royal courts, successfully asserting jurisdiction in advowson cases depended on at least some claimants having a reason to prefer that their cases be heard before the king's justices.

Both economists and historians have long been interested in the role of jurisdictional competition in shaping the English common law. On the one hand, when courts compete for business, the resulting system might be expected to favor plaintiffs, who choose where to sue.[1] Based on reported cases, it appears that forum shopping in English courts did produce plaintiff-friendly rules until the enactment of a 1799 statute that took fees away from justices.[2] On the other hand, the common law had an eye from the beginning toward the traditional prerogatives of secular and ecclesiastical lords. As previously discussed, King Henry II and his advisers carefully limited the early writs to situations in which a plaintiff alleged that the seigneurial court had failed to provide justice. Before the emergence of the modern state, the existence of competing centers of authority could serve as both a check on innovation and an impetus toward reform.

Scholars have expressed a wide range of opinion on the extent to which the *ius commune* might have influenced the early English common law, but they generally agree that the great European reception of Roman law in the later Middle Ages did not cross the English Channel. Charles Sherman, whose maximalist case has yet to be matched, nonetheless acknowledged that the impact of Roman law in England was "limited in character as compared with the Continental reception." The best explanation for this may be the timing thesis offered by Raoul van Caenegem: because England had developed an efficient, centralized legal system at such an early stage, the increasingly sophisticated commentaries and glosses on canon and Roman law texts that emerged in the thirteenth century and later were of limited use to the English royal justices.

If one assumes that the precocious development of the English common-law system explains its resistance to the continental reception, that does not mean the entrenchment of royal justice in England was a foregone conclusion by the thirteenth century. The Angevin legal reforms were not universally popular. Criticism of royal justice became particularly strong during the reign of King John, whose persistent presence in England after the loss of his continental possessions and assertive style of governance led to frequent personal interventions in the operation of the royal courts. Paradoxically, John's actions may have contributed to the development of the concept of rule of law, as evidence points to a backlash by some royal justices who may have resented the king's interference with their work. Of course, the most famous product of John's ineffective leadership was the Great Charter of 1215, several clauses of which addressed the need for fairness in judicial proceedings.

It is ironic that the king who agreed to what may be the world's most important constitutional document is nonetheless remembered as one of England's least effective rulers. This might be partly explained if key features of Magna Carta reflect neither a recognition of restraints on royal power nor ancient English customs but a reception of certain principles from the *ius commune*. Richard Helmholz has vigorously argued that the *ius commune* played a significant role in shaping Magna Carta, particularly with regard to clause 22, dealing with the amercement of clerks; clause 27, regarding the disposition of chattels on intestacy; and clause 55, dealing with unjust fines and amercements.[3] If the *ius commune* did play a role in the development of Magna Carta, this prompts two questions. First, why was this critical constitutional moment not an occasion for the English royal courts to embrace more features of Roman and canon law? Second, why did the ecclesiastical courts not seize this opportunity during the years leading up to the Great Charter to claim jurisdiction over matters that were subject to overlap between the two systems?

I have suggested a partial answer to the second of these questions, which may be connected to the first. With regard to advowsons, the surviving records from Lincoln, one of England's most important dioceses, suggest that what might have been an opportunity for an ecclesiastical court to seize more power during the king's moment of weakness was instead marked by a deliberate abdication of responsibility, an abdication that was made possible by the king's shrewd appointment of a compliant bishop.[4] The register of Hugh of Wells reveals traces of what may have been a more aggressive approach of his predecessor bishops of Lincoln in patronage disputes. A less loyal bishop might have built on that precedent to successfully lure lay plaintiffs back into the episcopal court. Instead Hugh of Wells deferred to the jurisdiction of the king's courts and did not attempt to reassert his ancient episcopal privileges. After the constitutional crisis provoked by King John had passed, the supremacy of the king's courts over important patronage disputes was permanently secured.

Canon Law and the King's Courts

Beginning in the mid-twelfth century with Gratian's *Decretum* and continuing into the latter half of the twelfth century and the early thirteenth, popes and canon lawyers developed an elaborate system of rules relating to advowsons.[5] The main features of this system have been outlined by Peter Landau, who comprehensively studied the relevant papal legislation and juristic commentary.[6] Landau did not, however, devote much attention to whether the rules of canon law were actually applied in practice. Given the nature of the surviving sources, this question is not easy to answer. For present purposes, the relevant issue is whether the English royal courts heeded canon law rules in deciding advowson disputes. A brief discussion follows of these rules and how they were applied (or ignored) in the English royal courts in the late twelfth and early thirteenth centuries.

Under canon law, a lay patron's ability to receive income from the church of which he held the advowson was restricted. Laymen were not permitted to appropriate the church's revenue (tithes) for their own purposes.[7] Any clerk who paid money in exchange for ecclesiastical office committed the grave sin of simony, for which he could be deprived of his benefice.[8] With limited exceptions, the patron could not receive any income from the church.[9] Nevertheless, advowsons could have great value to medieval English litigants. Several plaintiffs in the early thirteenth century described their advowson as the "head of their honor" or "chief part of their inheritance."[10] Certain pleas required plaintiffs to state the damages they had suffered by the loss of their advowson, and they were generally able to name a monetary value, accurate or otherwise.[11] The ultimate source of the advowson's value lay in the tithes that pertained to the church, as well as its glebe, offerings, and mortuaries. Litigants who sued in ecclesiastical court concerning the tithes often faced a countersuit in the royal court on the grounds that they were effectively claiming the advowson.[12] When a bishop's refusal to institute a priest presented by a layman was challenged in the royal courts, it was a valid defense to say that the house of worship in question was a chapel to which no tithes pertained.[13]

The mere fact that advowsons derived their value from the church's tithes and other assets, however, does not mean that simony was widespread in medieval England or that the lay patrons of churches were directly controlling the tithes. Advowsons were a valuable source of patronage, which could be used to reward a clerk who had provided faithful service, to encourage future assistance, or both. A great lord needed, in effect, his own personal civil service,[14] of which clerks who had taken holy orders formed a significant part.[15] Men who could read and count were in great demand on estates with complex legal and financial entanglements and responsibilities. There was no better way to attract such men than to hold the key to a permanent source of income down the line.

While the value of the advowson ultimately lay in the tithes, the lay patron could benefit from the advowson without laying claim to those tithes directly. A patron who brought a writ of prohibition to halt an ecclesiastical suit concerning tithes might simply be protecting his clerk. The early plea rolls give no indication that lay patrons were flouting canon law by taking direct management of churches.

A lay patron might also value an advowson as a possible opportunity to advance the career of a younger son or other male relative. Nepotism in the exercise of advowsons was not strictly prohibited, although two decretals of Alexander III appear to discourage it.[16] The early English plea rolls contain many cases in which the patron had presented his brother[17] or son[18] to the parsonage. Under the system of primogeniture, the father's eldest son inherited all land that the father held by knight's service, leaving the younger sons with no land to inherit unless the father held some land in a form of tenure known as socage.[19] Providing a younger son or younger brother with a parsonage ensured him a source of income, relieving the eldest son of any obligation to support the younger.

For the most part, this advantage could be realized without violating canon law. A case from Michaelmas Term 1217, however, is strangely close to the specific exception in canon law to the permissibility of presenting sons. In a lawsuit brought against the prior of Kenilworth concerning the church of Hampton in Arden (Warks), William of Hampton in Arden alleged that his father Roger had presented William to the church when William was a clerk. When Roger died, William became a knight, resigned the church, and presented his brother, also named Roger, to the church. No judgment is recorded, so we do not know whether this plea was acceptable.[20] The circumstances also differ from the case presented by the canonists in that William presented his brother rather than his son. Even so, the fact that William considered it appropriate to tell the court that he presented his brother after resigning the church suggests that the English royal courts may have been more comfortable with quasi-hereditary benefices than were contemporary canonists.

Although canon law prohibited hereditary benefices, the canonists generally understood the advowson itself to be an inheritable right.[21] Some dispute, however, arose regarding whether the advowson could be transferred to individuals other than "blood heirs" (*heredes sanguinis*). Rufinus (fl. 1150–91) opined that only blood heirs could inherit an advowson, and no gifts were permitted except to "churches of equal or greater religion."[22] Other early decretists echoed this view.[23] By the early thirteenth century, however, most canonists had come around to the opinion of Huguccio (fl. 1180–1210), who thought that all heirs ought to be allowed to inherit an advowson.[24] Huguccio's view thus left open the possibility that an advowson could be devised to a stranger.[25]

The inheritability of advowsons was taken for granted in the English royal courts, and extremely specific rules dictated who inherited an advowson when the patron died. Devises, however, were not permitted. The inheritance rules for advowsons tended to mirror those for the land to which the advowsons were or had been appurtenant, which generally meant the rules for military tenure. If the patron had any sons, the first-born son would inherit the advowson.[26] If the patron had no sons but had daughters, the daughters would collectively inherit the advowson.[27] If the patron had no children, the advowson would descend to the patron's siblings in a similar manner. Central to the scheme was the rule that the patron could not direct the disposition of the advowson by will, for as *Glanvill* says, "God alone, and not man, can make an heir."[28] Thus the English royal courts did not adopt the liberal position of Huguccio; one could not devise an advowson to strangers. As will be discussed, however, lifetime gifts were a different matter.

When an advowson was held in common by several individuals, such as daughters who inherited in the absence of a male heir, a disagreement might arise among the co-patrons. The Third Lateran Council provided in canon 17 that if the "founders" of a church preferred different candidates, "the one would be preferred who has the greater merit and is chosen and approved by the greater number."[29] Huguccio interpreted this to be an endorsement of majority rule, except in case of a tie, when the benefice would go to the worthiest candidate.[30] Other canonists, however, rejected the idea of majority rule and would leave the choice up to the bishop in all cases of disagreement.[31]

The English royal courts applied the principle of majority rule. When a co-patron had only one-third of the advowson, he could not impede the presentation of the other two patrons, and the parson would be admitted at the presentation of the majority.[32] The royal courts did not, however, take any position on what should happen when the co-patrons were equally divided. In that circumstance, the royal courts would give the litigants a writ to the bishop that he admit a candidate at the presentation of the co-patrons in common.[33] This comported with the rule of canon law that the bishop should choose the worthiest candidate when the patrons were equally divided.

Canon law also delineated a period within which a vacancy had to be filled. Canon 17 of the Third Lateran Council originally provided that when a legal controversy arose concerning the patronage and no decision was arrived at within a certain time, the bishop would automatically choose the parson himself.[34] Two months may have been the time limit expressed by the council, but later canonists referred to three or four months, and four months was the limit referred to when the canon was included in the *Compilatio I* and the *Liber Extra*.[35] More significantly, a decretal of Alexander III issued after the Third Lateran Council and directed to the archbishop of Canterbury specified that, in a controversy over the patronage, the bishop, six months after the vacancy occurred, could himself fill the church.[36] Canonists offered different explanations for the contradiction between the six-month period of the decretal and the four-month period of the council. Bernard of Pavia, who taught at Bologna during the 1170s, believed that the shorter period applied when the disputing parties were responsible for the failure of the process to conclude, whereas the longer period applied when the judge was responsible for the delay.[37] Other writers contended that the six-month period was reckoned from the time when the church became vacant, whereas the four-month period was counted from the beginning of the controversy between the rival patrons.[38] Eventually the canonists settled on the theory that the four-month limit applied to secular patrons, and the six-month period applied to spiritual patrons.[39]

Records of the English royal courts do not refer to two different time limits. Occasionally the plea rolls do report that a benefice was filled by the bishop of the diocese "by authority of the council" (auctoritate concilii) because of a lapse of time.[40] However, if the time in question is specified, it is always said to be six months.[41] The English plea rolls never refer to a four-month period, nor do they give any indication that separate time periods existed for secular and spiritual patrons. The English royal court records leave the impression that the English royal judges interpreted the Third Lateran Council as establishing a fixed six-month time limit for all patronage disputes. No canonist writing during this period shared that opinion, thus raising the question of how the English royal judges reached this conclusion.

One possibility is that the English bishops made a practice of waiting six months before instituting a clerk pursuant to the council, and the plea rolls simply reflected the behavior of the bishops in practice. If the bishops followed such a practice, however, they probably did so out of deference to the jurisdiction of the royal courts in advowson disputes. It seems unlikely that the bishops would have relinquished their rights under canon law in the absence of pressure from the king and his judges.[42] The most likely explanation is that the bishops cooperated with the royal courts to allow more time for darrein presentment actions to run their course. To persuade the bishops to wait six months, however, the royal judges must have had some basis for their interpretation of the council.

Although the provision of the Third Lateran Council dealing with advowson disputes referred to a time limit of two months (extended to four months in the *Compilatio Prima* and the *Liber Extra*), another provision of the council does refer to a six-month period. Under canon 8, when ecclesiastical prebends or other offices in a church became vacant, they were not to remain unfilled, but within six months they were to be conferred on persons who could suitably administer them.[43] This provision, unlike canon 17, was not specifically aimed at controversies over patronage. It seems, however, that the English interpretation viewed the shorter limit of canon 17 as yielding precedence to the six-month limit of canon 8. The decretal of Alexander III that spoke of a six-month limit, which may even have been interpreted by the English bishops (including the addressee, the archbishop of Canterbury) as a special concession directed to England, undoubtedly reinforced this interpretation, though the decretal itself did not make that clear.[44]

Perhaps the most significant thing about the English interpretation of the council's provisions is that the perspective of the secular courts apparently mattered more than the theories of the leading canonists. Four months left the king's judges very little time to hold an assize of darrein presentment, but six months gave them a bit more flexibility. The English bishops were thus somehow persuaded to refrain from exercising the rights that may theoretically have been granted to them under an aggressive interpretation of canon law. On the other hand, the royal judges did not attempt to disregard the rule of the Third Lateran Council entirely, however attractive that option might have been to the lay lords who claimed rights of patronage in the royal courts. The royal courts acknowledged the authority of canon law, but the bishops did not press the issue quite as far as they might have.

One question of great interest to canonists in the late twelfth and early thirteenth centuries was whether an advowson could be transferred from one patron to another. The answer depended on the circumstances. Was the advowson to be transferred as a separate item or as an appurtenance to an estate? Was the transfer by sale or by donation? Did the bishop give his approval? Some of these scenarios gave rise to controversy among the canonists.

By the 1180s, canonists generally accepted that an advowson could be transferred as an appurtenance to a whole property (*universitas*). We see some early disagreement on the issue, but two decretals of Alexander III dating to the late 1170s established that an advowson could be acquired through the purchase of an estate to which the advowson was appurtenant.[45] The famous canonist Huguccio emphasized that in any transfer of a whole property, whether by sale, gift, or enfeoffment, the advowson would be included unless specifically excepted.[46] The bishop's approval was not required for the transfer, nor did it matter whether the transfer was to or from a layman or a religious house. Notably, in Roman law, when one estate was servient to another, the servitude was considered to follow the sale of either estate, as did a building on either property.[47] That canon law applied this basic principle to advowsons should not surprise us.

When an advowson was transferred by itself, not as an appurtenance, the permissibility of the transfer depended on the circumstances. The decretal law on the subject of whether an advowson could be transferred by gift was unclear at the death of Alexander III (1181), providing rich material for controversies among the canonists.[48] One point of contention was whether the bishop's consent must be obtained for the transfer. Alanus Anglicus, who taught and wrote circa 1190 to 1215, thought that a gift to a layman required episcopal consent but a gift to a monastery did not, while the author of the apparatus *Ecce vicit Leo* (1202/1210) conversely believed that episcopal consent was necessary for a gift to a monastery, but not for a gift to a layman.[49] By contrast, Huguccio reasoned that the consent of the bishop was never necessary.[50] Tancred (ca. 1185–1236), Vincentius Hispanus (fl. ca. 1210–48), and Innocent IV (jurist and pope, lived ca. 1200–1254) followed the view of Huguccio, while Johannes Teutonicus (ca. 1170–1245) followed the apparatus *Ecce vicit Leo*.[51] Edited by Bernard of Parma (ca. 1200–1266), the ordinary gloss to the *Liber Extra* expressed the view that episcopal consent was always necessary for any gift.[52] It was not until the second half of the thirteenth century that the view of Alanus Anglicus gradually prevailed.[53]

One type of transfer was always considered unacceptable. An advowson could not be sold as independent property under canon law. Only when the advowson was appurtenant to an estate and sold with the estate was a sale permissible.[54] Peter the Chanter (d. 1197) was the lone dissenter on this point, but his view was summarily rejected by other authors who discussed it.[55] Debates among canonists on this topic mainly concerned what would happen to the advowson after an illegal sale, with some offering the view that the patronage would come to an end, and others allowing the seller or his heirs to reclaim the advowson.[56]

Plea rolls from the late twelfth and early thirteenth centuries contain scores of references to gifts of advowsons. Laymen and religious houses both received gifts. However, as a general rule, an advowson was given to a layman only as an appurtenance to an estate (which was also given to the donee), while advowsons were given to religious houses separately from the land. Published royal court records from 1194 to 1250 reveal more than four dozen gifts to laymen of land with an advowson, but only a half-dozen gifts to laymen of an advowson where land was not mentioned.[57] In none of the latter six cases was judgment given for the donee.[58] On the other hand, a survey of the same records revealed only twenty-six gifts to religious houses of land with an advowson, but close to two hundred advowson gifts to religious houses that do not mention land.[59] It appears to have been customary, when making a gift to a religious house, to give the advowson separately from the land, whereas lay donees usually acquired the advowson as part of some estate. In general, lay patrons made gifts to religious houses with the hope that the religious order and its associated saint would help them gain admission to heaven while also enhancing their own earthly reputation.[60]

It is no coincidence that gifts were frequently the subject of litigation. Before the proprietary church system had been eradicated and while hereditary benefices were still common, laymen in the twelfth century frequently gave their churches to religious houses, encouraged by the reform-minded policies of the church. The practice continued through the early decades of the thirteenth century but then became less common as advowsons became more valuable owing to the end of the hereditary benefice and the expansion of seigneurial administration.[61] The late twelfth and early thirteenth centuries were a period of transition. Religious houses received fewer gifts of advowsons, as laymen saw increasing value in this form of patronage. To be sure, many laymen still wanted to make gifts to religious houses, especially if the patron had a younger son whom he wanted to send to the religious house as a monk or canon,[62] or if he wanted to become a monk or canon himself.[63] However, we also see signs of a less favorable attitude toward the monasteries.[64] For example, one patron allowed a priest to make a single presentation to a church, "provided that he not confer it on any religious house and do nothing to the prejudice of the right of his heirs."[65] Laymen in the thirteenth century often wished to repudiate gifts of advowsons made to religious houses by their ancestors in an earlier period, when the advowsons were less valuable. Lawsuits often resulted.

When religious houses acquired advowsons by gift, their leaders were typically careful to secure the approval or at least the acknowledgment of the bishop. The plea rolls reveal over sixty instances in which a religious house offered a confirmatory charter of the bishop to support its gift, and more than a dozen instances in which a charter of institution or other acknowledgment was offered.[66] However, one also finds over a hundred instances in which a religious house claimed a gift and the record includes no reference to an episcopal charter.[67] In twenty-two of these cases, the royal courts gave judgment for the religious house claiming by gift despite the lack of recorded episcopal confirmation.[68] Donees prevailed in these cases for various reasons, but it seems clear that the royal courts did not require a confirmatory charter from the bishop.

Donees also sometimes offered confirmatory charters of popes as well as bishops,[69] even though canon law required no papal confirmation for the gift of an advowson. Offering confirmatory charters of kings was also common, regardless of whether the king had a special interest in the advowson in question.[70] These confirmatory charters were generally optional as far as the royal courts were concerned, but such charters offered important evidence of authenticity in a world where forgery was common and difficult to detect.[71]

The canon law rules concerning gifts do not seem to have been of much consequence for litigants in the royal courts, but the canonical prohibition on sale does not appear to have been violated regularly, if at all. Setting aside cases where an advowson is alleged to have been sold with some land, the plea rolls from the late twelfth and early thirteenth centuries contain only one instance in which an advowson or moiety thereof is adjudged to a party who acquired it by virtue of a sale.[72] Thomas of Burgh claimed a moiety of the advowson of Penistone (Yorks) from Richard de Alencun in 1227. According to the jurors, a moiety of the advowson had been sold to William de Neville, father of Sarah, who was Thomas's mother and whose heir Thomas was; the other moiety had been sold to Roger de Munbegun, whose heirs were Eudes de Lungvillers and Geoffrey de Neville.[73] The court awarded Thomas the presentation of the moiety in question and amerced Richard.[74]

The case between Thomas and Richard does suggest that the royal courts might overlook the canonical prohibition on sale. It is worth noting, however, that the sale is referenced only in the jury's verdict and was not alleged by either of the parties. It is possible that the sale had included land as well as a moiety of the advowson, and the jury simply neglected to mention this fact (or it was not reported on the roll). In any event, one contrary instance does not mean that the royal judges generally failed to respect the canonical prohibition. It must be emphasized, on the other hand, that the standard language for charters did not distinguish between sales and gratuitous transfers. Unless the charter mentioned the consideration, or it came up during the litigation, a sale could be mistaken for a gift. Nevertheless, the surviving evidence gives us no reason to think that advowsons were being sold in violation of canon law.

In short, the rules of canon law regarding advowsons appear to have generally been respected in the royal courts. The plea rolls show no toleration for simony or refusal to adhere to the prohibition on sale. Questions relating to the presentation time limit under the council and the necessity of episcopal approval for gifts were controversial among the canonists, and the English positions on these questions were not indefensible. Whether by coincidence or by design, the royal courts generally stayed in line with the canons, at least to the extent that they were consistent with the exercise of royal jurisdiction over advowsons. It was in the interest of the two competing sources of power and judicial authority in England to reach a compromise, however uneasy that compromise may have been.

Patronage Disputes in the Ecclesiastical Courts

When it came to rights of presentation, the English courts disregarded canon law in one important way. In the view of the popes and canon lawyers, advowson disputes fell under the jurisdiction of the ecclesiastical courts, except when the advowson was appurtenant to an estate over which a secular court had jurisdiction.[75] The English royal courts were not willing to cede control of advowson disputes to the church, regardless of what the church leaders and jurists said. Moreover, England was not alone in taking the position that advowson disputes belonged in secular courts, at least in some circumstances. Normandy preserved a modified secular jurisdiction over advowsons after Philip Augustus conquered the region, and other parts of France later adopted the same.[76]

In clause 1 of the Constitutions of Clarendon, promulgated in 1164, Henry II proclaimed that all controversies concerning advowsons and presentation to churches, be they between laymen, clerks, or a combination thereof, were to be decided in his own royal courts.[77] Although Henry's bold statement was not well received by the church in England or in Rome, it was the preamble to hundreds of years of advowson litigation in the royal courts. Jurisdiction over advowsons reinforced the king's power and authority, and the kings of England were not about to give up their jurisdiction simply because the church objected. Members of the

English church hierarchy recognized this, and thus one finds priests, bishops, abbots, and priors suing for advowsons in the royal courts throughout the period.

Nevertheless, the English ecclesiastical courts continued to play an important role in patronage matters throughout the early period of the common law, although the nature and extent of ecclesiastical involvement are subject to dispute. As the common law developed, the two parallel English legal systems worked out a rough compromise, whereby the church courts would retain jurisdiction over disputes involving possession of benefices, and the royal courts would deal with advowsons. Policing this boundary, however, was not always an easy task, and one cannot entirely isolate the story of advowson writs and litigation in the royal courts from the broader story of church-state (and clerical-lay) relations in the late twelfth and early thirteenth centuries.

Although the preface to the Constitutions of Clarendon stated that Henry II was merely recording "some part of the customs, liberties, and dignities of his ancestors, that is, King Henry his grandfather and others,"[78] certain provisions, particularly those dealing with ecclesiastical appeals and royal jurisdiction over clerks accused of crimes, represented a much more significant interference with ecclesiastical affairs than had been attempted under previous English kings.[79] Henry II's provocation of the church met with strong episcopal and papal resistance, at least in some quarters. After the martyrdom of Thomas Becket, in the Compromise of Avranches of 1172, Henry agreed to "abolish customs prejudicial to the Church which had been introduced in his reign."[80] Admittedly, the compromise did not restore exclusive jurisdiction over advowsons to the ecclesiastical courts, even though Pope Alexander III made his opposition to clause 1 of the Constitutions of Clarendon clear in his decretal *Quanto*.[81] If Henry II meant to exclude the church courts from all disputes involving vacant benefices, however, he did not succeed. As J. W. Gray demonstrated in a 1952 article, the Constitutions of Clarendon did not entirely strip the ecclesiastical courts of their role in patronage disputes.[82]

We find some early evidence of the role that the ecclesiastical courts could play in advowson disputes, both before and after the Constitutions of Clarendon, in the chronicle of Battle Abbey. The chronicler discusses lawsuits the abbey brought in the mid-twelfth century concerning certain churches that had been given to the abbey by William the Conqueror and his son William Rufus.[83] Most of the parsons who occupied these churches during the reign of William Rufus survived into the reign of King Stephen. When the churches finally became vacant, certain laymen claimed that they, not the abbey, were entitled to the advowsons by royal gift.[84] Churches given by William Rufus included Mildenhall and Thurlow, in Suffolk.[85] With respect to these two churches, the abbey brought suit against laymen in both the royal and the ecclesiastical courts. The conflicts illustrate how royal and church court litigation might be intertwined.

During the so-called Anarchy, King Stephen granted the fee of Mildenhall to Robert de Crèvecœur, a powerful Kentish baron. Although the abbey claimed the church by gift of William Rufus, Robert granted it to the canons of Leeds, a Kentish priory. During the reign of Stephen, the abbey commenced suit against both Robert and the canons, the former suit "for unjust disseisin" (super injusta invasione), and the latter "for violent intrusion" (super violenta intrusione).[86] The chronicler says that the abbey sued in both royal and ecclesiastical court, but neither suit succeeded. After Henry II came to power, however, the abbey once again sought justice *nunc in curia regali, nunc in ecclesiastica*. Both sides appealed to the pope, who appointed the bishops of London and Salisbury as judges delegate. When the canons failed to appear before a court composed of the bishop of Salisbury and clerks of the bishop of London, the court ruled in favor of the abbey, subject to the condition that if the canons instituted further litigation within the year, the abbot would resign the church into the hands of the judges. The canons did not pursue the matter further, and the abbot took possession of the church and granted it to a certain Robert "the philosopher" subject to a fixed pension.[87]

The royal courts played a more significant role in the litigation concerning Thurlow, but the ecclesiastical courts were involved in that litigation as well. The dispute arose because, during the reign of Henry II, an important baron named Hamo Peche claimed the advowson as lord of the manor and granted the church to a clerk named William de Orbec.[88] Hamo obtained a royal mandate ordering the bishop to institute the clerk at Hamo's presentation.[89] According to the chronicler, William came to the abbey seeking confirmation of his appointment, but the abbot was not pleased, and "first from the royal, then from the ecclesiastical courts he sought that full justice be done him, complaining in the former about the violence of the knight, in the latter about the intrusion of the clerk."[90] The bishop of London, exercising jurisdiction pursuant to a papal mandate, ruled in favor of the abbot, who subsequently granted the church to Robert "the philosopher." After Robert's death, however, when the abbot attempted to grant the church to a clerk named Thomas, William de Orbec again occupied the church. This time the abbot decided not to sue William, "who had already long since been totally removed from the church by apostolic authority,"[91] but rather sued his putative patron, Hamo Peche, in the royal court. Hamo attempted to essoin, but the royal court seized the advowson into the king's hand. Hamo then sent his son Geoffrey to appear on his behalf. Geoffrey, to the abbot's surprise, conceded the suit and renounced the advowson on his father's and his own behalf. William continued to remain in the church but eventually renounced his right before the bishop of Norwich. The bishop then instituted Thomas as parson at the presentation of the abbot and monks of Battle; Thomas subsequently held the church for an annual pension.[92]

These two cases show how the ecclesiastical courts could play a role in disputes over the right to present a parson. In both cases, the dispute arose from the actions of a layman, who claimed the advowson of the church and either gave it to another religious house or presented a clerk to the bishop. The issue for the royal courts was whether the layman had held the advowson. Nevertheless, a second issue was involved: whether the church's current occupant(s) had been legitimately instituted parson. The latter issue was apparently thought of as lying within the province of the ecclesiastical courts, or at least it seemed plausible to the abbot and the ecclesiastical judges that the matter was subject to the church's jurisdiction. To cover all his bases, therefore, the abbot brought parallel lawsuits in both the royal and ecclesiastical courts, suing the lay claimants to the patronage in royal court and the clerical claimants to the parsonage in ecclesiastical court.

Another prominent case in the Battle chronicle concerns the church of Wye (Kent), the manor appurtenant to which had been given to the abbey by William the Conqueror. A priest named William held half of this church by grant of the abbey. When William died, during the vacancy of the abbacy, Richard de Lucy, chief justiciar of England, asked the prior and convent to grant the church to his son Godfrey de Lucy. The brothers of the abbey agreed but specified in their reply that Godfrey was only to have the moiety that William had held. Godfrey, however, obtained from the king the grant of the whole church, and Richard of Dover, the archbishop-elect, admitted, instituted, and confirmed Godfrey in the whole church. When Richard's election as archbishop was confirmed by the pope, Richard confirmed his prior acts regarding the church.[93]

In 1176, Godfrey brought a lawsuit before the legatine council at Westminster.[94] The abbey was represented by the distinguished canonist Gerard Pucelle.[95] Gerard made the bold argument that "in ecclesiastical matters the secular power possesses no right."[96] Because the king acted not as patron but as custodian of the abbey, the grant was invalid.[97] The presentation and institution, moreover, were invalid because the archbishop-elect had not been consecrated, and the archbishop could not retroactively confirm the invalid acts after his consecration.[98] It is likely that Gerard made these ambitious arguments to encourage a favorable settlement, and a settlement was in fact ordered by the judges delegate.[99] It is nonetheless interesting to see an ecclesiastical court after Clarendon hearing a challenge to the king's right to present a clerk to a benefice.

The dispute over Mildenhall was probably resolved around 1162,[100] before Henry II promulgated the Constitutions of Clarendon. Although the other Battle cases seem to have been concluded after Clarendon (Thurlow ca. 1164–70,[101] and Wye ca. 1176[102]), it is not clear whether, how, or to what extent any effort was made during the period immediately before and after the Compromise of Avranches to enforce the rule of Clarendon that advowson disputes ought to be litigated in the royal courts. By the end of Henry II's reign, however, litigants could invoke the crown's authority to call a halt to ecclesiastical litigation that encroached on the king's prerogative over advowsons.[103] A defendant in an ecclesiastical case that touched on a right of presentation could sue for a royal writ of prohibition to stay the ecclesiastical proceedings. Should the writ not be obeyed, the defendant could set in motion a prohibition plea in the royal court, compelling the plaintiff to explain why he sued, and the judges to explain why they held, a plea of advowson in the ecclesiastical court.[104]

Glanvill contains two writs of prohibition relating to advowson disputes.[105] The first deals with the case in which one putative patron is suing another; it orders the ecclesiastical judges to cease holding such a plea, "because pleas concerning the advowsons of churches appertain to my crown, and dignity."[106] This writ appears relatively infrequently in the early plea rolls.[107] The second writ, which would be known as an *indicavit*, deals with a situation in which clerk N (who claims the church by the presentation of someone other than the plaintiff) has impleaded clerk I (the plaintiff's clerk, who currently holds the benefice) in an ecclesiastical court. The writ explains that success by N in the ecclesiastical plea would have the effect of depriving the plaintiff of his advowson, violating the principle that advowson disputes pertain to the king's crown and dignity. Thus the ecclesiastical judges are directed not to hold the plea "until it be proved in my court, to which of them the advowson of such church belongs."[108] This clause shows the interlocutory nature of the writ: the royal court did not claim jurisdiction over the matter at issue but sought to interrupt the proceeding until the collateral issue of the patronage was decided.[109]

The writ of *indicavit* could be used to call a halt to ecclesiastical court litigation between clerks that infringed on a patron's claim to the advowson. Such litigation might concern the identity of the rightful parson of the church, as in the case of the lawsuits involving Battle Abbey. At some point during the 1220s, the action was extended to litigation over tithes: a plaintiff could seek a royal prohibition on the grounds that a pending ecclesiastical dispute over tithes would lead to the loss of his advowson.[110] In this way, the royal courts were able to protect their jurisdiction over advowsons, but only by asserting jurisdiction over matters that were traditionally the province of the church courts.

While the availability of the writ of *indicavit* ensured the primacy of royal court jurisdiction in matters concerning advowsons, the ecclesiastical courts continued to hear pleas in which a clerk claimed that another clerk had intruded on his benefice. The royal courts did not attempt to make inroads into this jurisdiction. In Michaelmas Term 1219, Ralph of Willoughby sued the prior of Lenton in the royal court for breach of a prohibition he had obtained concerning the church of Pleasley (Derbys). Ralph claimed that when his brother William held the church by gift of Ralph and John de Aincourt,[111] a certain Roger brought an ecclesiastical plea against William concerning the church and sought it by gift of King John. The prior responded that Roger's plea related to the benefice, not the advowson. According to the prior, when the church was vacant in time of war, King John presented Roger to the church by reason of the land of Ralph and John, which was then in the king's hand because they were against the king. However, the bishop did not admit Roger but rather admitted a clerk presented by Ralph and John. Roger accordingly impleaded William *per breve domini pape de intrusione;* that is, he appealed to Rome, and the case was referred to papal judges delegate, including the prior of Lenton.[112] Having heard this story, the king's court simply ordered the prior not to hold any plea in which an advowson was mentioned.[113] Provided that the ecclesiastical plea did not use the word *advocatio,* disputes such as that between Ralph and William could continue to be heard before ecclesiastical authorities.[114]

Lawsuits over benefices were not the only context in which the ecclesiastical authorities continued to exercise authority in disputes over parish churches. By the thirteenth century, if not earlier, it was standard procedure for the bishop to order an inquest concerning the right of patronage (*de iure patronatus*) every time a church became vacant.[115] This inquest, which bore some resemblance to trial by jury in the royal courts, seems to have been designed to prevent error in the admission of the parson.[116] References to the procedure appear in the plea rolls from the reign of John. In a 1213 lawsuit over the church of Brampton (Suffolk), for example, Thomas fitz William argued that the church was not vacant, because Ralph of Barsham was parson. Thomas offered letters of the official of the bishop of Norwich, saying that an inquest had been made, and when no one appeared to vindicate his or her right, the official instituted Ralph in the church by presentation of Thomas.[117] An inquest was also referred to in an entry from 1214 relating to a dispute over the church of Clifton Maybank (Dorset). Philip of Hawkchurch, a canon of Salisbury, asserted that when the bishop held the inquisition, Philip "appeared and made an appeal that nothing be done contrary to the liberty of his prebend" of Yetminster.[118] Philip's "appeal" may have been directed at the pope or the archbishop of Canterbury, but his appearance shows that the parties were allowed to come before the bishop during the inquisition and assert their claims concerning the church.

An inquest by the bishop or his official therefore might precede any dispute concerning an advowson in the royal courts. It could also be a sequel to such litigation. In 1206 the bishop of Hereford was summoned to explain why he did not admit a candidate presented by Cecily de Ebroicis to the church of Putley (Hereford) after Cecily recovered the advowson in the royal court against the chapter of Hereford. The bishop's attorney said that, upon receiving the royal mandate, the bishop "convened his clerks so that he might do what ought to be done."[119] The dean and chapter of Hereford appeared before the bishop and said they were parsons. The bishop held an inquisition and learned that the dean and chapter were indeed parsons of the church, as pertaining to a mother church of which they were parsons. The dean and chapter appealed for their right, and the bishop "did not dare to admit a parson" to a church that already had one.[120] This suggests that regardless of what the king's writ ordered, the bishop had to make his own determination about whether an institution would be valid under canon law.[121]

In general, the early plea rolls show that English bishops and church courts continued to play a vital role in disputes concerning advowsons well into the thirteenth century and long after the Constitutions of Clarendon. Despite the statement in the constitutions that the royal courts should be the forum for advowson disputes, important qualifications to that rule existed, given the recognized role of the church courts in hearing disputes about possession of a benefice between clerks and the administrative proceedings held by the bishop at the death of a parson. The fact remains, however, that the king's courts became extensively involved in advowson disputes in the decades after Clarendon. With very few exceptions, pleas between rival patrons were not held in the ecclesiastical courts, and the ecclesiastical courts generally recognized the "English custom" of allowing the right of advowson to be adjudicated in the royal courts.[122]

Jurisdictional Competition in the Plea Rolls of Richard I

The oldest surviving plea rolls of the English royal courts date to Trinity Term 1194, the fifth year of the reign of Richard I. From that point onward, the plea rolls survive in a more or less continuous series, although many rolls are missing, particularly from the late twelfth century and the early thirteenth. No equivalent series of continuous ecclesiastical court records survives for this early period, and therefore we must base any conclusions about the activity of ecclesiastical courts regarding vacant churches on other sources. Royal records sometimes helpfully refer to specific proceedings in the church courts. Even if the plea rolls do not specifically mention a prior dispute before the bishop, the parameters of a royal dispute may allow us to make an educated guess about what preceded it.

Forum shopping could occur even in cases where the church was not yet vacant. For example, when the current occupant of the church was expected to die soon owing to sickness, old age, or both, a putative patron who did not expect the bishop to view his claim favorably might bring a writ of right in the royal court to resolve the issue before the bishop would have an opportunity to act. However, parties might have had reasons to invoke the jurisdiction of the royal courts other than the possibility of episcopal bias. For example, in the event that an assize of darrein presentment involving the church in question had already been held, the losing party could feel compelled to bring a royal writ of right even if he would have preferred to have the bishop resolve the case. In some cases, moreover, a party might bring a writ of prohibition in the king's court in an effort to preclude further litigation in the ecclesiastical courts.

The clerks who transcribed the early English plea rolls carefully noted the county from which each case arose. In studying advowson cases, however, knowing the county offers less help than knowing the diocese in which the church was located. The patron exercised the advowson by presenting a clerk to the bishop, who would then decide whether to institute the clerk as parson of the church. By the thirteenth century, if not before, it was standard practice for the bishop to order an inquest concerning the right of patronage (*de iure patronatus*) whenever a church became vacant. In the event that no rival patron put in a claim, and the bishop accepted the patron's candidate, there would be no cause for dispute. However, a party who was pessimistic about how the bishop might conduct the inquest would have good reason to seek a remedy in the royal courts.

To investigate possible forum shopping in the early common law, one must first consider how many royal court cases came out of particular dioceses during the part of Richard I's reign for which plea rolls survive, who the parties were in those disputes, and which bishops would have been involved. The earliest rolls deserve careful study, as they give us some clues about what jurisdictional competition might have looked like before royal justice became a matter of routine.

The following tables are based on a survey of all disputes in the royal courts regarding advowson cases from Trinity Term 1194 through Hilary Term 1199.[123] I have included only those cases that mention the name of the church, to avoid possibly double counting disputes between the same parties over different churches. One way to view these data is to compare the percentage of cases brought in each diocese to its number of benefices and total valuation in the *Taxatio Ecclesiastica* of 1291. Table 1 classifies the provenance of royal court advowson disputes by diocese during this period, compared with (1) the number of benefices in each diocese according to the *Taxatio* as a percentage of the total for these dioceses,[124] and (2) the valuation of spiritualties in each diocese as a percentage of the total.[125] As seen in table 1, most royal advowson disputes during this period involved churches from one of two dioceses: Lincoln and Norwich. No other diocese in England came near to producing as many royal advowson cases; the diocese of York, which follows next in the ranking, produced only twelve cases.

Given the high percentage of benefices recorded in the 1291 *Taxatio Ecclesiastica* as being situated in the dioceses of Lincoln and Norwich, and the high valuation recorded for those dioceses, we would expect them to have generated a high percentage of the advowson litigation in the royal courts. However, table 1 shows that the percentage is even higher than what we might expect based on the number of benefices or the valuation of the dioceses, although the discrepancy is more pronounced in Norwich than in Lincoln. In any case, since the data from this period are insufficient to draw any significant conclusions about the other dioceses, the remainder of this discussion of the earliest cases will accordingly focus on cases from Lincoln and Norwich.

Tables 2 and 3 provide information on the identity of the parties to these cases: in particular, whether a monastery or other religious house was involved in the litigation and, if so, on which side of the case. These tables exclude *quo warranto* cases brought by the king as well as cases in which it is not possible to determine one or more of the parties

TABLE I.

Advowson cases by diocese, 1194–99 (compared with benefices and valuation in *Taxatio Ecclesiastica* 1291)

Diocese	# of 1194–99 cases	% of 1194–99 cases	% of 1291 benefices	% of 1291 valuation
Lincoln	37	27.60	21.50	21.70
Norwich	37	27.60	14.90	12.30
York	12	9.00	8.90	14.90
Salisbury	7	5.20	7.10	6.20
Exeter	6	4.50	7.30	3.20
Ely	5	3.70	1.80	2.30
London	5	3.70	5.80	4.20
Canterbury	4	3.00	2.80	3.80
Chichester	4	3.00	4.00	3.70
Coventry and Lichfield	4	3.00	5.10	5.00
Winchester	4	3.00	4.40	5.20
Worcester	4	3.00	5.20	3.80
Bath and Wells	2	1.50	4.20	3.20
Carlisle	1	0.70	1.20	2.00
Durham	1	0.70	2.00	5.30
Hereford	1	0.70	3.90	3.00

in interest. Table 2 categorizes the cases in which the identity of the parties can be determined, even if it is not possible to determine who is the plaintiff. Table 2 shows a clear difference between these two dioceses. Of the cases from the diocese of Norwich, 69.2 percent involve laymen on both sides and no religious house. By contrast, 60 percent of the cases from the diocese of Lincoln involve one or more laymen on one side and one or more religious houses on the other.

Table 3 further disaggregates the data from cases involving religious houses and laymen (which I term "mixed cases") according to which

TABLE 2.

Advowson cases by litigant type, Lincoln and Norwich
dioceses, 1194–99

Types of litigants	Lincoln	Norwich
Lay only	12 (34.3%)	18 (69.2%)
Lay and religious	21 (60%)	8 (30.8%)
Religious only	2 (5.7%)	0 (0.0%)
Total	35 (100%)	26 (100%)

TABLE 3.

Identity of plaintiff in mixed advowson cases, Lincoln and
Norwich dioceses, 1194–99

Types of litigants	Lincoln	Norwich
Lay plaintiff–religious defendant(s)	12 (80%)	4 (66.7%)
Religious plaintiff–lay defendant(s)	3 (20%)	0 (0.0%)
Lay plaintiff–lay and religious defendants	0 (0.0%)	2 (33.3%)
Religious plaintiff–lay and religious defendants	0 (0.0%)	0 (0.0%)
Total	15 (100%)	6 (100%)

party is the plaintiff, to the extent we can determine this information
from the surviving records. As table 3 shows, when the plaintiff can be
identified in cases between laymen and religious houses, the religious
house is usually, but not always, the defendant or one of the defendants.

The final table, table 4, introduces one additional factor: the various religious orders that were represented in lawsuits involving religious
houses.[126] In cases where a particular monastery was involved in lawsuits
over multiple churches, the table counts each dispute separately. Table 4
makes clear that the advowson cases from the diocese of Lincoln were
much more evenly distributed among the various religious orders than
the cases from the diocese of Norwich. That discrepancy becomes even

TABLE 4.

Representation of religious orders in advowson cases, Lincoln
and Norwich dioceses, 1194–99

Religious order	Lincoln	Norwich
Augustinian canons	6 (26.1%)	0 (0.0%)
Benedictine (cathed. chapter)	0 (0.0%)	2 (28.6%)
Benedictine (Cluniac)	0 (0.0%)	3 (42.9%)
Benedictine (nuns)	3 (13.1%)	0 (0.0%)
Benedictine (other)	8 (34.8%)	2 (28.6%)
Cistercian	2 (8.7%)	0 (0.0%)
Hospitallers	1 (4.3%)	0 (0.0%)
Gilbertine	2 (8.7%)	0 (0.0%)
Knights Templar	1 (4.3%)	0 (0.0%)
Total	23 (100%)	7 (100%)

starker when one considers the specific religious houses involved in the Norwich cases. All the religious houses implicated in disputes from Norwich diocese were Benedictine, but two actually involved the cathedral chapter of Norwich, and three involved Cluniac houses. One of the two remaining Norwich cases involved the French abbey of Saint-Pierre-sur-Dives. Only one case involved a non-Cluniac English religious house other than the cathedral chapter, the abbey of Saint Benet of Hulme. Nevertheless, given the small number of cases from Norwich involving religious houses, the distribution among types of houses there may simply be a coincidence.

The discrepancies between the types of cases brought to the royal courts from the dioceses of Lincoln and Norwich prompt the obvious question of who the bishops of those two dioceses were during the period. John of Oxford became bishop of Norwich in 1175, and Hugh of Avalon became bishop of Lincoln in 1186. Both held their sees until death, and both died in 1200. The two men shared some similarities, but also marked differences.

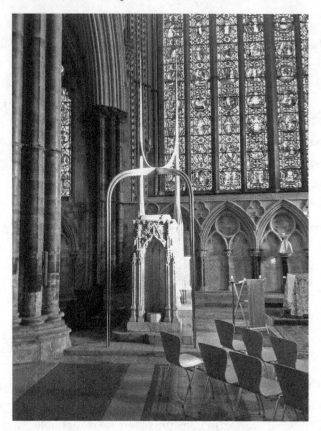

FIG. 6. Shrine of Saint Hugh, Lincoln Cathedral,
England. Photo by Joshua Tate.

As one would expect from his name, Hugh was born in Avalon, in
Burgundy. When Hugh was around eight years old, he and his father
joined a community of Augustinian canons.[127] However, Hugh decided to
join the Carthusian order in his early twenties, entering its head monastery, the Grande Chartreuse.[128] Through the intervention of Henry II,
Hugh became prior of the new charterhouse at Witham in 1180. King
Henry was said to have founded the priory as an alternative to fulfilling a
pilgrimage vow he took after Becket's murder.[129] Henry's later decision to
promote Hugh to bishop of Lincoln is supposed to have been motivated
by a different vow, made while the king was afraid of drowning during a
storm.[130] Henry's patronage of Bishop Hugh may also reflect the king's
more general concern for his soul as he approached the end of his life.[131]

Given Bishop Hugh's monastic background, it is unsurprising that he was a frequent thorn in the side of Henry II and his sons. Nevertheless, Bishop Hugh proved to be skilled in the art of diplomacy and, unlike Thomas Becket, seemed to know what lines should not be crossed in negotiating with Henry. Soon after Hugh became bishop, for example, he excommunicated a royal chief forester and refused to grant a prebend to one of the king's *curiales*. King Henry was furious, and Hugh rode to Woodstock to meet him. The king at first refused to speak, except to request a needle and thread to sew a bandage around his finger. Observing this, Bishop Hugh wryly noted the king's similarity to his "kinsmen from Falaise," a reference to the lowly origins of the mother of William the Conqueror. The king supposedly burst out laughing at the supposed insult, and Hugh was forgiven after explaining that he did not consult the king because he was certain the king would approve of Hugh's actions. If this anecdote is true, Hugh's joke was quite clever: although seemingly a mild insult, it emphasized the legitimacy of the Angevin dynastic claim.[132] Hugh shared the distinction of being canonized after his death with Thomas Becket, but Hugh managed to achieve this posthumous honor without being murdered in the process.

Compared to Hugh of Lincoln, John of Oxford was no holy man. The son of an Oxford sheriff, John spent much of his early career in diplomatic missions on behalf of Henry II in opposition to the subsequently martyred archbishop of Canterbury. Becket's contemporary supporters particularly reviled John for swearing an oath in which he pledged the king's aid and counsel to Frederick Barbarossa against Pope Alexander III, for which he earned the epithet *jurator*.[133] After being promoted to bishop of Norwich, John continued to serve as Henry II's adviser and diplomat, witnessing at least sixty of Henry's royal charters and serving as a royal justice for multiple eyres.[134] Bishop John was not, however, always a dutiful servant of the Angevin kings. Like Hugh of Lincoln, Bishop John was reprimanded at one point by Henry II for excommunicating a royal official without the king's consent.[135] In 1190, John obtained an absolution from Pope Clement III from his vow of pilgrimage, leading an obviously displeased King Richard I to require John to pay a thousand marks to the Templars.[136]

Bishop John's biggest conflicts were not with Henry and Richard but with his own monastic cathedral chapter of Norwich. Under Henry II, royal administrators tended in their own foundations to favor secular canons rather than Benedictine monasteries.[137] John of Oxford was no exception, offering to help the Augustinian canons of Holy Trinity Ipswich financially when their church and conventual buildings were damaged in a fire.[138] Bishop John's poisonous relationship with his chapter of Norwich, however, may have had less to do with his secular background than with his view of the monastic chapter as a mere dependency of his bishopric.[139] The Norwich monks regularly complained to successive popes that the bishop inflicted financial harm on the chapter, and some of the issues raised involved advowsons of churches.[140]

How might the respective backgrounds of Hugh of Lincoln and John of Oxford have affected preferences of rival claimants in advowson disputes? Perhaps the most simple explanation for the large number of royal cases involving disputes between laymen and religious houses from the diocese of Lincoln is that the laymen simply did not trust Bishop Hugh, with his monastic background and reputation as a holy man, to be impartial in disputes involving monasteries. It should be noted, however, that two of the cases brought to the royal courts from Lincoln diocese during this period involved religious houses on both sides. Moreover, the large number of religious houses involved in cases from the diocese of Lincoln could simply reflect the large number of foundations there. According to this theory, fewer royal cases involving religious houses were heard in the diocese of Norwich because there were simply fewer monasteries there.

In general, this argument might hold some weight. The total absence of cases from the diocese of Norwich involving houses of Augustinian canons, however, is difficult to explain by a dearth of such foundations there, as nearly two dozen houses of Augustinian canons existed in Norfolk and Suffolk at the beginning of the period.[141] Although Bishop John personally favored the Augustinian canons of Ipswich and was more partial to secular canons than to the religious orders, in this respect he was not unlike other royal administrators. In contrast, Bishop Hugh probably had a deeper relationship with the canons, having been one himself for much of his childhood. It may be that lay claimants to patronage of churches who had disputes with the Augustinian houses trusted Bishop John to resolve their issues but preferred to seek the aid of the king's courts rather than await the judgment of Bishop Hugh.[142]

As noted earlier, with one exception, the religious houses involved in royal advowson disputes from the diocese of Norwich were either Cluniac foundations or the cathedral chapter of Norwich itself. It is easy to see why the cathedral chapter of Norwich would not trust Bishop John, given the long-standing animosity between the bishop and his chapter. Less obvious is why Cluniac monasteries might have found themselves sued in the king's court. Two of those cases involved the priory of Lewes, the first and largest Cluniac monastery in England.[143] The other case involved the priory of Castle Acre.[144] Bishop John may have fallen from King Richard's favor after he received an absolution from his crusading vow, but it is hard to see how that would drive litigants into the royal courts in cases against Cluniac priories in particular.

Because we lack a regular series of day-to-day ecclesiastical court records comparable to the early plea rolls, it is not possible to confirm or refute the hypothesis that ecclesiastical court litigation in Lincoln declined in proportion to the increase in royal cases. With respect to one case from this period, however, it is possible to see forum shopping by direct rather than circumstantial evidence.[145] One of the earliest surviving entries from the plea rolls tells us that "the bishop of Lincoln seeks his court" in a dispute in Trinity Term 1194 between Fulk d'Oyri and the abbot of Crowland, a Benedictine monastery in Lincolnshire.[146] The records are fragmentary, but it appears that Fulk sought the presentation of the vicar of the church of Gedney, offering a charter that he claimed evidenced an agreement between himself and the abbot whereby Fulk would present a clerk and the abbey would receive a pension. The abbot's reply is revealing: he did not want to respond in the royal court, because Fulk spoke of a pension and vicarage, and those matters pertained to the ecclesiastical court.[147]

It would indeed be a mistake to claim a vicarage rather than an advowson by an action in the king's court. However, the broader point is that Fulk wanted the king to hear his dispute, and the abbot wanted the dispute to be heard by Bishop Hugh. The earliest surviving entry in the case makes it clear that Bishop Hugh also thought that the matter ought to be heard in his own court. Fulk did not lose the case, however; the parties were given license of agreement with a notation that the bishop of Lincoln would need to be present for any concord.[148] From a practical and political standpoint, Fulk's decision to initiate the case before the king's court was probably wise.[149]

Jurisdictional Competition in the Early Thirteenth Century

Had King John been content to allow the royal courts to follow their standard procedures, the triumph of the royal courts in the jurisdictional conflict over advowson disputes could easily be understood. However, as in other contexts, John was prone to intervene personally in certain advowson cases of particular interest to him.[150] In Easter Term 1201, for example, King John ordered his justices not to hear an assize of darrein presentment brought by Robert de Buillers and his wife Hillary against William of Firsby, archdeacon of Stow, until the king's preferred candidate, Roger de Beaumont, was accepted by the chapter of Lincoln as bishop to replace the recently deceased Hugh of Avalon.[151] In Hilary Term 1203, King John prohibited a lawsuit from being heard concerning the church of Saint Decuman's as long as the bishop of Bath had taken the sign of the cross.[152] Most transparently, in Trinity Term 1208, a dispute over the church of Wimpole in the diocese of Ely between Saer de Quenci, Earl of Winchester, and Robert de Insula was abruptly halted with the explanation that "the lord king does not want the lawsuit to proceed" (dominus rex non vult quod loquela illa procedat).[153]

Good reasons might have driven some of John's decisions.[154] It seems reasonable to wait for the appointment of a bishop of Lincoln before deciding an important dispute where the bishop had, as in the case from Easter Term 1201, been vouched to warrant. Other instances appear in the rolls in which a party was excused from appearance or given other relief on the grounds that he had taken the cross. Nevertheless, in light of his brother's absence from England during his reign, King John's personal involvement in these and other cases might have been perceived by the losing parties as an interference with the regular course of justice.[155] As Doris Stenton explained:

> John was but performing an ancient royal duty. But in the last ten years of the twelfth century the administration of justice had been carried on with but little reference to the king himself. It had been a time when the king's

court was growing rapidly in popularity. The practice of eyres had been elaborated and the court at Westminster had become the centre of a highly organised judicial system, which depended on the Justiciar whose writ ran as the king's. The accession of a king who knew England as well as Henry II had known it, who was as interested in legal problems as Henry II had been, meant that Justiciar and Judges alike found that they had a master.[156]

Perhaps the best evidence that John's involvement in the royal courts at the beginning of his reign was not perceived as a positive development is the Great Charter itself, which famously insists that John will not sell, deny, or delay right or justice to any person.[157] That famous line would have been unnecessary unless at least some of the losing parties in royal cases felt aggrieved by John's personal dispensation of justice, and such litigants would presumably have been open to a viable alternative. For some disputes, episcopal courts might not have been a practical option, but bishops who were able to offer justice in advowson disputes might have found willing customers in those subjects of King John who were frustrated by his rule. Why, then, did the ecclesiastical courts not seize the opportunity during the years leading up to the Great Charter to claim the jurisdiction granted to them under canon law? To answer this question, it is helpful to turn again to the diocese of Lincoln.

The medieval diocese of Lincoln was not the largest diocese in England, but it was nonetheless vast, including all or part of eight counties, and it probably contained the largest number of religious houses in England.[158] The *Taxatio Ecclesiastica* of 1291 records the diocese of Lincoln as having 1,747 benefices and a valuation of £27,435, approximately 20 percent of the total number of benefices, and 21 percent of the total valuation, for all of England and Wales.[159] It is therefore unsurprising that the diocese of Lincoln produced a high percentage of the ecclesiastical patronage disputes brought to the royal courts. As table 1 shows, of the advowson cases mentioned in the surviving plea rolls of Richard I, 27.6 percent involved churches in the diocese of Lincoln, which was tied with the diocese of Norwich. Taken together, the two dioceses accounted for the majority of the advowson disputes in the royal courts from 1194 to 1199, with the diocese of York a distant third at 9 percent.[160] As time passed, however, the percentage of cases involving churches from the

FIG. 7. View of Lincoln Cathedral from Steep Hill.
Photo by Joshua Tate.

diocese of Lincoln fell as other dioceses began to produce more litigation in the royal courts. By the time of the last rolls from King John's reign, the percentage of royal advowson cases involving churches in the diocese of Lincoln had dropped to 17.3 percent.[161] The diocese of Lincoln was no longer playing an outsize role in sending disputes to the royal courts.

As has already been noted, the high percentage of disputes between laymen and religious houses in the diocese of Lincoln during the last years of Richard I's reign may have reflected a perceived bias on the part of the saintly Bishop Hugh.[162] Lincoln continued to produce a high number of cases involving religious houses after the death of Saint Hugh in 1200, but by the end of John's reign, the diocese had ceased to be exceptional in that regard. Of the advowson disputes between religious houses

and laymen that first appear in the surviving plea rolls from Trinity Term
and Michaelmas Term 1214, five involve churches in the diocese of
Lincoln,[163] but six involve churches in the diocese of York,[164] four involve
churches in the diocese of Norwich,[165] and three involve churches in the
diocese of Bath.[166] One can most simply explain this change by concluding that, by the end of King John's reign, litigants initiated advowson disputes in the royal courts as a matter of course, not to avoid a perceived
bias on the part of particular bishops who presided over the ecclesiastical
courts.[167] Moreover, the steady stream of advowson disputes brought into
the royal courts by the Angevin reforms did not return to the ecclesiastical courts, notwithstanding the problems that some of King John's most
powerful subjects had with his dispensation of personal justice.

One way to track the changing caseload patterns in the early thirteenth
century is to focus on two statistics. First, what percentage of the overall
number of advowson cases with a lay plaintiff and religious defendant
came from each diocese? Second, what percentage of the total number
of advowson cases in the plea rolls consisted of cases with a lay plaintiff
and a religious defendant? The first metric shows the relative importance
of each diocese in producing the subcategory of cases that was most
likely to reflect jurisdictional competition, and the latter shows how important that type of case was in each diocese. Looking at both statistics
together enables us to see both national and local trends. Table 5 shows
the first metric.

Table 5 suggests significant variability over time, but notable trends
emerge.[168] Lincoln's importance in producing cases in this category
reached its zenith in the surviving rolls of Richard I, when the diocese accounted for more than half of the cases brought by laymen against religious houses. The diocese went back up to 44.44 percent from 1206 to
1210. After that period, the diocese did not account for more than one-
third of the cases. Meanwhile the diocese of York went from contributing
no cases in this category during Richard's surviving rolls to providing a
steady number of such cases thereafter, varying between 9.62 percent to
18.52 percent. Toward the end of John's reign and into the reign of
Henry III, the category "Other" (which includes all dioceses other than
those mentioned in the table) began to account for between one-fifth and
one-fourth of the cases. This trend shows a more widely diffused category

TABLE 5.

Percentage of lay plaintiff-religious defendant advowson cases by diocese, 1194–1225

Diocese	1194–99 (%)	1200–1202 (%)	1203–5 (%)	1206–10 (%)	1211–18 (%)	1219–22 (%)	1223–25 (%)
Cov. and Lich.	3.23	0.00	9.09	7.41	5.77	12.50	0.00
Exeter	6.45	4.76	0.00	0.00	9.62	1.56	8.33
Lincoln	54.84	33.33	24.24	44.44	23.08	28.13	19.44
London	3.23	9.52	6.06	3.70	3.85	3.13	8.33
Norwich	16.13	14.29	12.12	18.52	9.62	15.63	13.89
Worcester	6.45	4.76	3.03	0.00	5.77	3.13	11.11
York	0.00	23.81	15.15	11.11	9.62	14.06	13.89
Other	9.68	9.52	30.30	14.81	32.69	21.87	25.00

of litigation in which the diocese was less important in producing this specific type of case.

Table 6 shows how important the cases brought by laymen against religious houses were in each diocese, measured as a percentage of all advowson cases.[169] This metric shows how important this category of advowson cases was within each individual diocese. The trends in table 6 also point to Lincoln's becoming less of an anomaly over time. Throughout the period, the diocese of Lincoln always produced the highest percentage of cases involving lay plaintiffs and religious defendants. Over time, however, the percentage of cases produced in the other dioceses increased. By 1223 to 1225, the dioceses of Norwich and York were producing 3.9 percent of all cases in the category compared to 5.5 percent from Lincoln. The dioceses of Exeter, London, Winchester, and Worcester were producing between 2.4 percent and 3.1 percent of the cases, a notable increase over their percentages from 1194 to 1199.

Looking at these data, one can see that although the diocese of Lincoln continued to produce a large percentage of cases brought by lay plaintiffs against religious defendants, it was becoming less exceptional in that regard over time. By the period from 1223 to 1225, the percentage of lay plaintiff–religious defendant cases from the diocese of Lincoln had fallen to approximately one-fifth, similar to the proportion of benefices in that diocese and their valuation in the *Taxatio Ecclesiastica*. The reduction in the percentage of such cases from the diocese of Lincoln reflected a corresponding increase from other dioceses, most of which had sent few advowson cases of any kind to the royal courts at the end of the twelfth century. The observed trend could be explained if the royal courts had become the forum of choice for all lay plaintiffs suing religious houses, not just those who had some objection to the ecclesiastical courts. What might explain such a change?

The plea rolls are not our only source of information on possible changes in ecclesiastical courts with regard to patronage disputes by the end of King John's reign. Hugh of Wells, who became bishop of Lincoln in 1209, produced a series of rolls that form the earliest surviving episcopal register in England and provide a detailed record of the activities of the bishop and his archdeacons with regard to ecclesiastical vacancies.[170] Hugh's rolls show that it was routine to hold an ecclesiastical inquest *de*

TABLE 6.

Lay plaintiff–religious defendant cases by diocese as a percentage of all advowson cases, 1194–1225

Diocese	1194–99 (%)	1200–1202 (%)	1203–5 (%)	1206–10 (%)	1211–18 (%)	1219–22 (%)	1223–25 (%)
Bath	0.0	0.0	0.9	0.0	3.2	2.6	0.8
Canterbury	0.6	1.0	3.5	0.0	0.8	0.7	0.8
Cov. and Lich.	0.6	0.0	2.7	1.6	2.4	5.3	0.0
Exeter	1.3	1.0	0.0	0.0	4.0	0.7	2.4
Lincoln	11.0	6.8	7.1	9.7	9.5	11.8	5.5
London	0.6	1.9	1.8	0.8	1.6	1.3	2.4
Norwich	3.2	2.9	3.5	4.0	4.0	6.6	3.9
Salisbury	0.0	0.0	1.8	0.0	2.4	3.3	0.8
Winchester	0.6	0.0	0.0	0.0	2.4	1.3	2.4
Worcester	1.3	1.0	0.9	0.0	2.4	1.3	3.1
York	0.0	4.9	4.4	2.4	4.0	5.9	3.9
Other	0.6	1.0	2.7	3.2	4.8	1.3	2.4

iure patronatus whenever a benefice became vacant.[171] However, if the description in the rolls offers any guide to what procedure was followed in practice, the nature of the inquest seems to have evolved over time. Identified today by the reference number X but known during the episcopate of Bishop Hugh as the *Vetus Rotulus*, the earliest roll in the series consists of thirteen membranes in two different hands.[172] The careful research of David Smith demonstrated that the earliest entries on the roll are the first four entries on membrane 1 and the entries on membrane 2, which were written by a different scribe than the other entries on the roll. The latter scribe, whom Smith refers to as Scribe A, used a "small and untidy hand," while the other scribe, Scribe B, wrote in a hand that was "regular, neat, and more ornate." The entries written by Scribe A most likely date to 1214 and 1215.[173] One of the entries written by Scribe A relates to the institution of a parson to the church of Stibbington:

> Master Thomas of Tyrinton, presented by the abbot and convent of Thorney to the church of Stibbington, is admitted and instituted to that church. . . . And this was done after an inquest by the bishop, present in that very church, determined that the church was the subject of no controversy and the abbot and convent held the advowson.[174]

Many entries in the roll refer to an institution of a new parson, but the foregoing entry is the only one that refers to an inquest having been made by the bishop relating to the advowson. Some entries in membrane 2 refer to an inquest by the dean of Lincoln, one of the archdeacons, or another senior cleric, but those entries also typically state that the inquest determined that the advowson of the church belonged to a specific individual or religious house.[175] The formulaic language was soon changed, however, to a more ambiguous statement of what occurred at the inquest. The following entry from membrane 4 offers a good example: "William of Cennor, a clerk, having been presented by the abbess and convent of Godstow to the church of Easington . . . was admitted and instituted as parson since everything was made clear through an inquest by the archdeacon of Oxford."[176] Most subsequent entries report the archdeacon's inquest to have determined that "the matter was ready" (negotium fuit in expedito), giving the green light to the institution of the new parson while omitting any reference to a finding regarding the advowson. Even that is

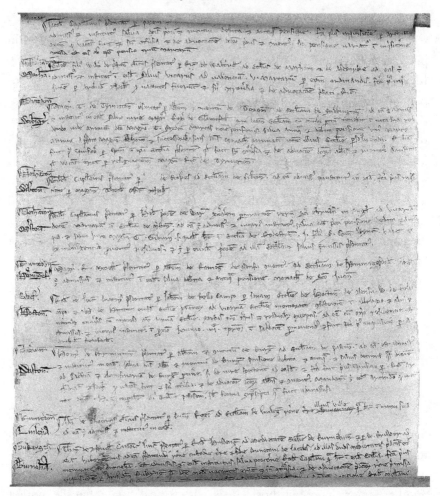

FIG. 8. Register of Hugh of Wells, roll 10, membrane 2. Photo by
Lincolnshire Archives, reprinted with kind permission of the Dean
and Chapter of Lincoln Cathedral.

more specific than some entries, which reduce the description of the inquest to a simple "etc."[177]

These changes in formulaic language, taken by themselves, might not
indicate any significant change in the procedures being followed in the diocese with regard to vacant churches. It is likely that neither Scribe A nor
Scribe B was present at the inquests he recorded. Perhaps Scribe B simply chose to be more concise in summarizing the returns he received

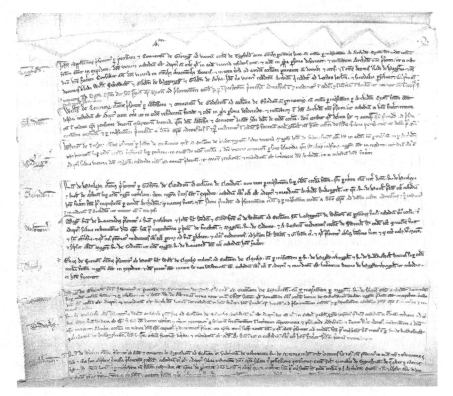

FIG. 9. Register of Hugh of Wells, roll 10, membrane 4. Photo by
Lincolnshire Archives, reprinted with kind permission of the Dean
and Chapter of Lincoln Cathedral.

from the clerks of the various archdeacons. However, in light of the significant drop in the percentage of royal advowson cases from the diocese
of Lincoln from the episcopate of Hugh of Avalon to that of Hugh of
Wells, it is at least possible that the entry relating to the church of
Stibbington might be the last trace of what was once a significant involvement by the bishop in patronage disputes.[178] When compared to
the neat and ornate hand of Scribe B, the hand of Scribe A, who was
responsible for the entries in membranes 1 and 2, suggests that he was either new to the role of keeping entries in the bishop's register or—more
likely, given the chronology of the entries—primarily trained to handle
other administrative matters and took on the role of scribe toward
the end of his career. Even if Hugh of Wells rarely intervened in such

matters, Scribe A could have remembered an earlier time when Hugh of Avalon as bishop took a more aggressive approach, making determinations about rights of presentation as a matter of course. At minimum, Scribe A regarded the church as playing some role in determining the ownership of the advowson, whether the inquest was made by the bishop or a lower official. Scribe B preferred instead to elide that aspect of the inquest, perhaps more sensitive to the fact that the royal courts considered advowson disputes to fall within their sole jurisdiction.

Setting aside the occasional revisionist historian, King John is not frequently mentioned as an effective administrator. In this one respect, however, John did have some success: he was able to appoint bishops to two of the most important dioceses in England who proved to be loyal allies or, at the least, not thorns in the king's side. One of those bishops was Hugh of Wells. Neither a holy man nor a scholar, Hugh joined the Chancery of King John in 1199 and continued to serve the king until his election to the bishopric of Lincoln in 1209. It is true that Hugh broke with John after the king's excommunication, which may have facilitated Hugh's confirmation, notwithstanding suspected election irregularities and other malicious rumors. Nevertheless, Hugh never caused the sort of problems for John that his predecessor Hugh of Avalon had caused for Henry II, and Hugh is remembered primarily as a competent administrator who served his diocese efficiently for many years. His loyalty may also be seen in the fact that Hugh served as a royal justice on several eyres during the reign of Henry III, John's successor.[179]

It comes as no surprise that a bishop with the background of Hugh of Wells would have little interest in reasserting claims under canon law that conflicted with the long-standing royal position that advowson disputes belonged in the king's courts.[180] Hugh of Wells was not the only loyal clerk whom King John was able to successfully appoint to a high ecclesiastical office. Like Hugh of Wells, John de Gray, bishop of Norwich from 1200 to his death in 1214, was a clerk in King John's service before being elevated to the episcopate. John de Gray was one of only two bishops to remain loyal to King John during his excommunication, the other being Peter des Roches, bishop of Winchester.[181] King John's confidence in the administration of his bishop of Norwich might explain a curt entry from the plea rolls of Hilary Term 1203 dismissing a lawsuit over the advowson of the church of Kettleston, in the diocese of Norwich, "by order of the lord king" (per preceptum domini regis), without further explanation.[182] A loyal bishop like John de Gray would have taken extra care to avoid decisions that might have incurred the king's displeasure. Thus the possibility of a jurisdictional conflict would have been of only theoretical importance in that relationship.

Despite their importance, disputes regarding advowsons constituted a small part of the business of the early royal courts. Had the bishops managed to seize jurisdiction over advowsons in the tumult leading up to Magna Carta, their victory would have been minor and possibly short-lived. Nevertheless, any account of the success of the English common law must take into account not only that the early common-law courts succeeded in attracting litigants but that they were able to keep that business through the end of the reign of one of England's least popular kings. If the common law had been less fair or efficient, the royal courts might have suffered the same fate as Star Chamber in a later age. The true genius of the Angevin legal reforms was their resilience in the face of the worst enemy of the rule of law: powerful men who do not understand the limits of their power.

CHAPTER SIX

CONCLUSION

At the time of the English common law's creation, it had one shared feature with any other innovation: to survive, it needed people to adopt it. If the king's new courts had no customers, they would have withered on the vine and been relegated to history's dustbin. What, then, made the common law succeed? The story of advowson litigation told in this book may help provide some answers.

In his classic work introducing the concept of early adopters, Everett Rogers identified compatibility and relative advantage as two key attributes of successful innovations.[1] Innovations become popular when they are not wholly incompatible with cultural values (compatibility) but are perceived as being better than existing alternatives (relative advantage). Did the common law, in the context of advowson litigation, show these attributes? At the risk of oversimplification, it is possible to call attention to two recurring themes in the preceding chapters that show how the common law rose to the challenge: the cumulative effect of various choices resulting in a balance between competing interests, and the tendency of the early common law to produce creative solutions to difficult problems.

The men responsible for developing the common law of advowsons do not seem to have feared the Roman and canon law taught in the schools, although at other times they made decisions quite foreign to the Romano-canonical tradition. We see the influence of Romano-canonical learning most clearly in the assize of darrein presentment, which was most likely created around 1180. The English government faced a problem: the writ of right took too long, and the courts needed a shorter method of resolving disputes. Darrein presentment was the solution, and it bears the hallmarks of Roman law influence.

Like the Roman interdicts *utrubi* and *uti possidetis,* the assize of darrein presentment looked to who was in control of the property in dispute at the time the lawsuit commenced, control in the advowson context being manifested in the last successful presentation. It was irrelevant who had the greater right in the advowson: that was a matter for the action of right, which might follow the conclusion of the assize. The relationship between the assize of darrein presentment and the writ of right of advowson may be said to parallel, at least to some extent, the relationship between the Roman interdict *uti possidetis* and the *rei vindicatio.*

At some point between 1180 and 1196, after the first two components of the English advowson scheme were already in place, a significant change occurred. Donees were given a remedy of their own: the writ of *quare impedit,* a remedy that seems to have been designed specifically to meet the needs of religious houses claiming by gift. This time, however, the royal advisers did not turn to Romano-canonical learning but crafted something distinctly English. *Bracton* said that the donee who brought *quare impedit* had quasi seisin, a category that in name recalled the quasi possession of Roman law but in substance blurred the line between ownership and possession that was traditionally a hallmark of the Roman legal system.

Nevertheless, the incongruity between *quare impedit* and Romano-canonical learning should not obscure the fact that the writ was essentially a concession to the church by the king's courts. Advowsons, and advowson disputes, lay at the intersection between the church and the secular world. Nothing could be more central to the operation of a parish church than the right to choose the parson, and yet this right was originally assigned to laymen, who exercised it at first without episcopal approval. By the twelfth century, the church hierarchy had successfully claimed a vote in the process, but laymen still had the crucial right to present the candidate. Although laymen could not be forced to give up this right, many of them parted with it voluntarily, giving advowsons to monasteries and convents. Over time, however, laymen began to realize the value that advowsons had, and some of the descendants of twelfth-century donors repented of their ancestors' gifts. It should not be surprising, therefore, that the king's advisers eventually developed a special writ for the benefit of donees.

Through papal legislation and canonist commentary, the church evolved its own set of rules regarding donations of advowsons. These rules were in flux in the late twelfth century and the early thirteenth, particularly with regard to the question of whether episcopal consent was required for a valid gift. On the one hand, some canonists thought that episcopal consent was always necessary; others thought that it was necessary only for gifts to laymen, and still others thought that it was necessary only for gifts to religious houses. On the other hand, canonists generally agreed that selling an advowson was prohibited unless the advowson was sold with an entire property (*universitas*).

According to canonistic doctrine, the English royal courts should not have been deciding many of the advowson cases discussed in these pages. The royal exercise of jurisdiction over advowson disputes was itself a rejection of canon law. In other respects, however, the English royal courts did not flagrantly violate canon law rules. The royal courts allowed the ecclesiastical courts to continue to hear lawsuits over intrusion, so long as they did not use the word "advowson." No evidence suggests that the royal courts tolerated simony or that laymen were allowed directly to control tithes. With regard to gifts, the royal courts do not seem to have required episcopal consent under any circumstances. This comported with the view of the eminent canonist Huguccio and was clearly a defensible view under canon law until the middle of the thirteenth century.

By not requiring episcopal consent, the English royal courts offered some assistance to the monasteries that claimed by gift. Nevertheless, until the late twelfth century, donees faced considerable obstacles in the royal courts. A donee could not bring the writ of right of advowson, nor (unless the other party was also a donee) could a donee bring the assize of darrein presentment. A donee could respond to an assize of darrein presentiment by pleading the exception of gift, but the exception was *in perso-nam* and could be pleaded only against the donor or his heir. When the donee claimed by gift from a third party, the donee would have no remedy in the royal court.

The creation of *quare impedit* in the late twelfth century, together with the absence of a requirement of episcopal consent, made it easy for a donee to sue on the basis of a gift of an advowson. Yet the ability to sue is not the same as the ability to win. At some point during the period, without fanfare, the royal courts adopted two significant rules that prevented some donees from successfully recovering their advowsons. One was the rule of subsequent presentation: when the donor, subsequent to the gift, presented another candidate who is instituted as parson, that subsequent presentation revokes the earlier gift. The other was the rule of subsequent transfer: when A gives to B, and B, without having presented, gives to C, C acquires nothing, but B gives up whatever B had. Both of these rules seem to reflect a skeptical attitude about the charters that donees offered as evidence of their gifts. When a charter was made before the institution of the last parson, or when a string of charters existed without additional evidence of transfer of seisin, the common-law courts would not trust the charters.

Quare impedit gave the donee something like an *in rem* claim, good against the world. Merely delivering the charter was enough to support a *quare impedit* action; no presentation was required. However, the justices applied the rule of subsequent presentation to the writ, meaning that the donee's claim was subject to the whims of the donor. Taken as a whole, these rules seem to reflect a balance between two competing interests: the king's lay subjects and the religious houses. The law favored the religious houses by creating the writ of *quare impedit*, granting an exception of gift to all three writs and not requiring evidence of episcopal consent. On the other hand, the law favored the laymen by virtue of the rules of subsequent presentation and subsequent transfer. Neither side would have chosen this regime, because it contained elements that favored both sides.

One might argue that granting the religious houses a remedy in court should have been a given from the start, not a prize to be fought for. Monks and canons, however, were experts in writing who could easily forge documents of gift. Allowing such parties to sue for their rights was a risky proposition, one that had to be balanced by some limitation on the kinds of charters that could be introduced in court. The rules of subsequent presentation and transfer represented a reasonable response to a very real problem of forgery, a response that acknowledged the validity of claims by religious houses without giving them a procedural advantage on account of their literacy. Overall, the picture that emerges from the early common law of advowsons is one of royal government (including the judiciary) gradually working out a compromise to mediate disputes between conflicting interest groups.

It is interesting to speculate on what might have happened had England been more zealous about following basic ideas of Roman law in this period. The assize of darrein presentment would certainly have been invented, but *quare impedit* would either not have been created or have been very different in nature. Had the royal courts wanted to give a remedy to the monasteries, the logical solution would have been to allow a donee to bring the writ of right, on the theory that delivering the charter constituted a valid *traditio.* The rule of subsequent presentation would not have applied to the writ of right under this scheme. The writ of right would have been different in any case: the plaintiff would probably have had to trace his ownership back to one of the acceptable natural or civil modes of acquisition, rather than simply recounting that his ancestor was seised in the reign of a specified king. By taking a more flexible approach, the common law eventually produced a system that may have been less intellectually coherent but allowed the compromise that was intended. The royal justices wanted the rule of subsequent presentation to apply to all gifts, and the ambiguous nature of *quare impedit* made this feasible.

No obvious counterpart to the rules of subsequent presentation and transfer exists in Romano-canonical learning. One might, however, see some parallel in the debates among the canonists over the extent to which advowsons might be transferred without episcopal consent and independently of an estate. Canonists, like the royal justices, were not entirely comfortable with the idea that advowsons were a transferable form of property separate from the land to which they were appurtenant. Thus, even though the common-law rules of subsequent presentation and transfer operated to bar claims made by religious houses, the skepticism of donations they represented might have been at least comprehensible to the canonists, who had been engaged in a controversy of their own on the subject. A contemporary canonist familiar with the emerging concepts of *ius ad rem petendam* and *quasi possessio*, moreover, might not have been surprised to see the common-law courts treat a gift of an incorporeal right of presentation differently from a gift of real or tangible property. Nevertheless, it seems highly unlikely that the idiosyncratic common-law rules of subsequent presentation and transfer were inspired by any developing Romano-canonical concepts.

Different branches of the royal government played a role in creating the common law of advowsons. We do not know exactly how the assize of darrein presentment was promulgated, but the means was probably some sort of royal decree. *Quare impedit*, on the other hand, was ultimately a product of Chancery, the branch of the king's government responsible for the creation of writs, although Chancery would not have been likely to act on an issue of such importance without a broader degree of approval. It was perhaps the royal justices themselves, however, who devised the rules of subsequent presentation and transfer that made *quare impedit* something less than a proprietary remedy and limited the exception of gift in the other writs. It was also the justices who declined to require proof of episcopal confirmation for gifts. Credit for the compromise worked out in the late twelfth and early thirteenth centuries goes to the royal government as a whole, but especially to the justices who put it into action.

Scholars have debated the extent to which kings, royal advisers, and judges consciously sought to create the English common law. Paul Brand thinks that, at least with regard to the overall functioning of the royal courts, it is "difficult to resist the conclusion that Henry II and his advisers possessed a vision of the legal system they wished to create in England."[2] In Milsom's view, by contrast, the making of the common law was a "series of accidents, of course, not really a human achievement: but still something was created."[3] The common law of advowsons shows many signs of creativity, but individual creative acts do not necessarily add up to a unified vision for the common law. One may raise legitimate doubts about whether the actors involved in this process knew what they were doing every step of the way.

The compromise concerning donees did not happen all at once. The first step in the process was the exception of gift, which was already part of the assize of darrein presentment by the time of *Glanvill*. It is likely that, from the beginning, the royal justices did not require evidence of episcopal consent from parties claiming by gift. Granting a separate remedy for donees happened after *Glanvill; quare impedit* was not part of the original plan. On the other side, the rules of subsequent presentation and transfer cannot be dated with certainty. Because they were, in all likelihood, judge-made rules, they probably evolved in response to particular cases heard in the years after the exception of gift was applied to darrein presentment. Unfortunately this process occurred before the period of the surviving plea rolls.

Perhaps the best way to see the development of the early common law of advowsons is as a series of creative responses to particular problems. The assize of darrein presentment, the writ of *quare impedit,* and the rules of subsequent presentation and transfer all fall under this description. But they were not all created at once, nor was a "master plan" likely to have existed at the outset. Nevertheless, when the last of these pieces was put into place—either *quare impedit* or the two rules—the result was a compromise that had some logic to it.

Of the pieces in this puzzle, *quare impedit* had the brightest future. After the early fourteenth century, the use of the other advowson writs became rare, and *quare impedit* became the dominant form of action.[4] By the time of William Blackstone, *quare impedit* was the sole action used by a plaintiff whose right of presentation had been disturbed.[5] The writ of *quare impedit* had its own treatise, written in the early eighteenth century.[6] *Quare impedit* was one of the few real actions to survive the Real Property Limitation Act of 1833, which abolished both the writ of right of advowson and the assize of darrein presentment.[7] Not until 1860 was *quare impedit* finally abolished, when the real actions were replaced by the writ of summons.[8]

Why *quare impedit* eventually supplanted the other advowson writs is a fascinating question, but beyond the scope of this book. It is interesting, however, to note that what appears to be the least Roman of the advowson writs proved to be the most resilient. If *quare impedit* was indeed a uniquely English creation, as the preliminary examination in this book has suggested, Chancery did well by thinking outside the box of Romano-canonical learning.

This book has sought to bring a little sunlight to a darkened corner of English legal history. A picture has emerged of a legal system struggling to find an appropriate solution for a significant social conflict and making innovative strides in the process. Although it is impossible to say for certain, the preponderance of the evidence suggests a real connection between Romano-canonical learning and the English common law of advowsons, but nothing close to transplantation.

We must do more work, however, to answer the difficult questions that follow from that conclusion. How precisely did the patronage conflict between religious houses and the laity play out on the European continent, and how does that compare to the English story? Did Chancery produce something as distinctive as *quare impedit* because of political or social conditions particular to England, or because the developing common law could not—or would not—fully internalize the Romano-canonical way of thinking? The advowson cases tell us as much about the history of the common law as any other branch of property litigation. But English law forms only one part of a larger puzzle, and that puzzle is far from being solved. At the least, we can say that the rules and institutions of medieval English law seem to have served their people well at the time. A legal system that fails to provide for the needs of its people will soon crumble on itself, but a system that strives for fair and impartial justice can survive even the most destructive of tyrants.

NOTES

Chapter One. Introduction

1. 12 CRR 219 no. 1071 (Mich. 1225).

2. *Id.*

3. Nicholas Vincent, "William de Warenne (*d.* 1240), Fifth Earl of Surrey," in *Oxford Dictionary of National Biography* (Oxford: Oxford University Press, 2004), http://www .oxforddnb.com/view/article/28739.

4. Roy Midmer, *English Medieval Monasteries (1066–1540): A Summary* (Athens: University of Georgia Press, 1979), 273; Antonia Gransden, *Legends, Tradition, and History in Medieval England* (London: Hambledon Press, 1992), 98.

5. 12 CRR 219 no. 1071 (Mich. 1225).

6. Nicholas Karn, "Geoffrey de Burgh (*d.* 1228), Bishop of Ely," in *Oxford Dictionary of National Biography* (Oxford: Oxford University Press, 2004), http://www.oxforddnb.com/ view/article/95140.

7. Confirmation by William, prior of Norwich, of the impropriation by Bishop Pandulf to Saint Benet's Abbey of the church of Ludham. Norfolk Record Office, DN/EST 5/6 (1220).

8. Nicholas Vincent, "Pandulf (*d.* 1226), Bishop of Norwich," in *Oxford Dictionary of National Biography* (Oxford: Oxford University Press, 2004), http://www.oxforddnb.com/ view/article/2717.

9. Christopher Harper-Bill, "Thomas de Blundeville (*d.* 1236), Bishop of Norwich and Papal Legate," in *Oxford Dictionary of National Biography* (Oxford: Oxford University Press, 2004), http://www.oxforddnb.com/view/article/21230.

10. 12 CRR 219 no. 1071 (Mich. 1225).

11. Daniel Lord Smail, *The Consumption of Justice: Emotions, Publicity, and Legal Culture in Marseille, 1264–1423* (Ithaca, N.Y.: Cornell University Press, 2003), 242.

12. See James Masschaele, *Jury, State, and Society in Medieval England* (New York: Palgrave Macmillan, 2008), 205 (explaining how the medieval English jury was a popular institution that gave the king an entrée into local structures of power).

13. For a discussion of this traditional view, see William Ewald, "Comparative Jurisprudence (II): The Logic of Legal Transplants," *Am. J. Comp. L.* 43 (1995): 489–90. Among its most notable proponents was the distinguished nineteenth-century German jurist Savigny, who associated positive law with the law of the people (*Volksrecht*), and thus with the *Volksgeist*, or "spirit of the people." Friedrich Carl von Savigny, *System des heutigen Römischen Rechts* (Berlin: Veit, 1840), vol. 1, p. 14. Savigny's vision of the German *Volksgeist*, however, was of one infused with the study of Roman law. See James Q. Whitman, *The Legacy of Roman Law in the German Romantic Era* (Princeton, N.J.: Princeton University Press, 1990), 110–12.

14. One suspects that a similar doubt in the universality of legal principles motivated Holmes's famous statement that "the common law is not a brooding omnipresence in the sky, but the articulate voice of some sovereign or quasi sovereign that can be identified." Southern Pac. Co. v. Jensen, 244 U.S. 205 (1917) (Holmes, J., dissenting).

15. Alan Watson, *Legal Transplants: An Approach to Comparative Law*, 2nd ed. (Athens: University of Georgia Press, 1993), 95–96. Others have expressed similar views. See Morris R. Cohen and Felix S. Cohen, *Readings in Jurisprudence and Legal Philosophy* (New York: Prentice Hall, 1951), 101 (noting that similarities among civil codes in different countries with respect to basic contract rules "offer a substantial challenge to the view that law reflects all the changes of changing economies and all the diversities of diverse civilizations"); Roscoe Pound, *The Formative Era of American Law* (New York: Peter Smith, 1950), 94 ("History of a system of law is largely a history of borrowings of legal materials from other legal systems and of assimilation of materials from outside of the law").

16. This may be a source of misunderstanding on the part of some of Watson's critics. See Ewald, "Comparative Jurisprudence (II)," at 504–8 (discussing criticisms made by the legal sociologist Richard Abel).

17. See Gunther Teubner, "Legal Irritants: Good Faith in British Law, or How Unifying Law Ends Up in New Divergences," *Modern L. Rev.* 61 (1998): 11–32.

18. See *id.* at 12.

19. Sir Thomas Smith, *De Republica Anglorum: A Discourse on the Commonwealth of England*, ed. L. Alston (1583; repr., Cambridge: Cambridge University Press, 1906), 142. As David Ibbetson has explained, Smith's position is one of three basic positions that continue to be pressed today, the others being that English law did in fact have a significant European

character or that "European law" is itself a misleading construct. See Ibbetson, *Common Law and* Ius Commune (London: Selden Society, 2001), 4.

20. Charles P. Sherman, "The Romanization of English Law," *Yale L.J.* 23 (1914): 329. Sixty years later, a legal historian writing in the same publication could confidently call Sherman's position "perhaps equally silly" as "the view that English law is exclusively a home-grown product of the British Isles." See Charles Donahue Jr., "The Civil Law in England," *Yale L.J.* 84 (1974): 168.

21. See, e.g., Charles Donahue Jr., "*Ius Commune,* Canon Law, and Common Law in England," *Tulane L. Rev.* 66 (1992): 1766–68, 1780; William M. Gordon, "A Comparison of the Influence of Roman Law in England and Scotland," in *The Civilian Tradition and Scots Law,* ed. David L. Carey Miller and Reinhard Zimmermann (Berlin: Duncker and Humblot, 1997), 147–48; R. H. Helmholz, *The* Ius Commune *in England: Four Studies* (Oxford: Oxford University Press, 2001), 3–9.

22. R. H. Helmholz, "Magna Carta and the *ius commune,*" *University of Chicago L. Rev.* 66 (1999): 370–71.

23. John L. Barton, *Roman Law in England,* in *Ius Romanum Medii Aevi,* pt. V.13a (Milan: Giuffrè, 1971), 24, 27–28, 95–96.

24. J. H. Baker, *An Introduction to English Legal History,* 4th ed. (Bath: LexisNexis, 2002), 29 (stating that "English law flourished in isolation from Europe"); S. F. C. Milsom, *A Natural History of the Common Law* (New York: Columbia University Press, 2003), 1 (contending that "there could not be much effect [of Roman law on English law] beyond whatever intangible force may have been exerted by language").

25. Reinhard Zimmermann, "Der europäische Charakter des englischen Rechts," *Zeitschrift für Europäisches Privatrecht* 1 (1993): 51 ("Es bestand ein ständiger intellektueller Kontakt mit dem kontinentalen Europa, der das englische Recht maßgeblich und charakteristisch geprägt hat").

26. This is not to discount the importance of earlier developments, such as the expansion of royal justice under Henry I and the earlier precedents of the Anglo-Saxon kings. See John Hudson, *The Formation of the English Common Law: Law and Society in England from King Alfred to Magna Carta,* 2nd ed. (London: Routledge, 2018), 70–71, 115–117 (discussing the concept of a "king's peace" in Henry I's Coronation Charter and his frequent intervention in land litigation); and Patrick Wormald, *The Making of English Law: King Alfred to the Twelfth Century* (Oxford: Blackwell, 1999), at 19 (comparing Henry II to the Anglo-Saxon legislating kings). However, it was during the reign of Henry II that royal involvement in adjudication became routine. See Hudson, *Formation of the English Common Law,* at 119–22.

27. Paul Brand, " '*Multis Vigiliis Excogitatam et Inventam*': Henry II and the Creation of the English Common Law," in *The Making of the Common Law* (London: Hambledon Press, 1992), 77.

28. See, e.g., Joseph Biancalana, "For Want of Justice: Legal Reforms of Henry II," *Columbia L. Rev.* 88 (1988): 435–41; Paul Brand, "The Origins of English Land Law: Milsom and After," in *The Making of the Common Law,* 203–25; S. F. C. Milsom, *The Legal*

Framework of English Feudalism (Cambridge: Cambridge University Press, 1976); Robert C. Palmer, "The Origins of Property in England," *Law and Hist. Rev.* 3 (1985): 1–50. A consensus seems to be emerging that although the assize of novel disseisin and other inventions of Henry II's reign may not originally have been intended to supplant the seigneurial courts, the creation of those inventions was a manifestation of royal authority. See John Hudson, *Land, Law, and Lordship in Anglo-Norman England* (Oxford: Oxford University Press, 1994), 254, 262–71; Biancalana, "For Want of Justice," at 435–36.

29. See chap. 5 *infra*.

30. F. Pollock and F. W. Maitland, *The History of English Law before the Time of Edward I*, 2nd ed. (1898; repr., Cambridge: Cambridge University Press, 1898), vol. 2, p. 136.

31. An advowson would eventually be classified as an "incorporeal hereditament" or "a right issuing out of a thing corporate." William Blackstone, *Commentaries on the Laws of England* (Chicago: University of Chicago Press, 1979, facsimile of 1st ed., 1765–69), vol. 2, pp. 20–21.

32. Blackstone describes this feature of advowsons in his treatise:

> The advowson is the object of neither the sight, nor the touch; and yet it perpetually exists in the mind's eye, and in contemplation of law. It cannot be delivered from man to man by any visible bodily transfer, nor can corporal possession be had of it. If the patron takes corporal possession of the church, the church-yard, the glebe or the like, he intrudes on another man's property; for to these the parson has the exclusive right. The patronage can therefore be only conveyed by operation of law, by verbal grant, either oral or written, which is a kind of invisible, mental transfer: and being so vested, it lies dormant and unnoticed, till occasion calls it forth; when it produces a visible, corporeal fruit, but intitling some clerk, whom the patron shall please to nominate, to enter and receive bodily possession of the lands and tenements of the church. (*Id.* at 21–22)

33. D. Whitelock, M. Brett, and C. N. L. Brooke, eds., *Councils and Synods with Other Documents Relating to the English Church*, vol. 1 (Oxford, 1981), pt. 2, pp. 878–79. The Constitutions of Clarendon are not to be confused with the assize of Clarendon from two years later, which created the jury of presentment that is an antecedent of the modern grand jury. On the assize of Clarendon and its role as a turning point in the criminal law of medieval England, see Elizabeth Papp Kamali, *Felony and the Guilty Mind in Medieval England* (Cambridge: Cambridge University Press, 2019), 21–22.

34. See Charlotte Whatley, "Edward III and the Fight for the Benefices of Exeter," in *Fourteenth Century England VIII*, ed. J. S. Hamilton (Woodbridge: Boydell Press, 2014), at 62 (noting that "advowson rights and papal provisions had been a source of conflict in England ever since the Norman Conquest").

35. On the changes to advowson litigation made by the Provisions of Westminster, see Paul Brand, *Kings, Barons, and Justices: The Making and Enforcement of Legislation in Thirteenth-Century England* (Cambridge: Cambridge University Press, 2003), at 71–75, 136.

36. The treatise was almost certainly not written (as was once thought) by the royal judge Henry of Bracton (or Bratton), although he may have been responsible for certain revisions. See Paul Brand, "The Age of Bracton," *Proceedings of the British Academy* 89 (1996): 66–73 (arguing that the treatise was written in the mid- to late 1230s); and Morris S. Arnold, "Book Review," *Harvard L. Rev.* 91 (1977): 519 (discussing the findings of Samuel Thorne). J. L. Barton, "The Mystery of Bracton," *Journal of Legal History* 14 (1993): 1–142, defends the traditional view. In his recent study, Thomas McSweeney dates the treatise as having been "written over several decades, between the 1220s and the 1260s," by royal justices who may have included Martin Pattishall, William of Raleigh, and Henry of Bratton. Thomas J. McSweeney, *Priests of the Law: Roman Law and the Making of the Common Law's First Professionals* (Oxford: Oxford University Press, 2019), 1–2.

37. Everett M. Rogers, *Diffusion of Innovations*, 3rd ed. (New York: Free Press, 1983), at 246.

38. Harold J. Berman, *Law and Revolution: The Formation of the Western Legal Tradition* (Cambridge, Mass.: Harvard University Press, 1983), 99–107, 116–18. The eleventh-century reform movement is also referred to as the Gregorian reform, after one of its principal proponents, Pope Gregory VII. However, the reform was a gradual process, and some have argued that its roots lay in the monastic reforms of the tenth century and earlier. See Uta-Renate Blumenthal, *The Investiture Controversy: Church and Monarchy from the Ninth to the Twelfth Century* (Philadelphia: University of Pennsylvania Press, 1988), 64–65.

39. For a recent assessment of the conflict, see Anne J. Duggan, "Henry II, the English Church and the Papacy, 1154–76," in *Henry II: New Interpretations*, ed. Christopher Harper-Bill and Nicholas Vincent (Woodbridge: Boydell Press, 2007), 154–83.

40. See chap. 3 *infra*.

41. On the concepts of possession and right in English law and how that framework compares to the Roman structure, see generally David J. Seipp, "Roman Legal Categories in the Early Common Law," in *Legal Record and Historical Reality: Proceedings of the Eighth British Legal History Conference Cardiff 1987*, ed. Thomas G. Watkin (London: Hambledon Press, 1989), 9–36.

Chapter Two. The Advowson Writs

1. Susan Wood, *The Proprietary Church in the Medieval West* (Oxford: Oxford University Press, 2006), 66–91.

2. Peter M. Smith, "The Advowson: The History and Development of a Most Peculiar Property," *Ecclesiastical L.J.* 5 (2000): 320–21.

3. Dietrich Kurze, *Pfarrerwahlen im Mittelalter* (Cologne: Böhlau, 1966), 519; G. W. O. Addleshaw, *Rectors, Vicars, and Patrons in Twelfth and Early Thirteenth Century Canon Law* (London: St. Anthony's Press, 1956), 17. Some advowsons may have retained this characteristic even into the modern period. Blackstone discusses advowsons donative, which were "merely in the gift or disposal of the patron, subject to his visitation only, and not to that of the ordinary." Advowsons donative, according to Blackstone, were created by the

king "or any subject by his license." Blackstone, *Commentaries*, vol. 2, 23. The advowsons referred to in the plea rolls from the late twelfth and early thirteenth centuries are invariably presentative, meaning that the patron must present his clerk to the bishop. However, examples of what Blackstone calls advowsons donative did exist during the medieval period, such as the royal free chapels, which were generally free of episcopal interference. See J. H. Denton, *English Royal Free Chapels, 1100–1300: A Constitutional Study* (Manchester: Manchester University Press, 1970), 15–19, 90.

4. Ulrich Stutz thought that the *Eigenkirchen* tradition originated in pagan German traditions of "house worship" (*Hauskult*). See Stutz, *Die Eigenkirche als Element des mittelalterilich-germanischen Kirchenrechts* (1895; repr., Darmstadt: Wissenschaftliche Buchgesellschaft, 1955), 22–23. More recently, some controversy has arisen regarding whether the *Eigenkirchen* were Germanic or Roman in origin, and whether landownership or a tradition of private temples provided the main impetus for their creation. See Bruno Steimer, ed., *Lexikon der Kirchengeschichte* (Freiburg im Breisgau: Herder, 2001), 394; Wood, *Proprietary Church*, 92–100.

5. N. J. G. Pounds, *A History of the English Parish* (Cambridge: Cambridge University Press, 2000), 25–26.

6. In theory, medieval priests were expected to be celibate, a centuries-old tradition in the Latin Church. Alfons Maria Cardinal Stickler, *The Case for Clerical Celibacy: Its Historical Development and Theological Foundations* (San Francisco: Ignatius Press, 1995), 21–41. Before the thirteenth century, however, the celibate tradition was not universally observed in practice, at least by Anglo-Norman priests. See Jennifer D. Thibodeaux, *The Manly Priest: Clerical Celibacy, Masculinity, and Reform in England and Normandy, 1066–1300* (Philadelphia: University of Pennsylvania Press, 2015), at 41–47; J. E. Newman, "Greater and Lesser Landowners and Parochial Patronage: Yorkshire in the Thirteenth Century," *English Hist. Rev.* 92 (1977): 281–82.

7. Harold J. Berman, *Law and Revolution: The Formation of the Western Legal Tradition* (Cambridge, Mass.: Harvard University Press, 1983), 99–107; Uta-Renate Blumenthal, *The Investiture Controversy: Church and Monarchy from the Ninth to the Twelfth Century* (Philadelphia: University of Pennsylvania Press, 1988), 64–65.

8. See, e.g., 1 Conc. Lat. c. 8 (1123), in *Conciliorum Oecumenicorum Decreta* [COD], ed. Giuseppe Alberigo et al. (Bologna: Edizioni Dehoniane, 1991), 191; 3 Conc. Lat. c. 14 (1179), COD 218–19 = X 3.38.4. These ecumenical councils were preceded by papal and local conciliar legislation.

9. Addleshaw, *Rectors, Vicars, and Patrons*, 17.

10. See Newman, "Greater and Lesser Landowners," at 281–82. The custom was not stamped out altogether, but inheritance was no longer automatic. See 7 CRR 84 (Hil. 1214) (lay patron presents son of the previous priest); 3 BNB no. 1072, p. 97 (Pas. 1225) (same).

11. This is the modern practice followed today in many English dioceses. See, e.g., "The Institution and Induction of a New Priest Authorized by the Bishop 1998," http://www.ely.anglican.org/liturgy/institution/institution.html (setting forth the rite as followed

in the diocese of Ely). During this service, the patron presents the candidate by saying to the bishop, "Reverend Father in God, I present to you *A.B.* to be admitted to the cure of souls in this parish(es)," and the bishop responds by thanking the patron for his presentation and proceeding to institute the new parson, after which the archdeacon inducts him into corporeal possession. The ceremony takes place in the parish church. However, holding the institution at the parish church is a recent innovation, and there has never been any requirement that the bishop actually come to the parish church for the institution, let alone the presentation.

12. 9 CRR 196–97 (Trin. 1220).

13. J. W. Gray, "The Ius Praesentandi in England from the Constitutions of Clarendon to Bracton," *English Hist. Rev.* 67 (1952): 492; Addleshaw, *Rectors, Vicars, and Patrons,* 19–20. References to letters of presentation are rare in the early plea rolls, probably because they were not accessible to litigants after they were sent to the bishop. In one case from the 1230s, a party arguing that a particular seal was indeed that of the donor noted that he had "presented clerks to many churches by that seal" (clericos presentavit per sigillum illud ad plures ecclesias). 15 CRR no. 1394, p. 357 (Trin. 1234–35).

14. Gray, "Ius Praesentandi," at 492. This task was generally delegated by the archdeacon or his official to the rural dean. *Id.*

15. 3 Conc. Lat, c. 3 (1179), COD 212 = X 1.6.7.

16. 9 CRR 196 (Trin. 1220). The case calls to mind a letter of Robert Grosseteste, the famous philosopher and bishop of Lincoln, to William of Raleigh, treasurer of Exeter and chief justice of the king's court, in which Robert declined to appoint a boy to a pastoral charge as recommended by William because the boy was "a minor and not sufficiently educated, still a boy, in fact, who thinks Ovid the greatest letter-writer!" F. A. C. Mantello and Joseph Goering, eds. and trans., *The Letters of Robert Grosseteste, Bishop of Lincoln* (Toronto: University of Toronto Press, 2010), 95.

17. See Addleshaw, *Rectors, Vicars, and Patrons,* 20–21, for an example of a letter of institution.

18. *Id.* at 21.

19. The sources do not define what this meant; most likely the priest took hold of the ring by which the door was opened, signifying that he could now enter the church as his own.

20. Norma Adams and Charles Donahue Jr., eds., *Select Cases from the Ecclesiastical Courts of the Province of Canterbury, c. 1200–1301,* Selden Society 95 (London, 1981), 277n1. The performative aspects of the induction ceremony were essentially unchanged by the Protestant Reformation. See John Johnson, *The Clergyman's Vade-Mecum* (London: Robert Knaplock and Sam. Ballard, 1731), 84–85.

21. The case was originally about the bishop of Worcester's refusal to admit William of Meriden to the church of Longborough. When William died, the bishop again refused to admit the next clerk presented by the patron, Richard of Pevensey; thus the case continued. *Select Cases from the Ecclesiastical Courts,* 95 Selden Soc. C.17, pp. 236–37.

22. *Select Cases from the Ecclesiastical Courts,* 95 Selden Soc. C.17, pp. 246, 248, 260.

23. *Id.* at 246 (*hoc vidit et audivit*).

24. *Id.* at 241 (*commune dictum patrie*); 244 (*per communem relatum patrie*).

25. The term "rector" was later used as well. Addleshaw, *Rectors, Vicars, and Patrons,* 7. The English royal court records from the period under discussion, however, generally refer to the priest in charge of the parish as the *persona.*

26. See *infra* text accompanying notes 41–42.

27. In one early case, a plaintiff tried to sue in the royal court for the right to present a vicar; his opponent responded that because a vicarage was involved, the plaintiff should have sued in the ecclesiastical court. No judgment is recorded. 14 PRS 10 (Trin. 1194).

28. It was also possible, however, for the same clerk to hold both moieties. See 17 CRR no. 2384, p. 486 (Pas. 1243) (patron presents separate clerks to two moieties, then, on the death of the clerk who held the second moiety, presents the other clerk to the second moiety, so that one clerk holds the whole church).

29. See, e.g., 1 CRR 122 (Hil. 1200); 5 CRR 178 (Pas. 1208).

30. For an early example, see 2 RCR 176 (Pas. 1200). The use of *pertinere* to refer to the ownership of the advowson by a party (as opposed to its connection to a church or some land) becomes more common in the mid-thirteenth-century rolls.

31. See *infra* text accompanying notes 82–84 (discussing the procedure in *Glanvill* for seizing an advowson into the king's hand).

32. On the requirement of being Christian, see Peter Landau, *Jus Patronatus: Studien zur Entwicklung des Patronats im Dekretalenrecht und der Kanonistik des 12. und 13. Jahrhunderts* (Cologne: Böhlau, 1975), 38–41.

33. For a few examples, see 5 CRR 174 (Pas. 1208); 6 CRR 28 (Pas. 1210); 6 CRR 93 (Mich. 1210); 7 CRR 46 (Mich. 1213).

34. See 8 CRR 121 (Mich. 1219) for one example; the scenario was quite common. While the woman could not sue without the husband, the converse was also true: a man had to sue with his wife if the advowson was part of her inheritance or dower. Staffs. 31 = 1 PKJ no. 2519, p. 230 (Mich. 1199); 6 CRR 21 (Hil. 1210).

35. In 1253, Cecilia widow of Gilbert sought to recover the advowson of Oxcombe in Lincolnshire from the prior of Bullington, arguing that she inherited it from her mother Matilda. She lost her suit, not because maternal inheritance was barred but because the prior successfully argued that Matilda had other heirs who were not named in the writ. TNA KB 26/149, m. 2 (Trin. 1253), http://aalt.law.uh.edu/H3/KB26_149/0002.htm (accessed December 21, 2020).

36. See, e.g., 5 CRR 84 (Mich. 1207); 11 CRR no. 378, p. 70 (Hil. 1223); 11 CRR no. 1450, p. 291 (Trin. 1224); 13 CRR no. 2752, p. 581 (Hil. 1230). Whether the woman could claim an advowson as part of her dower was subject to certain rules and could depend on whether the dower was nominated by the husband during his lifetime. *Glanvill,* VI, 17, Woodbine pp. 94–96; *Bracton,* ff. 243b–244, III, pp. 221–22; 13 CRR no. 266, p. 59 (Trin. 1227) (woman denied her recovery because she had only a third part of the manor and

failed to show that she had nominated dower). A man could also hold an advowson by curtesy. See 13 CRR no. 1495, p. 320 (Hil. 1229).

37. 6 CRR 187 (Mich. 1211).

38. 5 CRR 73 (Mich. 1207). Such distant patrons might present through an agent. 14 CRR no. 795, p. 158 (Mich. 1230).

39. 1 CRR 88 (Hil. 1199).

40. See, e.g., 4 CRR 91 (Pas. 1206); 8 CRR 121 (Mich. 1219); 9 CRR 101 (Trin. 1220). The argument was quite common. Generally the chaplain was regarded as subordinate to the rector and subject to dismissal by him. See C. H. Lawrence, "The English Parish and Its Clergy," in *The Medieval World*, 2nd ed., ed. Peter Linehan et al. (Abingdon: Routledge, 2018), 746–69, at 751.

41. See, e.g., 10 CRR 160 (Pas. 1221) (abbot claims that a priest is parson at the abbey's presentation).

42. This happened in 8 CRR 118 (Mich. 1219); the sources do not mention any pressure on the priest in question, but it seems unlikely that it was his idea to be demoted in this way.

43. According to R. A. R. Hartridge, the closer the monastery was to the church, the more subservient the vicar was likely to be to the monks, meaning that the tithes (or most of them) would belong to the monastery, and the vicar would be paid a salary. Hartridge, *A History of Vicarages in the Middle Ages* (Cambridge: Cambridge University Press, 1930), 46–48. The opposite arrangement, which gave more control and potential wealth to the vicar, was more common when the rector "was not a monastery, but an absentee or incapacitated individual." There are, however, examples of English vicars paying a pension to monastic parsons. See *id.* at 26, 48. For more on the practice of appointing vicars when churches were appropriated to religious houses, see Michael Burger, *Bishops, Clerks, and Diocesan Governance in Thirteenth-Century England* (Cambridge: Cambridge University Press, 2012), 26; and John R. H. Moorman, *Church Life in England in the Thirteenth Century* (Cambridge: Cambridge University Press, 1955), 44–45.

44. R. C. van Caenegem, ed., *English Lawsuits from William I to Richard I*, Selden Society 107 (London, 1991), no. 365, p. 328.

45. See *id.* at 329n5.

46. Warin fitz Gerold, who witnessed this advowson writ as royal chamberlain, held that office from 1155 to 1158. Robert William Eyton, *Court, Household, and Itinerary of King Henry II* (London: Taylor and Co., 1878), 315. J. R. West, the editor of the cartulary of Saint Benet's, proposed 1158 as the most likely date of issuance for the writ. J. R. West, ed., *Register of the Abbey of St. Benet of Holme, 1020–1210* (Norf. Record Society, 1932), vol. 3, pp. 254–55. Van Caenegem simply assigns the writ a date range of 1155–58. R. C. van Caenegem, *Royal Writs in England from the Conquest to Glanvill*, Selden Society 77 (London, 1959), no. 196, pp. 514–15. The writ thus dates to a period in which Henry II finally put an end to the military conflicts that had characterized Stephen's reign and stabilized the royal finances. Emilie Amt, *The Accession of Henry II in England: Royal Government Restored, 1149–1159* (Woodbridge: Boydell Press, 1993), 1–3, 187.

47. R. C. van Caenegem, *Royal Writs,* 77 Selden Soc. no. 196, pp. 514–15 (trans. Van Caenegem).

48. For the archbishop's letter, see West, *Register,* vol. 2, no. 22 ("euocato vicino capitulo et eo in quo prefata ecclesia sita fuit diligenti studio inquiratis in cuius territorio constructa fuerit ecclesia"); for the royal writ, see *id.,* vol. 2, no. 23 ("Si abbas de Hulmo potest diracionare ecclesiam de Randewrthe antiquitus fuisse constructam in feodo suo, et post mortem regis H. sine iudicio in alterius feodum fuisse remotam, tunc precipio quod iuste et sine dilacione facias eam esse ubi prius fuit"). For commentary, see *id.,* vol. 3, p. 255. The royal writ concerning the church's location does not imply an assertion of jurisdiction over the advowson dispute.

49. See *infra* chap. 5.

50. Van Caenegem, *English Lawsuits,* 107 Selden Soc. no. 445, p. 477.

51. The treatise makes clear (both in the prologue and in the substance of the discussion) that it was written during the reign of Henry II, and it includes two final concords dating from 1187, the later of which dates to November 29. Hall, introduction to *Glanvill,* p. xxxi.

52. *Id.;* Sarah Tullis, "*Glanvill Continued:* A Reassessment," in *Law in the City: Proceedings of the Seventeenth British Legal History Conference, London, 2005,* ed. Andrew Lewis et al. (Bodmin, Cornwall: MPG Books, 2007), 15n2.

53. Hall, introduction to *Glanvill,* xxxvi–xl.

54. The first words of *Glanvill* are "Regiam potestatem non solum armis . . . decoratam," which, replacing *Imperatoriam* for *Regiam,* are the first words of the prologue to the *Institutes. Glanvill,* prologue, Woodbine p. 23.

55. *Glanvill,* X, 3, Woodbine p. 134; Hall, introduction to *Glanvill,* xxv–xxvi, xxxvi–xxxviii.

56. "Leges namque Anglicanas licet non scriptas leges appellari non videatur absurdum. . . . Leges autem et iura regni scripto universaliter concludi nostris temporibus quidem omnino impossibile est, tum propter scribentium ignorantiam tum propter earum multitudinem confusam." *Glanvill,* prologue, Woodbine p. 24. See Joshua C. Tate, "Glanvill and the Development of the English Advowson Writs," in *Texts and Context in Legal History: Essays in Honor of Charles Donahue,* ed. Sara McDougall, Anna di Robilant, and John Witte Jr. (Berkeley, Calif.: Robbins Collection, 2016), 130.

57. Such an audience, moreover, would be familiar with the Third Lateran Council and its time limit for advowson disputes, which might account for the otherwise puzzling absence of any reference to the six-month collation period in *Glanvill's* discussion of the advowson writs. See *infra* text accompanying notes 106–125.

58. Paul Brand, "Legal Education in England before the Inns of Court," in *Learning the Law: Teaching and the Transmission of Law in England, 1150–1900,* ed. Jonathan A. Bush and Alain Wijffels (London: Hambledon Press, 1999), 53–55.

59. Pollock and Maitland, I, 166.

60. *Glanvill,* I, 1, Woodbine p. 42. Unless otherwise indicated, Latin quotations from *Glanvill* herein come from the Woodbine edition published in 1932 by Yale University

Press. English quotations (with my amendments in brackets and modernized capitalization) come from the 1812 translation by John Beames, which is in the public domain.

61. *Id.* I, 3, Woodbine p. 42 (trans. Beames, p. 4).

62. *Id.* (trans. Beames, p. 5).

63. *Id.* I, 6, Woodbine p. 43.

64. M. T. Clanchy, "Magna Carta, Clause Thirty-Four," *English Hist. Rev.* 79 (1964): 543.

65. *Glanvill*, I, 6, Woodbine p. 43.

66. *Id.* I, 10, Woodbine p. 44; I, 12, Woodbine p. 45; I, 18, Woodbine p. 47; I, 25, Woodbine p. 50; I, 29, Woodbine p. 52.

67. *Id.* I, 7, Woodbine pp. 43–44.

68. *Id.* I, 7, Woodbine p. 44.

69. *Id.* II, 3, Woodbine p. 58.

70. J. H. Round, "The Date of the Grand Assize," *English Hist. Rev.* 31 (1916): 268–69.

71. *Glanvill*, II, 3, Woodbine p. 58.

72. *Id.* II, 11–12, Woodbine pp. 64–66.

73. *Id.* XIII, 33, Woodbine p. 172; see also *infra* chap. 3.

74. *Id.* IV, 1, Woodbine p. 75 (trans. Beames, p. 83).

75. *Id.* (trans. Beames, p. 84).

76. *Id.* IV, 1, Woodbine p. 75. The assize in question is the assize of darrein presentment, discussed *infra*.

77. *Id.* IV, 1, Woodbine pp. 75–76 (trans. Beames, pp. 84–85).

78. *Id.* IV, 1, Woodbine p. 76.

79. Tate, "Glanvill and the Development of the English Advowson Writs," 132.

80. "Rex vicecomiti salutem. Praecipe N. quod iuste et sine dilatione dimittat R. advocationem ecclesiae in villa illa quam clamat ad se pertinere, et unde queritur quod ipse ei iniuste deforciat. Et nisi fecerit, summone eum per bonos summonitores quod sit ibi eo die coram me vel iustitiis meis ostensurus quare non fecerit. Et habeas ibi summonitores et hoc breve. Teste etc." *Glanvill*, IV, 2, Woodbine p. 76 (trans. Beames, pp. 85–85).

81. Tate, "Glanvill and the Development of the English Advowson Writs," 133.

82. *Glanvill*, I, 7, Woodbine pp. 43–44; IV, 3–6, Woodbine pp. 76–78.

83. On the origins of this phrase and its significance in medieval English governance, see Ian Forrest, *Trustworthy Men: How Inequality and Faith Made the Medieval Church* (Princeton, N.J.: Princeton University Press, 2018), 95–111.

84. *Glanvill*, IV, 5, Woodbine p. 77.

85. "Peto advocationem illius ecclesiae sicut ius meum et pertinentem ad hereditatem meam, et de qua advocatione ego fui saisatus [vel aliquis antecessorum meorum fuit saisatus] tempore Henrici regis avi domini Henrici regis, vel post coronationem domini regis; et ideo saisatus, quia ad eandem ecclesiam vacantem presentavi personam aliquo praedictorum temporum, et ita presentavi quod ad presentationem meam persona fuit in ecclesia illa instituta, et si quis hoc voluerit negare, habeo probos homines qui hoc viderunt et

audierunt, et parati sunt hoc dirationare secundum considerationem curiae, et maxime illum N. et illum et illum." *Id.* IV, 6, Woodbine pp. 77–78 (trans. Beames, p. 88).

86. *Id.* IV, 6, p. 78.

87. Tate, "Glanvill and the Development of the English Advowson Writs," 133–34.

88. *Id.* at 134.

89. *Id.*

90. *Glanvill,* IV, 8–14, Woodbine pp. 78–83.

91. *Infra* chap. 5.

92. *Glanvill,* IV, 7, Woodbine p. 78.

93. *Id.* IV, 8, Woodbine p. 78. The writ given in *Glanvill* actually summons both the clerk and the rival patron, but G. D. G. Hall has suggested that this form of writ might have been used after an earlier writ directed specifically against the clerk. Hall, *Glanvill,* 47n3.

94. *Id.* IV, 9, Woodbine p. 80. This is consistent with the compromise that I discuss in chap. 5, whereby the ecclesiastical courts were allowed to hold pleas that concerned the benefice and not the advowson.

95. *Id.* IV, 9, Woodbine p. 80.

96. "Et quidem in curia domini regis nil amplius de eo agetur, nisi quod de advocatione ipsa inter advocatos iudicabitur. Sed in curia christianitatis advocatus qui de nouo ius advocationis evicit versus clericum ipsum coram episcopo suo vel eius officiali placitabit, ita quod si tempore praesentationis credebatur is patronus per quem fuit praesentatus, tunc remanebit illi ecclesia illa omnibus diebus vitae sue." *Id.* IV, 10, Woodbine pp. 80–81 (trans. Beames, pp. 93–94).

97. "Statutum est etiam super hoc in regno domini regis de clericis illis qui ecclesias obtinent per tales advocatos qui se in advocationes ecclesiarum tempore guerrae violenter intruserunt, ne ecclesias illas quamdiu vixerint amittant." *Id.* IV, 10, Woodbine p. 81 (trans. Beames, p. 94). This may be a reference to the settlement reached at the beginning of Henry II's reign, or to a more recent settlement after the rebellion of the young king.

98. *Id.* IV, 11, Woodbine p. 82.

99. *Id.* XIII, Woodbine pp. 157–74.

100. *Id.* XIII, 19, Woodbine p. 167 (trans. Beames, pp. 324–25). The Latin word *villa* (which Beames renders into English as "vill") in this writ is difficult to translate, but here it seems to mean "village," although, in an earlier part of the writ, the king summons men *de visneto de illa villa,* "from the neighborhood of that village." Interestingly, book XIII of *Glanvill* does not mention the requirement found in later versions of the writ that the presentation have been made in time of peace (*tempore pacis*), although a reference is made to the requirement in *Glanvill,* IV, 1, Woodbine p. 75. For early examples of the writ with the *tempore pacis* requirement, see 1 PKJ nos. 3497, p. 373 (1199), 3533, p. 402 (1199), 3534, p. 403 (1199); see also Elsa de Haas and G. D. G. Hall, eds., *Early Registers of Writs,* Selden Society 87 (London, 1970), pp. 4 (Hib. no. 9); 28 (CA no. 40). It is not clear why the requirement was omitted from the discussion in *Glanvill.*

101. *Glanvill,* XIII, 3, Woodbine p. 158; 19, Woodbine p. 167; 33, Woodbine p. 172. Not all recognitions involved a jury of twelve: the recognition to determine whether a particular man was underage summoned a jury of eight. *Id.* XIII, 16, Woodbine p. 166.

102. *Id.* XIII, 7, Woodbine p. 160; XIII, 20, Woodbine p. 167.

103. *Id.* XIII, 20, Woodbine p. 168.

104. *Id.* XIII, 20–21, Woodbine p. 168.

105. *Id.* XIII, 20, Woodbine p. 167.

106. See *infra* chap. 5.

107. English attendees at the council included the bishops of Bath (Reginald fitz Jocelin), Hereford (Robert Foliot), Norwich (John of Oxford), and Durham (Hugh de Puiset), as well as Peter of Blois, archdeacon of Bath, and Walter Map. See *Councils and Synods* I, pt. 2, pp. 1011–12.

108. Charles Duggan, "Reginald *fitz* Jocelin (*c.* 1140–1191)," in *Oxford Dictionary of National Biography* (Oxford: Oxford University Press, 2004), http://www.oxforddnb.com/view/article/9613.

109. See Ralph V. Turner, *The English Judiciary in the Age of Glanvill and Bracton, c. 1176–1239* (Cambridge: Cambridge University Press, 1985), 19, 30, 45–48; Christopher Harper-Bill, "Oxford, John of (*d.* 1200)," in *Oxford Dictionary of National Biography* (Oxford: Oxford University Press, 2004), http://www.oxforddnb.com/view/article/21058.

110. Van Caenegem, *Royal Writs,* 77 Selden Soc. 332–33; Van Caenegem, *English Lawsuits,* 107 Selden Soc. no. 518. An 1182 entry in the pipe rolls may also refer to the assize of darrein presentment, though it could also refer to the grand assize. *Pipe Roll 28 Henry the Second,* 83 (1182) ("Radulfus Ferrariis reddit compotum de 10 marcis pro respectu de recognitione cujusdam ecclesie").

111. See, e.g., Van Caenegem, *Royal Writs,* 77 Selden Soc. 332.

112. Landau, *Jus Patronatus,* 195–98.

113. "Si aliquis clericus ab ordinario iudice in aliqua ecclesia fuerit institutus ad praesentationem illius, qui eiusdem ecclesiae credebatur esse patronus, et postea ius patronatus alius evicerit in iudicio, clericus, qui institutus est, non debet ab ipsa ecclesia propter hoc removeri, si tempore praesentationis suae ille, qui eum praesentavit, ius patronatus ecclesiae possidebat, cum ex hoc ei, qui de iure debet habere, nullum in posterum praeiudicium generetur. Si vero tunc non possidebat ius patronatus, sed tantum credebatur esse patronus, cum tamen non esset, nec possessionem patronatus haberet secundum consuetudinem Anglicanam poterit ab eadem ecclesia removeri." WH 184, 1 Comp. 3.33.23 = X 3.38.19 (1173–76).

The manuscripts indicate that the decretal was issued on April 8 at Anagni and addressed to Simon, abbot of Saint Alban's. Simon held that position from 1167 to 1183. Rodney M. Thompson, *Manuscripts from St. Alban's Abbey, 1066–1235* (Woodbridge: D. S. Brewer, 1982), 51. During that period, Pope Alexander was at Anagni on April 8 in 1173, 1174, and 1176, but not before 1173 or after 1176. *Regesta Pontificium Romanorum,* ed. Philip Jaffé (Leipzig, 1888), 265, 275, 293, 297. This means that the decretal must have been issued sometime during the period 1173–76.

114. WH 184, 1 Comp. 3.33.23 = X 3.38.19 (1173–76).

115. Peter Landau, *Jus Patronatus: Studien zur Entwicklung des Patronats im Dekretalenrecht und der Kanonistik des 12. und 13. Jahrhunderts* (Cologne: Böhlau, 1975), 196–98n696.

116. Thirteenth-century royal justices exercised discretion to expedite darrein present-ment (and *quare impedit*) actions to avoid collation under the council, a practice that was legislatively confirmed in the 1259 Provisions of Westminster. See Brand, *Kings, Barons, and Justices*, at 71–72.

117. Joshua C. Tate, "The Third Lateran Council and the *Ius Patronatus* in England," in *Proceedings of the Thirteenth International Congress of Medieval Canon Law: Esztergom, 3–8 August 2008*, ed. Peter Erdö and Sz. Anzelm Szuromi (Vatican City: Biblioteca Apostolica Vaticana, 2010), 589, 596.

118. *Id.* at 207–10. See also R. H. Helmholz, *The Oxford History of the Laws of England,* vol. 1, *The Canon Law and Ecclesiastical Jurisdiction from 597 to the 1640s* (Oxford: Oxford University Press, 2004), 478–79 (citing X 2.1.3).

119. See *infra* chap. 3.

120. W. J. Millor, S.J., and H. E. Butler, eds., *The Letters of John of Salisbury* (Oxford: Clarendon Press, 1986, rev. by C. N. L. Brooke), no. 72 (lawsuit held before Theobald, archbishop of Canterbury, in 1161). I discuss this case and other similar cases in chap. 3 *infra.*

121. D.11 c.4.

122. WH 244, 1 Comp. 3.26.4 = X 3.30.7 (1164–79) (*generalem Anglicanae ecclesiae consuetudinem*). Innocent III also uses this phrase. X 2.20.32 (*consuetudine generali Anglicanae ecclesiae*).

123. Landau, *Jus Patronatus,* 196n696.

124. Tate, "The Third Lateran Council," at 597–98.

125. *Glanvill,* IV, 10, Woodbine p. 81 (trans. Beames, p. 94). See Gray, "Ius Praesentandi," at 488n4.

126. Tate, "The Third Lateran Council," at 598.

127. Tate, "Glanvill and the Development of the English Advowson Writs," 137.

128. *Id.*

129. Van Caenegem deduces this date from the fact that the writ was witnessed by Simon fitz Peter (who appears in records from 1158 to 1166) at the castle of Portchester, where Henry II was in 1164 and 1166. Van Caenegem, *Royal Writs,* 77 Selden Soc. 286–87; Eyton, *Court, Household, and Itinerary,* 70, 91–92, 340. S. F. Hockey, the editor of the Carisbrooke cartulary, proposes an earlier date of 1155–58, but this seems unlikely. S. F. Hockey, *The Cartulary of Carisbrooke Priory* (Southampton: Camelot Press, 1981), 14.

130. Van Caenegem, *Royal Writs,* 77 Selden Soc. no. 97, p. 462; Van Caenegem, *English Lawsuits,* 107 Selden Soc. no. 433, p. 466 (trans. Van Caenegem).

131. The writ was issued at Verneuil, which means a date of August 9, 1173, or October 1, 1177. See Eyton, *Court, Household, and Itinerary,* 176, 220.

132. Van Caenegem, *English Lawsuits,* 107 Selden Soc. no. 500, p. 555 (trans. Van Caenegem).

133. Tate, "Glanvill and the Development of the English Advowson Writs," 138.

134. "Rex vicecomiti salutem. Praecipio tibi quod sine dilatione saisas M. de una hida terrae in villa illa quam petiit versus R. et unde idem R. posuit se in assisam meam, quia praedictus M. dirationavit terram illam in curia mea per recognitionem. Teste etc." *Glanvill,* II, 20, Woodbine p. 69 (trans. Beames, p. 69).

135. "Rex episcopo tali salutem. Sciatis quod N. disracionauit in curia nostra per recognicionem ultime presentacionis seisinam presentacionis sue ad ecclesiam de N. Et ideo uobis mandamus quod [ad] presentacionem ipsius ad ecclesiam illam idoneam personam admittatis. Teste etc." Haas and Hall, *Early Registers of Writs,* 87 Selden Soc. 5 ("Hib" no. 12) (trans. Haas and Hall).

136. Tate, "Glanvill and the Development of the English Advowson Writs," 139.

137. Compare *Glanvill's* writ for delivering seisin after a battle, which specifically notes that a battle has taken place. *Glanvill,* II, 4, Woodbine p. 60.

138. "Et nisi feceris, archiepiscopus Cantauriensis faciat fieri ne pro penuria recti vel plene justicie ius suum amittat." Van Caenegem, *Royal Writs,* 77 Selden Soc. no. 196, pp. 514–15.

139. Tate, "Glanvill and the Development of the English Advowson Writs," 140.

140. *Id.* at 283–87. For discussion of this ordinance, see *infra* chap. 3.

141. *Pipe Roll 13 Henry the Second,* 10; Van Caenegem, *Royal Writs,* 77 Selden Soc. at 287.

142. Van Caenegem, *Royal Writs,* 77 Selden Soc. at 287.

143. Tate, "Glanvill and the Development of the English Advowson Writs," 141.

144. See Tate, "The Third Lateran Council," at 595.

145. Tate, "Glanvill and the Development of the English Advowson Writs," 141–42.

146. *Id.* at 142.

147. *Glanvill,* XIII, 20, Woodbine p. 167.

148. *Id.* IV, 11, Woodbine p. 81 (trans. Beames, p. 95).

149. *Id.* at Woodbine pp. 81–82 (trans. Beames).

150. As previously discussed, other writs may have existed earlier in the twelfth century. The chronicle of Battle Abbey shows that a donee of an advowson could, early in the reign of Henry II, bring a suit to recover it in the royal courts. The chronicle, however, does not specify the nature of the writ(s) the abbey brought, if indeed the lawsuits in question were begun by writ.

151. 1 CRR 18 (Hil. 1196) ("placito impedicionis presentacionis ad ecclesiam"); 31 PRS 79 (Hil. 1196) ("placito impedicionis persone ad ecclesiam"); 31 PRS 90 (Hil. 1196) ("placito impedimenti presentare idoneas personas ad ecclesias").

152. Van Caenegem, *English Lawsuits,* vol. 2, 107 Selden Soc. no. 572, p. 619.

153. *Glanvill,* prologue, p. 3, Woodbine p. 24 (trans. Beames p. xl).

154. Breue quod dicitur impedit.

Vicecomiti salutem. Precipe tali quod iuste et sine dilatione permittat tali presentare idoneam personam ad ecclesiam talem que uacat ut dicitur, et unde queritur quod talis eum iniuste impedit; et nisi fecerit, et predictus talis fecerit te securum de clamore [suo] prosequendo, tunc summoneas per bonos summonitores predictum talem quod sit coram iusticiariis nostris apud Westmonasterium tali die ostensurus quare non fecerit, et habeas ibi summonitores et hoc breue.

Haas and Hall, *Early Registers of Writs,* 87 Selden Soc. xli, 31 (CA no. 52) (trans. Haas and Hall). Neither version of *quare impedit* appears in the Irish register "Hib." *Id.* at 364. As Paul Brand has argued, the Irish register "Hib." most likely dates to 1210, thus predating CA. Paul Brand, "Ireland and the Literature of the Early Common Law," in *The Making of the Common Law,* 450–56. The existence of *quare impedit* cases in the twelfth-century plea rolls, however, shows that the writ did exist by the date of the Irish register, even though it was not included.

155. G. J. Turner, introduction to *Brevia Placitata,* Selden Society 66 (London, 1951), xcvii.

156. *Bracton,* f. 247, III, pp. 229–30. Thorne's translation suggests that the word *impedit* is actually used in both writs, although the heading and the discussion make clear that the treatise authors thought of the second writ as *quare non permittit. Id.* at p. 230 (adopting the reading of the manuscripts which give *impedit* rather than *non permittit*).

157. *Id.* f. 247, III, p. 230.

158. "Rex vicecomiti salutem. Quia A fecit nos securos de clamore etcetera, pone per vadium et salvos plegios B. quod sit etcetera, ad respondendum eidem A. quare impedit eundem A. praesentare idoneam personam ad ecclesiam de N., cuius ecclesiae advocationem idem A. nuper in curia nostra . . . recuperavit versus eundem B. vel versus alium talem per assisam ultimae praesentationis inde inter eos captam, vel per iudicium curiae nostrae vel alio quocumque modo, unde idem A. queritur quod praedictus B. iniuste et contra coronam nostram vel in contemptum curiae nostrae eum inde impedit." *Id.* f. 247, III, pp. 229–3b (trans. Thorne).

159. *Id.* f. 247, III, p. 230 ("nullam omnino habuit . . . seisinam vel quasi") (trans. Thorne).

160. *Id.* ("ponere pedem in ius alienum") (trans. Thorne).

161. On the etymology, see Charlton T. Lewis and Charles Short, *A Latin Dictionary* (Oxford: Oxford University Press, 1879), 897.

162. 1 CRR 44 (Pas. 1198); see 2 RCR 53 (Mich. 1199) for reference to the gift. The facts of the lawsuit, between the abbot of Stanley and Matthew fitz Herbert, are discussed hereafter.

163. 13 CRR no. 1744, p. 367 (Pas. 1229) (*quare impedit*); 13 CRR no. 1903, p. 398 (Pas. 1229) (*non permittit*).

164. 13 CRR no. 1763, p. 371 (Pas. 1229). The defendants were Agnes of Walcot and her sisters, Lucy, Maud (sued with her husband David), and Juetta, along with the abbot of Peterborough. The prior claimed by gift of Hugh de Neville, father of the four women, offering his charter and a confirmation of the bishop (either Hugh of Avalon, d. 1200, or Hugh of Wells, d. 1235). The prior was awarded seisin when three of the sisters and the

abbot acknowledged that the advowson belonged to the prior, and the fourth sister, Lucy, failed to appear. *Id.*; 13 CRR no. 1903, p. 398; 13 CRR no. 1979, p. 415 (Pas. 1229).

165. There are several parishes named Stoke in Buckinghamshire, but the plaintiff's surname suggests Stoke Goldington.

166. 15 CRR no. 16, p. 5 (Hil. 1233). The defendant was Richard dean of Newport. Peter asserted that he had recovered the advowson before the royal justices at High Wycombe in a plea against the prior of Huntingdon. The outcome of the plea between Peter and Richard is not recorded. See also 8 CRR 121 (Mich. 1219) for another example.

167. 18 CRR no. 1387, p. 289 (Pas. 1244). The defendant, the prior of Prittlewell, responded that his predecessor William prior of Prittlewell, and not the king, presented Geoffrey. The prior and Margaret had brought parallel pleas, the prior's suit being an assize of darrein presentment; a jury of assize rendered a verdict in favor of the prior, who was given a writ to the bishop. 18 CRR no. 1690, p. 346. Hubert de Burgh, justiciar of England during the minority of Henry III, had been imprisoned in 1232 on charges of inciting riots against Italian clerks whom the pope had provided to English benefices. Hubert's marriage to Margaret, daughter of William the Lion, king of Scotland, "was the chief prize of his career." See D. A. Carpenter, "The Fall of Hubert de Burgh," in *The Reign of Henry III* (London: Hambledon Press, 1996), 45, 55–56.

168. 18 CRR no. 1387, p. 289 (Pas. 1244).

169. As McSweeney explains, the authors of *Bracton* can generally be seen as "trying to work out a way to describe the practices of the king's courts as entirely consistent with Roman law." McSweeney, *Priests of the Law*, at 134–35. Logical inconsistencies in the rolls, such as the varying references to *quare impedit* and *quare non permittit*, had to be rationalized or explained in some way.

170. Cholderton lies within the parish of Amport, and a chapel existed there by the twelfth century, if not earlier. *VCH, Hants*, vol. 4, 339–41, 344.

171. 1 CRR 111–12 (Hil. 1199). Adam, lord of Basing from 1172 until his death in 1213, was involved in parallel litigation concerning the chapel of Appleshaw, which he also claimed to be appurtenant to the church of Amport. See 1 CRR 191 (Trin. 1200); Sanders, *English Baronies*, 9. Henry's surname comes from one of two towns named Colombières in the region of Calvados in Normandy. Sanders, *English Baronies*, 67.

172. 1 CRR 192 (Trin. 1200) ("dies datus est . . . de capiendo cirographo suo"). A chirograph is part of an indented document known as a final concord, or fine, recording a formal settlement between parties reached in the king's court. The "foot" of the fine was retained in the king's treasury, and the other two parts were delivered to the litigants. Pollock and Maitland, II, 97. In 1209 the mother church of Amport was acquired by Richard Poore, bishop of Chichester, on behalf of the dean and chapter. *VCH, Hants*, vol. 4, 344.

173. On the Clare family genealogy, see Sanders, *English Baronies*, 35. Richard III de Clare died in 1217, leaving his son and heir Gilbert III de Clare, who was recognized as Earl of Gloucester in 1218.

174. Gilbert initially refers to Hugh's uncle as Richard of Saint Philbert, but Hugh then refers to him as Richard de Lucy; later in the entry, he is referred to as Godfrey de Lucy. It seems that the same person is meant throughout; perhaps the clerk transcribing the proceedings got confused. A Richard of Saint Philbert appears in the plea roll from Hilary 1221. 10 CRR 25.

175. Gilbert acknowledged that his ancestor Earl Roger had given land in Thaxted to an ancestor of Hugh until he might otherwise make provision for him, and that Earl Richard, Gilbert's father, had later assigned land in escambium in Wells to Hugh's uncle. According to Gilbert, however, his father had retained the advowsons in making the second assignment. Gilbert alleged that his father had presented Robert de Clare to the church of Caldecote before the assignment and presented the same Roger to the church of Shingham after the assignment. Gilbert noted that Hugh offered no proof that the advowsons were given with the land, and also asserted that Hugh's uncle had had a brother named Roger, whose daughter was the true heir of Hugh's uncle. (The daughter in question may have been Beatrice, whom we see to be involved in a suit against Hugh the following year. 14 CRR no. 206, p. 40 [Trin. 1230].)

176. Hugh also contended that he was the true heir of his uncle, as evidenced by the fact that he recovered the manor of Wells against Roger of Saint Philbert by fine in the king's court.

177. 13 CRR no. 1878, pp. 393-94 (Pas. 1229) ("quia summonitus fuit ad respondendum quare impedit et ipse sufficienter ostendit quare").

178. *Id.*

179. *Glanvill*, XIII, 20, Woodbine p. 168.

180. *Id.* XIII, 20, Woodbine p. 167 (is cui sui vel alicuius antecessorum suorum gratia adiudicabitur ultima [praesentatio], eo ipso saisinam ipsius advocationis intelligitur dirationasse) (trans. Beames, p. 325).

181. *Id.* IV, 1, Woodbine p. 76 (sine recognitione unam personam praesentabit ad minus) (trans. Beames, p. 85).

182. *Id.* IV, 6, Woodbine p. 78.

183. 1 CRR 44 (Pas. 1198). The facts of this case are discussed hereafter.

184. *Id.*

185. The name is spelled out in 1 CRR 386 (Hil. 1201).

186. The prior and monks also offered a confirmation of Roger de Pont l'Évêque (d. 1181), archbishop of York. After unsuccessfully challenging the writ on the grounds that it mentioned another defendant (Adam of Cuckfield) who was not present, William sought a jury on the grounds that his grandfather presented the last parson. The prior again referred to the charters of gift and confirmation. William countered that the charter was made on his grandfather's deathbed in his last illness and should therefore be disregarded. The prior responded that William's grandfather was in his liege power when he made the gift. A blank was left on the roll. 2 RCR 171 (Pas. 1200). In Michaelmas Term 1200, the parties were given a day three weeks from Easter. 1 CRR 327 (Mich. 1200). In Hilary Term 1201, William offered a mark for a jury; the request was granted, and the jury was set to come on the morrow of the close of

Easter wherever the king might be in England. 1 CRR 386–87 (Hil. 1201). The last entry dealing with the case records a postponement of the jury until the coming of the justices. 1 CRR 430–31 (Pas. 1201). For further discussion of the case, see 1 PKJ 77–78.

187. 2 RCR 171.

188. The prior offered John's charter and a confirmatory charter of Ranulph, former bishop of Bath. No bishop named Ranulph is listed for Bath in the Fryde handbook; perhaps this was an error for Reginald fitz Jocelin, d. 1191. E. B. Fryde et al., *Handbook of British Chronology*, 3rd ed. (Cambridge: Cambridge University Press, 1986), 228.

189. 7 CRR 67 (Hil. 1214). The roll does not record any response by Robert to the prior's charter.

190. Three William Pantolfs are mentioned in this case: William *senior*, William *junior*, and the defendant. The defendant claimed that William *junior* gave him the land of Dalby with the advowson for homage and service. The prioress claimed that William *senior* gave her church one virgate of land in Dalby with the advowson; she offered a charter of William *senior* and a confirmatory charter of Isolda Pantolf, daughter and heir of William *junior*. A William Pantolf was "one of the most important tenants-in-chief of Roger, Earl of Montgomery, at the end of the eleventh century." Sanders, *English Baronies*, 94. That William's second son and heir was named Robert; it is possible that the William *senior* mentioned in this case was a younger son.

191. 3 BNB no. 1295, pp. 305–6 (Mich. 1217).

192. It is noteworthy that this was apparently considered a valid exception to the rule that the church must be vacant for the assize to proceed.

193. Several powerful barons in medieval England bore the name Geoffrey de Mandeville. J. H. Round, *Geoffrey de Mandeville: A Study of the Anarchy* (London: Longmans, Green, 1892), 453–54. The Geoffrey in this case is the fifth earl of Essex, a contemporary of King John, and should not be confused with the earlier Geoffrey de Mandeville who was a significant player in the crisis of Stephen's reign. *Id.* at 39. Maud and Beatrice de Say were the two daughters of William de Say, and they married half brothers. Beatrice married Geoffrey fitz Peter, and their son, Geoffrey de Mandeville, became the fifth earl of Essex; Maud married William of Buckland, half brother of Geoffrey. See George Edward Cokayne, *The Complete Peerage of England, Scotland, Ireland, Great Britain, and the United Kingdom* (London: St. Catherine's Press, 1926), vol. 3, pp. 116–17; *Handbook of British Chronology*, 461; J. C. Holt, *Colonial England, 1066–1215* (Rio Grande, Ohio: Hambledon Press, 1997), 130, 311. Robert fitz Peter, mentioned in this grant, was the older brother of both Geoffrey fitz Peter and William of Buckland. The manor of Wellsworth belonged to William de Say in the time of Henry II and was inherited at his death by Maud of Buckland; at her death, the manor passed to Geoffrey fitz Peter and thence to Geoffrey de Mandeville. *VCH, Hants*, vol. 3, p. 107.

194. 3 BNB no. 1570, pp. 452–53 (Mich. 1222). The prior began by asserting that the church was not vacant because a certain William was parson. Geoffrey de Lucy responded

that William was not admitted at the presentation of the prior, but rather the bishop of Winchester conferred the church on William by reason of the council. Geoffrey de Lucy subsequently asserted that, before the war between King John and the barons of England, Geoffrey de Mandeville, the fifth earl of Essex, had brought an assize of darrein presentment concerning the church, but the assize was not taken because the war intervened. Subsequently, Geoffrey de Lucy claimed, the earl gave him his right in the advowson. The prior then offered a charter of Maud of Buckland and her brother-in-law Robert fitz Peter (who were respectively the aunt and uncle of Geoffrey de Mandeville, see *supra* note 193) purporting to grant the church to Southwick priory. Geoffrey de Lucy responded that Maud had nothing in Wellsworth except dower and that Robert fitz Peter was never seised of Wellsworth. The prior's attorney then argued that the prior had presented parsons after the gift, and that he had presented Roger, the last parson who died before William. Geoffrey de Lucy responded that Earl Geoffrey had presented Roger and sought his assize; the prior conceded the assize, but it was postponed for default of recognitors. The last entry dates to Hilary Term 1223 and records a subsequent postponement. 11 CRR no. 133, p. 24 (Hil. 1223).

195. *Glanvill*, XIII, 20, Woodbine p. 167.

196. The prior's charter in fact stated that Thurstan gave to the priory everything that remained in his hand after his gift to the abbey. The prior argued that since Thurstan presented another clerk to the church after the gift to the abbey, the advowson of the church was in Thurstan's hand when he made the gift to the priory. On the rule of subsequent presentation, see *infra* chap. 4.

197. 4 CRR 97–98 (Pas. 1206), 164 (Trin. 1206); 5 CRR 64 (Mich. 1207), 230 (Trin. 1208), 235, 253–54 (Trin. 1208), 305 (Mich. 1208). 5 CRR 235 suggests that the lawsuit was of interest to King John.

198. According to Gilbert, William Chaplain was parson by consent of Herbert Poore, predecessor of Gilbert. Because William Pantolf lived far from the church of Oakham and the area of Knossington was poor, Gilbert explained, William Pantolf often lost his service. William Pantolf accordingly went to Herbert and asked him to permit him (William Pantolf) to find a chaplain at his expense. Herbert agreed, and thus William Chaplain came to be in the church. Gilbert further alleged that the church was not vacant but was in the bishop's hand because of the lawsuit Ralph brought.

199. The jury said that the parson of Knossington gave a mark to the church of Oakham because of a settlement of a dispute concerning some tithes.

200. 13 CRR no. 1675, pp. 354–55 (Pas. 1229).

201. "Aliis autem qui tenent per feoffamentum et non per descensum numquam competit antequam semel praesentaverint, quia de seisina eorum quorum heredes non sunt petere non possunt per assisam non magis quam per breve de recto." *Bracton*, f. 238, III, p. 205.

202. See *supra* text accompanying notes 196–97.

203. *Bracton*, f. 238, III, p. 205.

204. 1 CRR 471 (Pas. 1201). The church is usually spelled Warden, although the manor is spelled Old Wardon. William II de Bussy held the estate of Old Wardon in the mid-twelfth century and died before 1166, leaving Bartholomew (d.s.p. ca. 1178–79) and Walter (d.s.p. ca. 1182) as his heirs. Their heirs were their sisters Cecily and Maud. Cecily married John de Builly (d. 1213), and Maud married Hugh Wake (d. 1194–99). Sanders, *English Baronies*, 133. Although the text of 1 CRR 471 is corrupt, it appears that William and Beatrice vouched to warrant Maud, Cecily, and Cecily's husband John de Builly. The lawsuit between the abbot and William and Beatrice was one of three pleas that the abbot brought concerning different moieties of the church of Warden, the others being brought against John de Builly and Cecily his wife and Maud de Bussy respectively. 2 RCR 201–2 (Pas. 1200), 1 CRR 238 (Trin. 1200). It is likely that all three pleas were brought by writ of right, although only the suit against William and Beatrice uses the telltale phrase *sicut ius ecclesie sue*. The relationship between Beatrice and the others is not specified, but it seems probable that Beatrice was the widow of Bartholomew de Bussy and sister-in-law of Cecily and Maud, and that Bartholomew endowed her with a third part of the advowson of Warden. Beatrice was the daughter of Anselm de Stuteville. 2 CRR 232 (Pas. 1203).

205. The priory of Merton was an independent house of Augustinian canons in Surrey, founded in the early twelfth century. David Knowles and R. Neville Hadcock, *Medieval Religious Houses: England and Wales* (London: Longman, 1971), 142.

206. 4 CRR 126 (Pas. 1206). Brian and Gunnora offered twenty shillings for an inquisition whether the charter was made after Eudes became a canon. The prior said that he did not defend against the charter at an earlier time and sought judgment about whether he could defend against it now. The entry ends there, and no record exists of an earlier appearance in which Eudes failed to object to the charter. The dispute between the prior and Brian and Gunnora involved land as well as the advowson; Brian and Gunnora can be seen bringing the writ of right against the prior concerning one hide of land in Malden during the same term. 4 CRR 133, 148–49 (Pas. 1206). Gunnora was the daughter of Eudes, who allegedly gave the land and advowson to the priory. 4 CRR 149 (Pas. 1206).

207. 4 CRR 217 (Mich. 1206).

208. 2 BNB no. 39, pp. 33–35 (Pas.–Trin. 1219); 8 CRR 51, 134 (Mich. 1219); 9 CRR 84 (Trin. 1220); 10 CRR 37, 91 (Pas. 1221); 11 CRR no. 496, p. 94 (Hil. 1223); 11 CRR no. 1541, p. 308 (Trin. 1224). The donee in question was the abbot of Valmont, and his opponent was Nicholas II de Stuteville. Nicholas was the son and heir of Nicholas I de Stuteville, who died soon after the battle of Lincoln in 1217. Sanders, *English Baronies*, 37. Nicholas II brought an assize of darrein presentment against the abbot to recover the church of Kimberley (Norf). The abbot excepted to the assize on the basis of a gift from Nicholas I, offering a charter of Nicholas I and a confirmation of John of Gray, bishop of Norwich. Nicholas II replied that the charter was null because King John later presented by reason of his (Nicholas II's) wardship, and offered charters showing that King John had presented William of Kimberly to the vicarage and John archdeacon of Worcester to the parsonage. The abbot acknowledged that King John had presented the last parson,

but said he did so unjustly and *per voluntatem suam,* vouching Nicholas II to warrant his father's charter. The court awarded seisin to Nicholas in the darrein presentment action. In the subsequent action of right, however, the abbot prevailed after multiple defaults by Nicholas.

209. 2 CRR 173 (Hil. 1203) (quia ipse prior petit alterius ius per cartam sibi datam et non suum ius proprium). An earlier entry shows that the Templars brought an assize of darrein presentment against the prior concerning the same church. 2 CRR 78 (Mich. 1201). The most likely explanation is that the prior lost the assize and subsequently brought a writ of right. The plea between the prior and the Templars was one of at least three lawsuits concerning the church of Donington over a span of seven years or more. A lawsuit between the prior and David of Scotland, Earl of Huntingdon, was heard in the royal courts circa 1196–99. 1 CRR 22 (Hil. 1196); 2 RCR 14 (Mich. 1199). In Easter Term 1203, William Russell can be seen bringing a writ of right against the Templars, also claiming the advowson of Donington. 2 CRR 229 (Pas. 1203).

210. 11 CRR no. 121, p. 21 = 3 BNB no. 1578, p. 457 (Hil. 1223) (loquitur de alieno iure et alterius seisina quam antecessorum suorum). The quoted language comes from BNB; the plea roll has *sequitur* instead of *loquitur.*

211. This chapel and the associated lost hamlet of Alsthorpe were in the parish of Burley to the northeast of Oakham. *VCH, Rutland,* vol. 2, 112, 119.

212. 2 BNB no. 488, pp. 383–84 (Hil. 1231).

213. A favorable judgment in a *quare impedit* suit would also bar a subsequent action of darrein presentment, as seen in an entry from 1253 in a case involving the church of Eyeworth in Bedfordshire. John de Gravenel had brought an assize of darrein presentment against the prioress of Saint Helen's, London, claiming that he had the advowson by inheritance from his ancestor Walter of Tresley. The prioress argued that she had previously been awarded a moiety of the advowson in a lawsuit brought by *quare impedit* by a third party, and asked the court to consult the rolls of Martin of Pattishall. The court did so, determined that the prioress was correct, and ruled in her favor. TNA KB 26/149, m. 21 (Trin. 1253), http://aalt.law.uh.edu/H3/KB26_149/0021.htm (accessed December 21, 2020).

214. 2 CRR 228 (Pas. 1203).

215. 3 CRR 241 (Mich. 1204).

216. Ralph had initially sued Robert of Bedingham, but Ralph brought another writ after Robert (the vicar) said he had nothing except through the archdeacon. 4 CRR 119 (Pas. 1206), 170 (Trin. 1206).

217. 5 CRR 84 (Mich. 1207). The record gives no explanation for the judgment; perhaps the defendants could not contradict the plaintiffs' claim.

218. 13 CRR no. 1495, pp. 320–21 (= 2 BNB no. 319, p. 268) (Hil. 1229). The prior said that a certain brother "from Melksham" appealed against Richard's presentation, not in the name of the prior but in the name of John Bauzan, who was underage and in the prior's wardship. The prior denied that any ancestor of Richard ever presented, and the un-

derage John said the presentation pertained to him. The assize proceeded. The jurors said that Roger Constantin presented the last parson, Thomas. Asked who was heir of Roger, they said that Roger had a son named William, who had a son Roger and a daughter Amicia. Roger died without an heir, and the inheritance descended to Amicia, who was the wife of Richard the plaintiff and had children by him. The jurors also explained that William fitz Roger sold the land of Hargrave to a certain Frumbald to be held of him. Having heard this, the court awarded seisin to Richard but pardoned the prior's amercement because he sued on behalf of John.

219. *Bracton*, f. 244, III, p. 222.

220. Pollock and Maitland, II, 139.

221. Joshua C. Tate, "The Origins of Quare Impedit," *Journal of Legal History* 25 (2004): 203–19, 212.

222. 1 CRR 18 (Hil. 1196); 31 PRS 79 (Hil. 1196); 31 PRS 90 (Hil. 1196); and 1 CRR 44 (Pas. 1198) all involve a religious house; in all but 31 PRS 79, the religious house is the plaintiff. 1 CRR 101 (Hil. 1199) and 1 CRR 111 (Hil. 1199) do not involve a religious house. This count excludes 1 CRR 19 (Hil. 1196), which cannot definitely be identified as *quare impedit*, although it looks like it; a religious house is also plaintiff in that case.

223. 1 CRR 44 (Pas. 1198). For the details of this case, see D. M. Stenton's description at 1 PKJ 8 and 352–53. Stenton states that Matthew fitz Herbert "was a powerful royal servant as well as an important baron." 1 PKJ 8. It is possible that Matthew's wife Joan was the daughter of William of Mandeville, Baron of Erlestoke in Wiltshire. See Sanders, *English Baronies*, 42.

224. 1 PKJ no. 3475, pp. 351–52 (circa 1199).

225. 1 CRR 142 (Hil. 1200).

226. 2 RCR 226 (Pas. 1200). This procedure differs from the usual practice of the thirteenth century, in which the knights are sent simply to determine whether the person is actually sick; here they are sent to determine *si vellet warantizare donum suum*, the substantive issue in the lawsuit.

227. The record does not indicate which queen is meant, but Eleanor of Aquitaine is likely.

228. "Dicunt quod ipsa dixit quod ipsa, postquam Matheus filius Hereberti duxerat in uxorem filiam suam et de ipsa liberos habuerit, prece domine regine fecit cartam monachis predictis et eo tempore quo terra ad quam abbatia [recte advocatio] illa pertinet non fuit in manu sua, et quod ipsa non vult coram iusticiariis venire nec aliquem loco suo attornare." 1 CRR 201 (Trin. 1200).

229. The last entry involving Matthew and the abbot records a postponement by the king's command in what appears to be a separate case involving the advowson of Chillington. 1 CRR 301 (Mich. 1200).

230. See, e.g., the dispute between the prior of Lenton and William of Saint Patrick, discussed *supra;* and 5 CRR 145 (Hil. 1208), where the prior of Alvingham claimed by gift from the defendant's uncle, and the defendant responded that the charter was sealed after

his uncle's death. The pattern is extremely common in early cases of darrein present-ment, although the parties are usually reversed, and the religious house is the defendant. Sometimes both the layman and the religious house claimed by charter, as in 2 RCR 200 (Pas. 1200).

231. Generally, such a dispute would occur between the religious house and the donor's heir; the abbot of Stanley's case is unusual in that the donor was still alive and was not a party to the original lawsuit.

232. Religious houses were not the only donees who could bring *quare impedit*. For exam-ple, in one *quare impedit* action brought toward the end of the period, the plaintiff, William of Wyville, claimed that his ancestor had been given the advowson of Barnby (in Nottinghamshire) in *maritagium* by the ancestor of the defendant, John of Neville. The judgment is omitted from the entry. See TNA KB 26/217, m. 2 (Hil. 1259), http://aalt.law.uh.edu/AALT1/H3/KB26no217/IMG_3568.htm (accessed December 31, 2020). On the branches of the Neville family, which included several generations of high-ranking royal officials, see Charles R. Young, *The Making of the Neville Family in England, 1166–1400* (Woodbridge: Boydell Press, 1996), at x–xiii. Lay plaintiffs claiming by gift were, however, far outnumbered by religious houses throughout the period.

233. See Moorman, *Church Life in England,* 38–42 (noting that appropriation of churches by monasteries became "very common" in the twelfth century, and "at least half of the parish churches of England" were appropriated by the end of the thirteenth). In most cases, the primary motivation for appropriation seems to have been financial, since many religious houses fell into debt in the thirteenth century. See Lawrence, "The English Parish and Its Clergy," at 749.

234. See *infra* chap. 5.

Chapter Three. Ownership and Possession

1. H. F. Jolowicz and Barry Nicholas, *Historical Introduction to the Study of Roman Law,* 3rd ed. (Cambridge: Cambridge University Press, 1972), 259.

2. W. W. Buckland and Arnold D. McNair, *Roman Law and Common Law: A Comparison in Outline,* 2nd ed., rev. F. H. Lawson (Cambridge: Cambridge University Press, 1952), 62.

3. Dig. 41.2.12.1.

4. *Bracton,* f. 39, II, p. 122. On the efforts by the authors of *Bracton* to reconcile the Roman law of ownership and possession with English law, see McSweeney, *Priests of the Law,* at 114–30.

5. See 3 BNB 330 (Mich. 1354) (quoting a letter of the former bishop of Salisbury ordering a certain clerk to be put "in corporalem possessionem" of the church of Warminster); 9 CRR 52 (Trin. 1220) (quoting a letter of the legate "super possessione ca-pelle" of Alderton). We find a rare example of the term *possessio* being used in the plea rolls in a dispute between laymen (and not in a quotation from a bishop's letter) in a 1252 entry from a dispute over the advowson of Gedding, in Suffolk, which William and Adam

of Rickinghall brought against Adam of Gedding. When the defendant offered a deed of quitclaim from the father of the plaintiffs, the plaintiffs responded that the quitclaim was ineffective because it was not a charter of feoffment or donation, and "nec potest jus advocationis vel possessio transire de persona in personam nisi per viam donationis vel redditionis in curia que recordum habet." TNA KB 26/147B, m. 21d (Mich. 1252), http://aalt.law.uh.edu/H3/KB26_147B/0021d.htm (accessed December 21, 2020). That this reference dates from the 1250s, when Roman legal concepts arguably reached the peak of their influence on the medieval English judiciary, is unlikely to be a coincidence.

6. Joshua C. Tate, "Ownership and Possession in the Early Common Law," *American Journal of Legal History* 48 (2006): 280–313, 282.

7. Pollock and Maitland, II, 33.

8. *Id.* II, p. 62.

9. *Id.* II, p. 47.

10. Milsom, *Legal Framework*, 39–40.

11. *Id.* at 71.

12. Milsom, *Natural History*, 1.

13. Mary Cheney, "The Litigation between John Marshal and Archbishop Thomas Becket in 1164: A Pointer to the Origin of Novel Disseisin?" in *Law and Social Change in British History*, ed. J. A. Guy and H. G. Beale (London: Royal Historical Society, 1984), 9, 25–26.

14. Sutherland cited Milsom's introduction to the revised edition of Pollock and Maitland's *History of English Law*, published in 1968.

15. Donald W. Sutherland, *The Assize of Novel Disseisin* (Oxford: Clarendon Press, 1973), 22–23.

16. *Id.* at 23.

17. *Id.* at 41–42.

18. Mary Cheney, "*Possessio/proprietas* in Ecclesiastical Courts in Mid-twelfth Century England," in *Law and Government in Medieval England and Normandy: Essays in Honour of Sir James Holt*, ed. George Garnett and John Hudson (Cambridge: Cambridge University Press, 1994), 245–54.

19. Tate, "Ownership and Possession," at 283.

20. *Id.* at 284.

21. Francis de Zulueta and Peter Stein, *The Teaching of Roman Law in England around 1200*, Selden Society Supp. Series 8 (London, 1990), 1 ff. I refer to the English commentary in this source as the *Lectura*.

22. LP.

23. See, e.g., Peter Stein, "Vacarius (*c.* 1120–*c.* 1200)," in *Oxford Dictionary of National Biography* (Oxford: Oxford University Press, 2004), http://www.oxforddnb.com/view/article/28048; De Zulueta and Stein, 8 Selden Soc. Supp. Series pp. xxxiii, xxxvii. Contrary to the traditional view, a "continuing academic tradition" probably did not exist at Oxford "until the last years of the twelfth century." R. W. Southern, "Master Vacarius

and the Beginning of an English Academic Tradition," in *Medieval Learning and Literature: Essays Presented to Richard William Hunt,* ed. J. J. G. Alexander and M. T. Gibson (Oxford: Clarendon Press, 1976), 282; see also Leonard E. Boyle, "The Beginnings of Legal Studies at Oxford," *Viator: Medieval and Renaissance Studies* 14 (1983): 109–11 (suggesting that Oxford's transformation into an "open school of law" may have occurred between 1189 and 1196, although legal studies there probably began in the late 1170s). For a recent summary of modern research on the *Liber Pauperum,* see Jason Taliadoros, *Law and Theology in Twelfth-Century England: The Works of Master Vacarius (c. 1115/1120–c. 1200)* (Turnhout, Belgium: Brepols, 2006), 31–35.

24. Because the *Liber Pauperum* does not excerpt passages from the *Institutes,* one may surmise that the former was meant to complement the latter. The purpose of the *Liber Pauperum* was to allow students to advance from the *Institutes* to writings contained in the *Digest* and *Code.* Francis de Zulueta, *The "Liber Pauperum" of Vacarius,* Selden Society 44 (London, 1927), li. Vacarius seems to have intended the *Liber Pauperum* to serve as a textbook for students planning to enter a career in canon law, who needed some knowledge of basic legal principles not covered by the *Decretum* or subsequent papal decretals. See Leonard E. Boyle, "Canon Law before 1380," in *The History of the University of Oxford,* ed. J. J. Catto (Oxford: Clarendon Press, 1984), vol. 1, p. 533.

25. See Boyle, "The Beginnings," at 119–26 (arguing that the *Liber Pauperum* survives only in a later and expanded recension, and the lost original Vacarian manuscript would likely have dated to the 1170s and have been unglossed).

26. See W. Senior, "Roman Law in England before Vacarius," *Law Q. Rev.* 46 (1930): 191–92; Ralph V. Turner, "Roman Law in England before the Time of Bracton," *J. Brit. Stud.* 15 (1975): 1.

27. See Turner, "Roman Law," at 2.

28. De Zulueta and Stein, 8 Selden Soc. Supp. Series p. xxii.

29. John of Salisbury, "Policraticus," in *The Statesman's Book of John of Salisbury,* ed. and trans. John Dickinson (New York: A. A. Knopf, 1963), viii, 22; Turner, "Roman Law," at 6.

30. See Peter Stein, "Vacarius (c. 1120–c. 1200)."

31. Turner, "Roman Law," at 7.

32. See Beryl Smalley, *The Becket Conflict and the Schools: A Study of Intellectuals in Politics* (Totowa, N.J.: Rowman and Littlefield, 1973), 162–63.

33. W. Senior, "Roman Law Mss. in England," *Law Q. Rev.* 47 (1931): 337.

34. Turner, "Roman Law," at 23.

35. See Eleanor Rathbone, "Roman Law in the Anglo-Norman Realm," *Studia Gratiana* 11 (1967): 263 (finding "evidence of some degree of familiarity with the principles and doctrines of Roman law in a fairly wide stratum of the educated class in England about 1180 and of a marked infiltration in court and council by men with specialist knowledge"). On the contributions of the secular clergy to royal administration and lay administration more generally during this period, see Hugh M. Thomas, *The Secular Clergy in England, 1066–1216* (Oxford: Oxford University Press, 2014), 122–25.

36. Dig. 41.2.12.1 (LP 7.17). See also Dig. 41.2.17.1 (LP 7.17) (explaining that one can lose possession by intent alone, but ownership can only be lost by an act such as delivery).

37. Inst. 2.1.12 and *Lectura* gloss to 2.1.17.

38. Inst. 2.1.18 and *Lectura* gloss. The reference to *inventio* in the *Lectura* may have been intended as shorthand for *thesauri inventio,* a concept similar to, but distinct from, *occupatio.* For a discussion of *thesauri inventio* in Roman law, see W. W. Buckland, *A Textbook of Roman Law from Augustus to Justinian,* ed. Peter Stein (Cambridge: Cambridge University Press, 1963), 218–21.

39. Inst. 2.1.25 and *Lectura* gloss to 2.1.27.

40. Inst. 2.1.40.

41. *Id.* 2.1.41.

42. *Id.* This particular rule seems to have been introduced by Justinian and was not the classical position. See D. L. Carey Miller, "Property," in *A Companion to Justinian's Institutes,* ed. Ernest Metzger (Ithaca, N.Y.: Cornell University Press, 1998), 55.

43. Inst. 3.1.ff.

44. *Id.* 2.6.pr. The three-year period for movables was a reform of Justinian; classical law had provided a one-year usucapion period for movables and two years for immovables. See *id.*

45. "Distinguitur causa ex qua solet dominium transferri, Puta ex emptione, permutatione etc. similibus. Distinguitur etiam initium, ut sit iustum." *Lectura* gloss to 2.6.pr. (trans. de Zulueta and Stein). This allowed property to be acquired in good faith and by normal means from a nonowner, which was not possible by *traditio.*

46. "Mala fide uero possessa non minus xxx. annorum spatio adquiruntur." *Id.* (trans. de Zulueta and Stein).

47. Dig. 6.1.1 (LP 3.27).

48. *Id.*; Inst. 4.6.1.

49. Dig. 6.1.36.pr. (LP 3.27).

50. "Nota enim actione in rem persequimur quod nostrum est. Nemini enim sua res debetur." *Lectura* gloss to Inst. 4.6 (trans. de Zulueta and Stein).

51. Dig. 41.2.1.pr. (LP 7.17).

52. Dig. 41.2.3.1 (LP 7.17). A gloss on this rubric in the *Liber Pauperum* distinguishes between civil and corporeal possession: the former can only be lost when someone strong and powerful takes possession and I cannot repel him, while the latter can be lost simply when another takes possession in his own name. LP gloss *ad rubricam* 7.17.

53. See Giuseppe Brini, *Possesso delle Cose e Possesso dei Diritti nel Diritto Romano* (1906; repr., Rome: G. Bretschneider, 1978), 28–38; see also Enrico Finzi, *Il Possesso dei Diritti* (1915; repr., Milan: A Giuffrè, 1968).

54. Dig. 8.2.20.pr. (LP 3.39) ("quia in tuo aliquid utor et si quasi facto quodam possideo").

55. Dig. 8.5.10 (LP 3.42) ("Si quis diuturno usu et longa quasi possessione ius aquae ducendae nactus sit, non est ei necesse docere de iure, quo aqua constituta est . . . sed utilem

habet actionem, ut ostendat per annos forte tot usum se non vi non clam non precario possedisse").

56. *Lectura* gloss to Inst. 4.15 (trans. de Zulueta and Stein), 132.

57. Apparatus *Materia auctoris,* gloss to 1 Comp. 3.33.23, v. *non possidebat,* cited in Landau, *Jus Patronatus,* 203n714.

58. Bernard of Parma, *Glossa ordinaria* to X 3.38.19, v. *credebatur* ("et erat in quasi possessione iuris patronatus").

59. WH 184, JL 12636, 1 Comp. 3.33.23 = X 3.38.19 ("ius patronatus ecclesiae possidebat . . . secundum consuetudinem Anglicanam"). The reference to the English custom, however, was deleted in the *Liber Extra,* although it appears in the *Compilatio Prima.*

60. Inst. 4.15.pr.

61. Dig. 6.1.24 (LP 3.27) ("Is qui destinavit rem petere animadvertere debet, an aliquo interdicto posit nancisci possessionem, quia longe commodius est ipsum possidere et adversarium ad onera petitoris compellere quam alio possidente petere").

62. "Plerumque et fere semper ingens existit contentio de ipsa possessione." Inst. 4.15.4 (trans. Birks and McLeod).

63. Inst. 4.15.2.

64. Inst. 4.15.3.

65. "Namque nisi ante exploratum fuerit, utrius eorum possessio sit, non potest petitoria actio institui, quia et civilis et naturalis ratio facit, ut alius possideat, alius a possidente petat." Inst. 4.15.4 (trans. Birks and McLeod).

66. "Uti possidetis interdicto is vincebat, qui interdicti tempore possidebat, si modo nec vi nec clam nec precario nanctus fuerat ab adversario possessionem, etiamsi alium vi expulerit aut clam abripuerit alienam possessionem aut precario rogaverat aliquem, ut sibi possidere liceret: utrubi vero interdicto is vincebat, qui maiore parte eius anni nec vi nec clam nec precario ab adversario possidebat." Inst. 4.15.4a. (trans. Birks and McLeod).

67. "Hodie tamen aliter observatur: nam utriusque interdicti potestas quantum ad possessionem pertinet exaequata est, ut ille vincat et in re soli et in re mobile, qui possessionem nec vi nec clam nec precario ab adversario litis contestationis tempore detinet." *Id.* (trans. Birks and McLeod).

68. Dig. 43.17.2 (LP 8.14).

69. *Id.*; Dig. 43.31.1 (LP 8.28).

70. "Ait praetor: 'Uti eas aedes, quibus de agitur, nec vi nec clam nec precario alter ab altero possidetis, quo minus ita possideatis, vim fieri veto.' " Dig. 43.17.1.pr. (LP 8.14) (trans. Fritz Schulz). See Fritz Schulz, *Classical Roman Law* (Oxford: Clarendon Press, 1951), § 781.

71. Dig. 43.17.1.1 (LP 8.14).

72. Lucien Masmejan, *La protection possessoire en droit romano-canonique médiéval (XIIIe–XVe siècles)* (Montpellier: Société d'histoire du droit et des institutions des anciens pays de droit écrit, 1990), 261.

73. *Id.* at 261–62.

74. "Hoc interdicto uincit ille qui tempore interdicti possidebat, et competit pro rebus soli. . . . Sed quia maxima oritur questio de iure possessionis, ideo necessarium est huius-modi ordinari ut expressum sit uter agens et uter reus dici debeat. Sed quia frequenter melior solet esse pars possidentis, circa huiusmodi interdicta maxima inter partes solet esse de possessione contentio; uterque namque se possidere defendit. unde uterque actor et uterque defensor esse uidetur. unde etiam, ut in sequenti habetur, duplicia dicuntur huiusmodi interdicta, quia duplicia uidentur partes agere." *Lectura* gloss to Inst. 4.15.4 (trans. de Zulueta and Stein).

75. "Est autem retinende possessionis clam perdite, est etiam prohibitorium quo pos-sessor aduersarium ne sibi possidendi uis fiat proh(ibet)." LP gloss *ad rubricam* 8.14 (*Uti pos-sidetis*).

76. "Sed hoc interdictum propter uim proditum est; sed illud supra ad uim ulciscen-dam, hoc autem ad propulsandam pertinet." *Id.*

77. Dig. 43.16.1 (LP 8.12). Classical law knew a separate interdict *de vi armata*, but the distinction between the two had collapsed by the time of Justinian. See Ernest Metzger, "Actions," in *A Companion to Justinian's Institutes*, 211.

78. "Per quod is qui deiecit cogitur ei restituere possessionem, licet is ab eo qui vi dei-ecit vi vel clam vel precario possidebat." Inst. 4.15.6.

79. Dig. 43.16.1.3 (LP 8.12).

80. Dig. 43.16.1.26 (LP 8.12).

81. Dig. 6.1.24 (LP 3.27).

82. Francesco Ruffini, *L'actio spolii: Studio storico-giuridico* (1889; repr., Rome: L'Erma di Bretschneider, 1972), 329, 337.

83. This was not settled until the end of the fourteenth century, however. Masmejan, *La protection possessoire*, 187–91.

84. Pollock and Maitland, I, 135; II, 48n1.

85. *Id.* II, 48n1.

86. W. S. Holdsworth, *A History of English Law*, vol. 2, 3rd ed. (London: Methuen, 1923), 204.

87. Pollock and Maitland, I, 135.

88. H. G. Richardson and G. O. Sayles, *Select Cases of Procedure without Writ under Henry III*, Selden Society 60 (London, 1941), cxxviii–cxxix.

89. C.3 q.1 c.3–4.

90. Ruffini, *L'actio spolii*, 329, 337.

91. Not until the end of the fourteenth century would it be finally settled that laymen as well as churchmen could avail themselves of the *condictio ex canone Redintegranda* (see Masmejan, *La protection possessoire*, 198), and canonists would argue for centuries over whether the action could be successfully brought against a third party who had received the property in good faith.

92. "Saepe contingit, quod spoliatus iniuste, per spoliatorem in alium re translata, dum adversus possessorem non subvenitur per restitutionis beneficium spoliato, commodo

possessionis amisso, propter difficultatem probationum iuris proprietatis amittit effectum. Unde, non obstante iuris civilis rigore, sancimus, ut, si quis de cetero scienter rem talem receperit, cum spoliatori quasi succedat in vitium eo, quod non multum intersit, [praesertim] quoad periculum animae, iniuste detinere ac invadere alienum, contra possessorem huiusmodi spoliato per restitutionis beneficium succuratur." 4 Conc. Lat. c. 39 = X 2.13.18 (1215).

93. Masmejan, *La protection possessoire,* 188–94.

94. Van Caenegem, *Royal Writs,* 77 Selden Soc. 388 (quoting Ruffini, *L'actio spolii,* 288).

95. C.2 q. 2; C.3 q. 1.

96. Van Caenegem, *Royal Writs,* 77 Selden Soc. 368 (listing Gratian's *Decretum* among books acquired by Lincoln Cathedral ca. 1150–58). The principles were also well known through the False Decretals themselves, which circulated in England as part of "Lanfranc's Collection." *Id.* at 389n1.

97. *Id.* at 388–89.

98. Linda Fowler-Magerl, Ordines Iudiciarii *and* Libelli de Ordine Iudiciorum *(From the Middle of the Twelfth to the End of the Fifteenth Century)* (Turnhout, Belgium: Brepols, 1994), 61.

99. Gustav Hänel, ed., *Incerti auctoris ordo iudiciorum (Ulpianus de edendo)* (Leipzig: B. G. Teubneri, 1838), 31 (quoting CJ 4.19.2).

100. A gloss found in some manuscripts of *Ulpianus de edendo* does distinguish between possessory and proprietary actions; however, these manuscripts apparently date to the fourteenth century, and it is not clear when the gloss was written. See *id.* at pp. xv–xvi, 52n173.

101. Ludwig Wahrmund, ed., *Quellen zur Geschichte der Römisch-Kanonischen Processes im Mittelalter* (Innsbruck: Waguer, 1925), vol. 4, pp. 4–5. On the date, see Fowler-Magerl, Ordines Iudiciarii, 63.

102. Wahrmund used Vat. lat. 2691, fol. 49r–58v, as one of the manuscripts for his edition. This manuscript is taken to represent the English version of Ricardus's *ordo.* See Kenneth Pennington, *Legal History Sources,* http://legalhistorysources.com/1140a-z.htm (accessed December 31, 2020). Wahrmund gives several alternate readings from this manuscript in the passage devoted to ownership and possession. Ludwig Wahrmund, ed., *Quellen zur Geschichte der Römisch-Kanonischen Processes im Mittelalter* (Innsbruck: Waguer, 1915), vol. 2:3, pp. 4–6. The alternate readings do not affect the gist of the passage, which describes separate remedies for ownership and possession, compares the *in rem* remedy to the Roman *vindicatio,* and distinguishes between actions for recovering and retaining possession.

103. See Stephan Kuttner and Eleanor Rathbone, "Anglo-Norman Canonists of the Twelfth Century: An Introductory Study," *Traditio* 7 (1949–51): 290.

104. Robert L. Benson, *The Bishop-Elect: A Study in Medieval Ecclesiastical Office* (Princeton, N.J.: Princeton University Press, 1968), 142–43; Harry Dondorp, "*Ius ad Rem* als Recht, Einsetzung in ein Amt zu Verlangen," *Tijdschrift voor Rechtsgeschiedenis* 59 (1991): 302; Landau, *Jus Patronatus,* 165–68.

105. *Summa Animal est substantia,* gloss to D. 23 c.1 v. *sicut* (quoted in Benson, *The Bishop-Elect,* 143n21).

106. On the relationship between *Animal est substantia* and the decretal *Pastoralis*, see Peter Landau, "Zum Ursprung des 'Ius ad rem' in der Kanonistik," in *Proceedings of the Third International Congress of Medieval Canon Law*, ed. Stephan Kuttner (Vatican: Biblioteca Apostolica Vaticana, 1971), 95–96.

107. 3 Comp. 3.30.4 = X 3.38.29 (1204).

108. 3 Comp. 2.18.8 = X 2.27.18 (1205).

109. Johannes Teutonicus, gloss to 3 Comp. 2.18.8, v. *aduersus*, in *Apparatus glossarum in Compilationem tertiam*, ed. Kenneth Pennington (Vatican City: Biblioteca Apostolica Vaticana, 1981), xii, 321. On the Roman law concept of a *procurator in rem suam*, see Reinhard Zimmermann, *The Law of Obligations: Roman Foundations of the Civilian Tradition*, paperback ed. (1990; Oxford: Clarendon Press, 1996), 60–64.

110. Tancred, gloss *Appellaverit* to 3 Comp. 3.33.4, quoted in Dondorp, *"Ius ad Rem,"* at 316. On the date of Tancred's gloss, see Pennington, *Legal History Sources*, http://legalhis torysources.com/1140a-z.htm (accessed December 31, 2020).

111. On this basis, Dondorp disagrees with the notion that *ius ad rem* had already developed into a hybrid real and personal right by the time of Tancred. See Dondorp, *"Ius ad Rem,"* at 317 (noting that "die frühen Dekretisten haben der Wahl und Präsentation jede Wirkung gegen Dritten abgesprochen"). For the opposing view, see Landau, *Jus Patronatus*, 170 ("Es steht auch bei Tankred bereits zwischen persönlichen und dinglichen Rechten").

112. Tate, "Ownership and Possession," at 292.

113. See Cheney, *"Possessio/proprietas,"* at 245–54; see also Hudson, *Land, Law, and Lordship*, 104, 267 (discussing a case recorded in a charter of Archbishop Theobald); Biancalana, "For Want of Justice," at 500–501 (discussing this case and another from the same period).

114. "Omisso iudicio possessorio, petitorium instituit asserens ecclesiam suam esse et se personam eius a tempore Mauritii bonae memoriae Lond(oniensis) episcopi extitisse." *Letters of John of Salisbury*, no. 72. For a discussion of this case, see Biancalana, "For Want of Justice," at 501.

115. Marion Gibbs, ed., *Early Charters of the Cathedral Church of St. Paul, London* (London: Royal Historical Society, 1939), no. 163.

116. E. O. Blake, ed., *Liber Eliensis* (Woodbridge: Boydell, 1962), 352–53.

117. Hans-Eberhard Lohmann, ed., "*Collectio Wigorniensis*," sec. 7.72, *Zeitschrift der Savigny-Stiftung für Rechtsgeschichte, Kanonistische Abteilung* 22 (1933): 143–44.

118. 180 PL, col. 1095 no. 72.

119. *Id.* col. 1153 no. 127 ("Facta autem restitutione, si clerici . . . de proprietate agere voluerint . . . causa audiatur").

120. *Letters of John of Salisbury*, no. 102.

121. Cheney, *"Possessio/proprietas,"* at 253.

122. A. Chédeville, ed., *Liber Controversarium Sancti Vincentii Cenomannensis* (Paris, 1968), no. 251 (translation by Cheney, *"Possessio/proprietas,"* at 250) ("tum quia super sola possessione fiebat, tum quia iam tertio multis laboribus et sumptibus ipsius abbatis producta fuerat").

123. Tate, "Ownership and Possession," at 295.

124. Cheney, *"Possessio/proprietas,"* at 252.

125. *Id.* at 247.

126. Pollock and Maitland, II, 47, 62; *Bracton,* f. 39, II, p. 122; *Glanvill,* I, 3, Woodbine p. 42. Maitland may have been influenced by his study of *Bracton.*

127. *Glanvill,* XII, 3, Woodbine p. 149 (trans. Beames, p. 286).

128. *Id.* XII, 6–7, Woodbine pp. 151–52; Biancalana, "For Want of Justice," at 443.

129. *Glanvill,* VI, Woodbine p. 90.

130. Biancalana, "For Want of Justice," at 466.

131. See chap. 2 *supra.*

132. Sutherland, *The Assize,* 35–36.

133. *Glanvill,* XIII, 33, Woodbine p. 172 (trans. Beames, pp. 335–36).

134. *Id.* XIII, 38, Woodbine pp. 173–74.

135. Pollock and Maitland, I, 145.

136. *Pipe Roll 12 Henry II,* 4, 7, 10, 14, 65.

137. See Sutherland, *The Assize,* 7–8; see also Doris M. Stenton, *English Justice between the Norman Conquest and the Great Charter, 1066–1215* (Philadelphia: American Philosophical Society, 1964), 39.

138. S. F. C. Milsom, *Historical Foundations of the Common Law,* 2nd ed. (London: Butterworths, 1981), 138–39.

139. J. E. A. Joliffe, *Angevin Kingship* (London: A. and C. Black, 1955), 46–47.

140. Sutherland, *The Assize,* 17–18; but see Palmer, "The Origins of Property in England," at 22 (suggesting that the assize was "formalized into a standardized writ shortly before 1188").

141. Van Caenegem, *Royal Writs,* 77 Selden Soc. 267–303, 444–64.

142. Stenton, *English Justice,* 33–34.

143. *Bracton,* f. 164b, III, p. 25 ("multis vigiliis excogitatam et inventam") (trans. Samuel E. Thorne).

144. Pollock and Maitland, II, 46–47.

145. Milsom, *Legal Framework,* 14.

146. *Id.* at 11.

147. Milsom, *Legal Framework,* 11.

148. *Id.* at 12. In distraining the animals, the lord had to keep them in a certain place, and thus the sheriff would know where to find them. See Hudson, *Land, Law, and Lordship,* 31.

149. Milsom, *Legal Framework,* 13.

150. *Id.* at 178.

151. Milsom, *Historical Foundations,* 128–29.

152. *Id.* at 129.

153. Robert C. Palmer, "The Feudal Framework of English Law," *Mich. L. Rev.* 79 (1981): 1143–45.

154. See Palmer, "Origins," at 13, 22.

155. See 2 RCR 22–23 (Mich. 1199); 3 CRR 133 (Trin. 1204). For this plea to work, the defendant had to produce his court; if he did not, judgment would be given for the plaintiff. 3 CRR 161–62 (Trin. 1204); 3 PKJ no. 932, pp. 139–40 (York 1204); Milsom, *Legal Framework*, 13.

156. 1 CRR 86 (Hil. 1199).

157. 1 RCR 422 (Pas./Trin. 1199). This entry says "Trim" instead of "Grim," but it is probably the same defendant. Milsom, *Legal Framework*, 18n1.

158. 1 RCR 177 (Herts. 1198) (the assize); 2 CRR 259–60 (Trin. 1203) (the writ *de homagio capiendo*).

159. 2 CRR 55, 60 (Mich. 1201). The second entry does not mention the land, but both entries are from Hampshire.

160. See Paul Brand, "The Origins of English Land Law," at 221–24 (offering various counterarguments); Sutherland, *The Assize*, 31. Even if the assize of novel disseisin and other inventions of Henry II's reign were in fact intended to serve as a check on seigneurial courts, the imposition of such a check was itself a manifestation of royal authority and may reflect an attempt to aggrandize the king's power vis-à-vis that of the intermediate lords. See Hudson, *Land, Law, and Lordship*, 254, 262–71; Biancalana, "For Want of Justice," at 435–36. About ten years after the assize of novel disseisin was created, Henry II and his advisers created the assize of mort d'ancestor, designed for situations where a lord prevented an heir from inheriting land of which his ancestor had been seised. Biancalana, "For Want of Justice," at 484–85. Another important innovation of the reign of Henry II was the *precipe* writ of dower, which gave widows who had none of their dower a remedy in the royal courts. Biancalana, "For Want of Justice," at 514. Thus, in several different contexts, Henry II and his advisers intervened in matters that had previously been the province of the seigneurial courts. Such actions increased the authority of the king and the royal courts while strengthening the hand of freeholders against intermediate lords.

161. Milsom, *Legal Framework*, 13.

162. *Glanvill*, IX, 11, Woodbine p. 132 (tenant against lord); IX, 13, Woodbine p. 133 (neighbor against neighbor).

163. Cheney, "The Litigation."

164. *Id.* at 16–17 (trans. Cheney).

165. *Id.* at 19, citing Walther Holtzmann, ed., *Papsturkunden in England* (Berlin: Weidmannsche Buchhandlung, 1935), nos. 54 (Salisbury), 57 (Chichester), 78 (Exeter, misdated 1153 for 1146). The special emphasis in these letters on recovering lost property is probably related to the chaos caused by King Stephen's reign, but the duty to recover lost possessions was an ancient canonical duty "impressed upon each prelate at the time of his blessing or consecration." *Id.* At any time during the twelfth or thirteenth centuries, prelates would have sought to recover church land that had fallen into lay hands.

166. Mike Macnair, "Vicinage and the Antecedents of the Jury," *Law and Hist. Rev.* 17 (1999): 581–82.

167. If the assize rolls from the early thirteenth century give any indication, churchmen were more likely to appear as defendants than as plaintiffs in novel disseisin cases. A

survey of assize records from six counties (Lincolnshire, Worcestershire, Yorkshire, Gloucestershire, Warwickshire, and Shropshire) from the early years of Henry III's reign, edited by the Selden Society in vols. 53, 56, and 59, revealed a total of 598 actions of novel disseisin. Of these, 98, or 16.39 percent, involved a member of the clergy either as a plaintiff or as a defendant; and 70, or 11.71 percent, involved a high-ranking clergyman such as an abbot, prior, or bishop. Of the total number of novel disseisin cases involving members of the clergy, 61, or 62.24 percent, were cases in which a member of the clergy was being sued by a layman or laymen; 29, or 29.59 percent, were cases in which a member of the clergy was suing a layman or laymen; and 8, or 8.16 percent, were cases involving members of the clergy on both sides. The figures are comparable if one considers only cases involving high-ranking clergymen: 45, or 64.29 percent, involved a high-ranking clergyman being sued by a layman or laymen; 29, or 27.14 percent, involved a high-ranking clergyman suing a layman or laymen; and the remaining 6, or 8.57 percent, were interclergy disputes. Notably, of the actions brought against higher-ranking clergy, the clergy were successful in thirty actions and unsuccessful in only seven. See Tate, "Ownership and Possession," at 303–4.

168. Macnair, "Vicinage," at 587. Macnair concludes, however, that "the king and his advisers and justices were not simply copying the developing canon law of proof, but rather stretching both canonical concepts and local practices to gain political advantage in the middle ground." *Id.*

169. Sutherland, *The Assize*, 22–23.

170. This principle was not stated in the language of the writ, but it is made clear by the discussion in *Glanvill*, which notes that the losing party is always subject to amercement *propter violentam desaisinam. Id.* at 27–30; *Glanvill*, XIII, 38, Woodbine p. 174.

171. Despite this rule, it was common in the early records to join the tenant who came in after the disseisin as a codefendant, and this became a requirement early in the thirteenth century. Sutherland, *The Assize*, 19n1.

172. *Id.* at 23–24.

173. *Id.* at 23. Sutherland downplays this difference on the grounds that the English system had no real counterpart to a Roman heir.

174. While the classical interdict *de vi non armata* applied only to dispossessions within the previous year, the interdict *de vi armata* did not contain this limitation. See Schulz, *Classical Roman Law*, §§ 779–80. The fusion of the two under Justinian allowed the interdict to be brought either within the year or afterward. Dig. 43.16.1.

175. Sutherland, *The Assize*, 22.

176. Milsom, *Natural History*, 1.

177. See *supra* chap. 2.

178. See Tate, "Ownership and Possession," at 308–9.

179. 1 CRR 175 (Trin. 1200).

180. 2 CRR 157 (Hil. 1203).

181. See Tate, "Ownership and Possession," at 309.

182. This response would suggest that Robert claimed the advowson by gift from Payn or his son, but he did not offer a charter or a confirmation of the bishop.

183. 1 CRR 332 (Mich. 1200).

184. 2 CRR 113 (Mich. 1202), 223, 236 (Pas. 1203).

185. Tate, "Ownership and Possession," at 309. See, e.g., (a) 12 CRR no. 1423, p. 289 (Mich. 1225) = 3 BNB no. 1685, p. 531 (the assize), and 13 CRR no. 26, p. 6 (Pas. 1227) = 2 BNB no. 248, p. 201 (the writ of right, with the parties reversed); (b) 13 CRR no. 1799, p. 377 (Pas. 1229) (defendant in action of right refers to earlier, successful darrein presentment action brought by his father); (c) 16 CRR no. 1942, p. 396 (Pas. 1242) (the assize), and 16 CRR no. 2463, p. 487 (Pas. 1242) (the writ of right, brought by the party who unsuccessfully claimed the last presentation at the assize).

186. 20 CRR no. 928, pp. 169–70 (Trin. 1250). The case involved a dispute over the advowson of Saint Benet Sherehog in London. In Trinity Term 1250, the prior of Saint Mary's Southwark brought an assize of darrein presentment against Stephen le Wimpler, alleging that the prior's predecessor Robert presented the last clerk, Walter le Petit, to the church in the reign of Henry III. Stephen responded that the advowson pertained to a tenement of which Peter le Cresp had enfeoffed him, and that Peter had presented the last clerk, Ralph, in the time of King John. Stephen denied that Walter had ever been parson of the church. The prior then noted that Peter had brought a writ of right against the prior during the reign of Henry III concerning the advowson and had died while the plea was pending. Since Peter had impleaded the prior by writ of right, the prior reasoned, so that he thereby conceded that the prior was in seisin ("desicut inplacitavit ipsum per breve de recto ita quod per consequens concessit quod idem prior inde fuit in seisina"), the prior sought a judgment whether Stephen could claim anything in the advowson. After consulting the mayor and aldermen, who confirmed the earlier lawsuit, the court ruled in favor of the prior and gave him a writ to the bishop; Stephen was amerced.

187. See 2 CRR 157 (Hil. 1203) and discussion *supra*.

188. When the defendant argued that a church was not vacant, it was a permissible response for the plaintiff to say that the current parson was admitted unjustly and over his appeal. See 3 BNB no. 1352, p. 328 (Mich. 1217); 3 BNB no. 1354, p. 330 (Mich. 1217). If the defendant conceded the plaintiff's presentation, however, it was immaterial whether the presentation was unjust. See 11 CRR no. 1662, p. 331 (Trin. 1224) (defendant concedes that the plaintiff presented the last parson, but says the presentation was unjust; summary judgment for plaintiff).

189. See Tate, "Ownership and Possession," at 309–10.

190. See *Glanvill*, XIII, 20, Woodbine p. 168, discussed in chap. 4 *infra*.

191. Tate, "Ownership and Possession," at 310.

192. See *infra* chap. 4.

193. See *supra* text accompanying notes 179–84.

194. Tate, "Ownership and Possession," at 311.

195. Richardson and Sayles, *Select Cases*, 60 Selden Soc., p. cxxix.

196. See Tate, "Ownership and Possession," at 311–12.

197. See *id.* at 312. The *tempore pacis* requirement appears in *Glanvill*, IV, 1, Woodbine p. 75, but not XIII, 19, Woodbine p. 167. See *supra* chap. 2. This may suggest either that XIII was completed before IV or that there was a clerical error in XIII.

198. "Ait praetor: 'Uti eas aedes, quibus de agitur, nec vi nec clam nec precario alter ab altero possidetis, quo minus ita possideatis, vim fieri veto.' " Dig. 43.17.1.pr. (LP 8.14).

199. See chap. 2 *supra*. The rule is stated plainly in 2 CRR 173 (Hil. 1203) ("alterius ius per cartam sibi datam et non suum ius proprium"); see also 11 CRR no. 121, p. 21 = 3 BNB no. 1578, p. 457 (Hil. 1223) (plaintiff amerced because "loquitur de alieno iure et alterius seisina quam antecessorum suorum"). The rule was not always applied in practice, however. See 1 CRR 471 (Pas. 1201) (plaintiff allowed to bring writ of right on basis of gift); 4 CRR 126 (Pas. 1206) (same); 2 BNB no. 39, pp. 33–35 (Pas.–Trin. 1219) (same).

200. Inst. 2.1.41.

201. Sutherland, *The Assize*, 41–42.

202. Tate, "Ownership and Possession," at 313.

203. *Glanvill*, I, 3, Woodbine p. 42.

204. If, as Paul Brand has suggested, the treatise was meant as a "conversion kit" for men with a Romano-canonical background who wished to enter the canon law, then the use of Romano-canonical terms is less surprising. See Brand, "Legal Education in England," at 53–55.

205. *Glanvill*, IV, 6, Woodbine p. 77 (trans. Beames, p. 88).

206. Milsom, *Legal Framework*, 40.

207. *Supra* chap. 2.

208. Van Caenegem, *Royal Writs*, 77 Selden Soc. no. 97, pp. 462–63; Van Caenegem, *English Lawsuits*, 107 Selden Soc. no. 500, p. 555. See *supra* chap. 2.

209. Milsom, *Legal Framework*, 40.

210. See, e.g., 3 BNB no. 1295, pp. 305–6 (Mich. 1217).

211. 18 CRR no. 242, p. 47 (Trin. 1242).

212. Parties might on occasion be allowed to continue pleading even after a jury's verdict, despite *Glanvill*'s statement to the contrary. See 4 CRR 97 (plaintiff in darrein presentment suit allowed to plead gift after jury verdict in favor of defendants).

213. 5 CRR 141–42 (Hil. 1208). For further discussion of this case, see *infra* chap. 4.

214. 7 CRR 280 (Mich. 1214).

215. 3 CRR 111 (Pas. 1204).

216. 3 CRR 293 (Pas. 1205).

217. See Sutherland, *The Assize*, 41–42.

218. *Bracton*, f. 245b, III, p. 226; f. 247, III, p. 230.

219. Dig. 8.2.20 (LP 3.39); 8.5.10 (LP 3.42).

220. In one of three advowson suits brought by the abbot of Warden in 1200, for example, the abbot claimed a moiety of the church of Warden from Maud de Bussy on the basis of a charter of gift from her father. Maud did not contradict the charter, and the court

awarded seisin to the abbot ("consideratum est quod abbas habeat seisinam suam"). See 1 CRR 238 (Trin. 1200); on the related litigation, see *supra* chap. 2.

221. The Romans did acknowledge that some kinds of possession were closer to owner-ship than others. The *actio Publiciana* offered a remedy for a plaintiff to claim property that was delivered for good cause by a nonowner and lacked only the relevant period of usu-capion to become the plaintiff's property. Dig. 6.2.1 (LP 3.28). This action, however, can-not be compared to the writ of *quare impedit*, which gives an *in rem* claim to one who has no possession.

222. *Infra* chap. 4.

223. S. F. C. Milsom, "Legal Introduction" to *Novae Narrationes*, Selden Society 80 (London, 1963), xli.

224. *Glanvill,* X, 9, Woodbine p. 140. This writ evolved into the writ of entry *ad terminum qui preteriit.* See Biancalana, "Origin and Early History," at 521–22.

225. Pollock and Maitland, II, 63–70.

226. See Biancalana, "Origin and Early History," at 519.

227. *Id.* at 518; Pollock and Maitland, II, 63.

228. It is theoretically possible, for example, that the canonistic development of the *ius ad rem* in the early thirteenth century, discussed earlier, influenced the development of common-law doctrines relating to *quare impedit.* However, since the latter doctrines appear in the plea rolls from the first decade of the thirteenth century, and the writ itself was much older, it seems highly unlikely that there was any such influence.

229. John Hudson, *The Oxford History of the Laws of England,* vol. 2, *871–1216* (Oxford: Oxford University Press, 2012).

Chapter Four. Pleading and Proof

1. For early examples, see 14 CRR no. 1227, p. 260 (Pas. 1231); 14 CRR no. 1496, p. 320 (Pas. 1231); and 15 CRR no. 349, p. 75 (Mich. 1233). The formula becomes standard in the late 1230s, apparently around 1238 or 1239, although the spotty survival of plea rolls from that period makes it difficult to pinpoint the exact moment of the change. See 16 CRR no. 176, p. 57 (Hil. 1238); 16 CRR no. 180, p. 58 (Hil. 1238); 16 CRR no. 195, p. 60 (Hil. 1238); 16 CRR no. 623, p. 128 (Trin. 1239); 16 CRR no. 681, p. 136 (Trin. 1239); 16 CRR nos. 851–52, p. 165 (Trin. 1239); 16 CRR no. 912, pp. 174–75 (Trin. 1239).

2. The dispute concerned the church of Tolleshunt Knights (Essex). In the plea, (1) Simon of Pattishall claimed the advowson as the heir of (2) his uncle Hugh of Pattishall, bishop of Coventry and Lichfield. Hugh, it was alleged, had purchased the advowson along with the appurtenant estate from (3) Wischard Ledet, son and heir of (4) Henry of Braybrooke, who in turn had purchased the land and advowson from (5) Richard de Eynefeud, nearest heir of (6) Gilbert son of Robert of Tolleshunt, whose guardian (7) Walter de Crepping had presented the last parson, Robert of Crepping. The defendant, the abbot of Saint Osyth, agreed that Walter of Crepping had presented the last parson

by reason of his wardship of Gilbert, but contended that Gilbert had died without an heir of his body and the right had descended to his two sisters, Juliana and Amice. Juliana and Amice, the abbot contended, had both married and after their respective marriages had, along with their husbands, given their rights in the advowson to the abbey. Simon responded that Gilbert had an elder half sister named Alice, daughter of Gilbert's father by his first wife, whose son and heir was Richard de Eynefeud. Richard, Simon alleged, had given certain lands to Juliana and Amice but had retained for himself the chief messuage with the advowson, which he sold to Henry of Braybrooke. The abbot for his part conceded that Alice was an older half sister of Gilbert and sought judgment about whether the presentation pertained to the abbot or to Simon, but the parties subsequently reached an agreement. 18 CRR no. 1265, pp. 266–67 (Pas. 1244). The Simon of Pattishall in the case is not the royal justice from the reigns of Richard and John but rather his grandson, who fought on the side of the barons against Henry III. Cokayne, *The Complete Peerage*, vol. 10, pp. 312–13.

3. *Bracton*, f. 240b, III, pp. 211–12, reports that the plaintiff was required to give a long count stating the basis for his seisin, his claim to the appurtenant fee (or, if there is no appurtenant fee, how he holds the advowson independently), and his descent from the ancestor who last presented, if he did not present himself.

4. On the early history of English law reporting, see Paul A. Brand, ed., *The Earliest English Law Reports*, Selden Society 123 (London, 2007), vol. 4, pp. xi–xxi. Yearbooks were unofficial records prepared either for practitioners or for young apprentices, written in the court dialect of Anglo-French and including the arguments made in court with the names of the speakers. Baker, *Introduction to English Legal History*, 179. No yearbooks survive, however, from before 1291–92. Brand, *Earliest English Law Reports*, vol. 4, p. xii.

5. See, e.g., 2 RCR 53 (Mich. 1199) (alleges gift from defendant's mother-in-law); 2 RCR 171 (Pas. 1200) (gift from defendant's grandfather); 5 CRR 54 (Mich. 1207) (gift from grandmother of defendants' warrantor); 5 CRR 145 (Hil. 1208) (gift from defendant's uncle); 6 CRR 162, 225 (Mich. 1211) (gift from grandfather of defendant's wife); 7 CRR 84 (Hil. 1214) (gift from defendant's ancestors); 8 CRR 288 (Pas. 1220) (gift from Hugh fitz Absalom, brother of one defendant and uncle of the other); 9 CRR 107 (Trin. 1220) (gift from defendants' cousin); 11 CRR no. 2789, pp. 560–61 (gift from defendants' grandfather); 13 CRR no. 192, p. 43 (gift from Philip de Colombières, father of one defendant and late husband of the other); 13 CRR no. 1763, p. 371 (gift from defendant's ancestor); 13 CRR no. 2761, pp. 583–84 (gift from defendant's father); 14 CRR no. 48, p. 7 (gift from common ancestor of defendants); 15 CRR no. 947, pp. 202–3 (gift to mother of defendant's late wife); 17 CRR no. 972, p. 183 (gift from brother of one of the defendants).

6. For examples of cases where the plaintiff claimed a gift either from a third party or from a person whose relationship to the defendant is not specified, see 5 CRR 141 (Hil. 1208); 7 CRR 280 (Mich. 1214); 7 CRR 294 (Mich. 1214); 9 CRR 26 (Trin. 1220); 12 CRR no. 372, pp. 70–71 (Hil. 1225); 3 BNB no. 1831, pp. 632–33 (Norf. 1227); 18 CRR no. 242, p. 47 (Trin. 1242); and 18 CRR no. 1106, p. 233 (Hil. 1244).

7. For examples of *quare impedit* suits where the plaintiff began by asserting that he or his ancestor or predecessor presented the last parson, see 11 CRR no. 1999, p. 400 (Mich. 1223) (plaintiff claims last presentation); 2 BNB no. 625, pp. 475–76 (Mich. 1231) (same); 2 BNB no. 692, pp. 531–32 (Pas. 1232) (plaintiff claims his father presented last parson); 18 CRR no. 1213, pp. 259–60 (plaintiff claims his predecessor presented last parson).

8. In 1244, Arnold de Ketelbergh brought a writ of *quare impedit* against John de Monewden concerning the church of Monewden (Suff), alleging that Henry de Monewden, brother of John, sold the advowson to Arnold along with twenty-four acres of land in Monewden. John responded that his brother had enfeoffed him with the manor of Monewden, including the advowson but excluding twenty-four acres of land, six years before he enfeoffed Arnold with those twenty-four acres. John vouched Henry to warrant, and he was summoned. 18 CRR no. 1267, pp. 267–68 (Pas. 1244).

9. In a *quare impedit* suit from 1250, Bartholomew Peche sued Philip de Cowley to recover the advowson of the church of Cowley (Middx). Bartholomew claimed that John de Sumery and his wife Lettice had presented the last parson, Stephen of Glaneford, and the right of presentation descended from Lettice to her daughter Juliana, who sold the advowson to Bartholomew. (The plea roll says that Lettice sold the advowson to Bartholomew, but this is likely a mistake for Juliana.) Philip responded that the church was not vacant because Stephen was still alive and parson in it; Bartholomew could not contradict this, and Philip went without day. 19 CRR no. 2230, p. 372 (Pas. 1250).

10. See, e.g., 4 CRR 174 (Trin. 1206); 19 CRR no. 877, p. 135 (Mich. 1249).

11. See, e.g., 6 CRR 170 (Mich. 1211); 6 CRR 352 (Trin. 1212); 18 CRR no. 890, pp. 183–84 (1243–44).

12. 2 BNB no. 395, p. 325 (Pas. 1230).

13. See, e.g., 8 CRR 121 (Mich. 1219) (recovery of advowson by plaintiffs' father in assize of darrein presentment); 15 CRR no. 16, p. 5 (recovery by plaintiff in grand assize); 15 CRR no. 453, p. 96 (recovery by plaintiff of moiety by assize of darrein presentment held five years prior); 15 CRR no. 528, pp. 110–11 (recent recovery by plaintiff by judgment against third parties).

14. In 1225, Bartholomew de Crek sued Robert de Crek by *quare impedit* to recover the advowson of the church of Morton on the Hill (Norf), asserting that he was entitled to present by reason of an agreement under which Robert gave up to Bartholomew all lands with appurtenances that he received from his mother's inheritance in return for Bartholomew's paying certain debts Robert owed to the king and to Jews. Robert acknowledged the agreement. 12 CRR no. 672, p. 136.

15. See 1 CRR 101 (Hil. 1199) (seisin of plaintiff's grandfather in time of Henry II); 10 CRR 41 (Pas. 1221) (seisin of plaintiff's father in time of Henry II).

16. The mid-thirteenth-century *Brevia Placitata* refers to tithes of corn, offerings, and oblations worth at least half a mark. G. J. Turner, ed., *Brevia Placitata*, Selden Society 66 (London, 1951), 159 ("Les esplez enpristrent cum en dimes de blez & de offrendes & de oblacions muntant a vn demi marc & a plus").

17. This last clause is frequently abbreviated in the rolls. If the defendant elected trial by battle, the plaintiff's champion and the defendant's champion would wage battle on the field. This was not merely a hypothetical possibility during the period. See 13 CRR no. 208, p. 47 (Pas. 1227) (battle waged to decide action of right). According to *Glanvill*, the plaintiff must state in his count whether he or his ancestor presented the parson, as the plaintiff in a *precipe* writ for land must state whether his father or grandfather was seised of the land. *Glanvill*, II, 3, Woodbine p. 57; IV, 6, Woodbine p. 77. The practice of tracing any intermediate steps of descent from the ancestor to the plaintiff, on the other hand, is not mentioned in *Glanvill* and was most likely introduced later. Compare Paul Brand, *The Origins of the English Legal Profession* (Oxford: Blackwell, 1992), 38–39 (discussing the evolution of pleading under the main *precipe* writ for land).

18. See, e.g., 11 CRR no. 2533, p. 503 (action of right brought by prior of Lenton on the basis of his predecessor's presentation).

19. See, e.g., 1 CRR 279 (Mich. 1200); 3 BNB no. 1336, pp. 321–22 (Mich. 1217); 9 CRR 142 (Trin. 1220); 9 CRR 237 (Mich. 1220); 3 BNB no. 1558, pp. 443–44 (Mich. 1222); 11 CRR no. 121, p. 21 (Hil. 1223); 11 CRR no. 524, p. 100 (Hil. 1223); 13 CRR no. 26, p. 6 (Pas. 1227). The reign of Henry I is sometimes designated as *tempore Henrici regis senioris* or *senis* or (during the reigns of Richard and John) *Henrici avi;* the rolls often further state that the ancestor was seised *anno et die quo obiit.* On the latter phrase, see Milsom, *Legal Framework*, 178–79; Brand, "Milsom and After," at 211. Contrary to Milsom's supposition, it does not seem to have been necessary during the reign of Henry II to state that the plaintiff was seised on the day Henry I was alive and dead. This practice apparently emerged around the year 1200, possibly in response to a legislative change in the limitation date. See Paul Brand, " 'Time Out of Mind': The Knowledge and Use of the Eleventh- and Twelfth-Century Past in Thirteenth-Century Litigation," in *Anglo Norman Studies XVI: Proceedings of the Battle Conference 1993*, ed. Marjorie Chibnall (Woodbridge: Boydell, 1994), 41–42.

20. See, e.g., 1 CRR 460 (Pas. 1201); 6 CRR 21 (Hil. 1210); Yorks. no. 1120, pp. 399–400 (1218–19); 8 CRR 159 (Mich. 1219); 8 CRR 353, 357 (Pas. 1220); 10 CRR 44 (Pas. 1221); 10 CRR 268 (Trin. 1222); 11 CRR no. 157, p. 28 (Hil. 1223); 11 CRR no. 2057, p. 416 (Mich. 1223); 11 CRR no. 2533 (Mich. 1224); 12 CRR no. 257, p. 45 (Hil. 1225); 13 CRR no. 208, pp. 46–47 (Pas. 1227); 13 CRR no. 1799, p. 377 (Pas. 1229); 14 CRR no. 169, p. 33 (Trin. 1230); 14 CRR no. 1356 (Pas. 1231); 14 CRR no. 1577, p. 337 (Trin. 1231); 19 CRR no. 1058, p. 168 (Mich. 1249).

21. See, e.g., 12 CRR no. 357, p. 66 (Hil. 1225); 3 BNB no. 1813, pp. 621–22 (Norf. 1227); 14 CRR no. 2242, pp. 480–81 (Mich. 1232); 2 BNB no. 843, pp. 660–62 (Pas. 1234).

22. In 1232 we find Henry de Drayton bringing a writ of right against Gervase de Islip concerning the chapel of Islip (Northants). Henry alleged that he was in seisin as of fee and right in the time of King John and presented a certain clerk Baldwin, who was admitted at his presentation. Gervase responded that he was parson of the mother church of Islip and the chapel in question had neither tithes nor a burial ground. Henry acknowledged this, and Gervase went without day. 2 BNB no. 693, pp. 532–33 (Pas. 1232).

23. In 1225 the prior of Newark sued the prior of Sherborne by writ of right to recover the advowson of Windlesham (Surrey). The prior of Newark asserted that he was seised of the advowson in the time of Henry III as a chapel pertaining to the mother church of Woking, which the prior of Newark held to his own use, receiving a pension from the chapel of three shillings. The prior of Sherborne's attorney responded that the church of Windlesham had long given three shillings to the church of Woking for burial rights, but the advowson of Windlesham belonged to a certain Hoppeshort, who gave that advowson to the prior and monks of Sherborne; the prior of Sherborne subsequently presented a parson, Richard Cucuel. After offering this explanation, the prior of Sherborne put himself on the grand assize. 12 CRR no. 1508, pp. 310–11 (Mich. 1225). The case was postponed when it became evident that the prior of Sherborne had also been impleaded concerning the same church by a third party, Alexander de Dorset, in an assize of darrein presentment. 14 CRR no. 335, p. 65 = 2 BNB no. 416, p. 339 (Trin. 1230). Alexander subsequently withdrew from his writ, 14 CRR no. 587, p. 116 (Mich. 1230), and the recognitors summoned to the grand assize reported their verdict in Trinity Term 1233. The recognitors related a long story, the upshot of which was that the prior of Newark had the greater right in the advowson; the prior of Newark recovered his seisin. 2 BNB no. 769, p. 586 (Trin. 1233). This isolated case, in which the plaintiff claimed to be parson of the mother church, does not mean that it was generally acceptable for plaintiffs in the early thirteenth century to bring the writ of right of advowson based on seisin in the reign of Henry III.

24. The references to more recent kings later in the thirteenth century most likely reflect that, as time passed, more parsons had intervened since the reign of Henry II.

25. In 1202, Reginald de Argenton brought a writ of right against the prior of Saint Neot's to claim the church of Everton (Beds). Reginald alleged that his grandmother Ticcia was seised as of right, but the entry does not name the king in whose reign Ticcia allegedly presented a parson. 2 CRR 135 (Mich. 1202). Similarly, in 1220, Ralph fitz Robert brought a writ of right against the prior of Dunstable to recover the advowson of Saint Peter's, Bedford (Beds). Ralph alleged that his ancestor Leofic was seised of the advowson and presented a clerk named Thomas who was instituted at his presentation, but the entry does not name the king within whose reign this occurred. The prior responded by offering a charter of gift of Henry I and a confirmation of Henry II and vouched the king to warrant; the case was postponed until Henry III came of age. 8 CRR 254 (Hil. 1220).

26. An entry from Easter 1205 may be an exception. The abbot of York brought a writ of right against the prior of Nocton (Lincs) seeking the advowson of Nocton. According to the entry, the abbot alleged that his predecessor abbot Clement, as lord of the fee, gave the church to a certain Robert *tempore pacis*. The prior put himself on the grand assize. 3 CRR 293 (Pas. 1205). The notation that the presentation occurred *tempore pacis* suggests that the abbot did not specify a king in whose reign the presentation had occurred. Because no further entries survive concerning the case, we cannot determine whether the abbot was allowed to recover without naming a king in his count.

27. See, e.g., 1 CRR 471 (Pas. 1201) and 4 CRR 126 (Pas. 1206), discussed in chap. 3 *supra*.

28. See, e.g., 2 BNB no. 488, pp. 383–84 (Hil. 1231), discussed in chap. 3 *supra*.

29. John Marshall brought a writ of right in 1220 against the prior of Lewes to recover the advowson of Stedham (Sussex). John alleged that Jocelin le Chastelein was seised of it in the time of Henry II and presented a clerk. Jocelin, John alleged, subsequently gave the land in which the church was situated to Richard de Percy, who gave the land to John for homage and service. The prior's attorney defended the right of the priory but stated that there was currently no prior; John replied that there was a prior when he brought his writ and that the attorney should respond despite the lack of a prior. 9 CRR 69 (Trin. 1220). The case was continued, but in the following term, John failed to appear and lost by default. 9 CRR 227 (Mich. 1220). Had the case been fully pleaded, it is likely that John would have lost. As a donee, he should not have been able to bring a writ of right, but even if this was overlooked, the justices would likely have ruled that John's donor Richard never had seisin of the advowson. On the rule of subsequent transfer, see hereafter.

30. See chap. 3 *supra*.

31. A defendant might offer the latter response when he claimed to be parson of the church rather than patron. See, e.g., 11 CRR no. 1708, p. 340 (Trin. 1224); 2 BNB no. 625, pp. 475–76 (Mich. 1231); *Bracton*, f. 247b, III, pp. 231–32.

32. *Supra* chap. 3.

33. Philip I de Colombières died circa 1185. His grandson Philip III died in 1257. See Sanders, *English Baronies*, 67.

34. Consecrated 1142; d. November 18, 1184. *Handbook of British Chronology*, 270.

35. Consecrated April 7, 1174; d. February 16, 1184. *Id.* at 232.

36. Ralph responded that Gervase was parson at the presentation of Philip I and died parson, and that Philip I presented Gervase after all the charters and confirmations offered by the prior. Ralph sought the assize. The prior said that he presented Gervase to the vicarage and sought the assize. The jurors said that after the charters offered by the prior, Philip I presented Gervase, who last died parson, to the church of Shaw. The jurors had heard that the prior and monks of Saint Fromund took forty shillings a year from the church, but they did not know whether the money was received in the name of a parsonage or in the name of a benefice; they were sure, however, that Gervase was parson in the church and at the presentation of Philip. Ralph prevailed and had a writ to the bishop. 2 BNB no. 636, pp. 488–89 (Mich. 1231). By "benefice," the jurors meant a payment that did not entail subjection to a mother church. See *Bracton*, f. 241b, III, p. 216.

37. Beaulieu, a.k.a. Beadlow, was a Benedictine priory in Bedfordshire, a cell of Saint Albans. *Medieval Religious Houses*, 52.

38. Consecrated September 21, 1186; d. November 16, 1200. *Handbook of British Chronology*, 255. The bishop is clearly Hugh of Avalon and not Hugh of Wells, as he is designated as *quondam episcopus*.

39. The case actually involved two defendants, the other being the prior of Ashby. Robert responded to the charter of Bishop Hugh introduced by the prior of Beaulieu by

saying that the bishop had been deceived because Cecily (presumably included as one of the *advocatorum* who allegedly consented to the institution of the monks) had died seven years before Hugh was bishop (which would put her death at or before 1179). Robert also offered his own letters from archdeacon A., which said that A. made an inquisition about whether the church of Milton was vacant and without controversy, and that the chapter reported that John was admitted to the church at the presentation of Cecily and that the prior of Beaulieu never received anything from the church. The prior of Ashby then appeared and claimed a fourth part of the church by gift of William Ursel, claiming that William was adjudged the advowson in the king's court and offering William's charter as well as a charter of Archdeacon Nicholas saying that John was instituted in the church at the presentation of William and Simon Basset. Robert replied that he claimed nothing on the part of William, and William had no right in the advowson to give, and the assize proceeded. 7 CRR 135–36 (Trin. 1214). Later in the term, the jury gave a verdict that Cecily presented the last parson, John, after she made the charter to the prior of Beaulieu. Robert was given a writ to the bishop to admit a clerk at his presentation; nothing more was said about the claim of the prior of Ashby. 7 CRR 215 (Trin. 1214).

40. Winterbourne was a chapel of Chieveley until 1866, when it became a separate civil parish. *Guide to the Local Administrative Units of England I: Southern England,* 27.

41. 12 CRR no. 1034, pp. 210–11 (Mich. 1225). Robert did subsequently bring a writ of right, claiming that Nicholas fitz Thorold, his ancestor, was seised in the time of Henry II and presented a clerk named John of Saint Lawrence, who was admitted at his presentation. The abbot responded that the advowson remained to his church of Abingdon by a fine in the court of King Henry II between Nicholas and the abbot, offering a chirograph. Robert acknowledged this and was amerced. 12 CRR no. 2023, p. 411 (Hil. 1226).

42. On the abbey, see *Medieval Religious Houses,* 265.

43. Confirmed June 27, 1217; translated Durham, May 14, 1228. *Handbook of British Chronology,* 270.

44. Consecrated June 5, 1194; d. January 7, 1217. *Id.*

45. Consecrated 1142, resigned 1184. *Id.*

46. The abbess's attorney said that a certain Ernulf of Hastings, ancestor of John, gave that church to the convent in alms with his daughter, and his son confirmed the gift. After the justices resolved some uncertainty about whether the attorney was properly attorned, he offered a charter from Ernulf of Hastings the younger confirming the gift of Ernulf his father, as well as confirmations from three kings. The justices determined that the church was not vacant and told John he could sue by writ of right. A marginal notation in *Bracton's Note Book* says that "in the king's court it can be discovered by charters and confirmations and by acts of the bishops whether or not a church is vacant" (Nota quod in curia domini Regis perpendi poterit per cartas et confirmationes et per facta episcoporum utrum ecclesia uacat uel non). 2 BNB no. 173, pp. 140–42. The *Bracton* treatise itself, however, notes that the bishop might not be consulted if he had an interest in the outcome, as when he had filled the vacancy at the presentation of a false patron. See *Bracton,* f. 241b, III, p. 216.

47. See *supra* chap. 3.

48. The prior claimed that Thomas gave the advowson of Aston to the priory by his charter, which he offered. John acknowledged that Thomas was his uncle, and he was his heir, but said that Thomas made the charter while he was underage and in the wardship of Hugh of Chalcombe, and at a time when he had no seisin of the land or advowson, although he later came into the land and was in seisin for five years. The prior said it was made when he was in seisin, and drew the court's attention to the fact that Thomas did not protest the charter. John responded that it was not possible for Thomas to reclaim the advowson while the clerk lived. Both parties put themselves on the charter witnesses. 10 CRR 316 = 2 BNB no. 205, p. 167 (Trin. 1222). Three charter witnesses eventually showed up in Easter 1224 and said that Thomas was of age and in seisin when he made the charter. The prior recovered his seisin. 3 BNB no. 975, pp. 25–26 (Pas. 1224).

49. Elected between July 18 and August 9, 1215; consecrated May 29, 1222; d. September 16, 1226. *Handbook of British Chronology*, 261. During the minority of Henry III, Pandulph "served as the chief mediator between the government of the boy king . . . and the papacy." Nicholas Vincent, "Pandulf (*d.* 1226)," in *Oxford Dictionary of National Biography* (Oxford: Oxford University Press, 2004), http://www.oxforddnb.com/view/article/21230.

50. 8 CRR 43 (Mich. 1219).

51. In addition to arguing that the church was vacant when she sued, Basilia alleged that she had presented three parsons after her husband's charter was made, if indeed it was genuine. The prior then claimed that all those clerks were vicars and that the prior had received two shillings' pension for forty years. Basilia responded that a certain Richard, who was parson, had paid those shillings to Richard *sine advocato* for the sake of peace. The justices decided that the assize would proceed, and the jurors rendered a verdict for Basilia. 9 CRR 361 (Mich. 1220) = 2 BNB no. 310, p. 258.

52. "Quaeri autem potest ab initio utrum aliquid dici possit quare assisa ista remaneret debeat. Et potest quidem ad hoc dici, scilicet tenentem ipsum concedere antecessorem petentis ultimam inde fecisse praesentationem sicut verum dominum et primogenitum heredem, sed postea feodum illud ex quo pendet advocatio ei vel antecessoribus suis contulisse aliquo vero titulo; et ita eo ipso remanet assisa, et placitum super exceptione ipsa inter ipsos litigantes deinde esse poterit." *Glanvill*, XIII, 20, Woodbine p. 168 (trans. Beames, p. 326). The reference to the ancestor as *verum dominum et primogenitum heredem* is puzzling, since it is not clear why the status of the ancestor would be relevant when the ancestor made the last presentation. It is possible that the tenant actually conceded that the plaintiff's ancestor presented as the true lord and that the plaintiff was the firstborn heir of the ancestor, but this statement became garbled in subsequent manuscripts of the treatise.

53. 4 CRR 254 (Mich. 1206).

54. Either Robert de Melun (consecrated December 22, 1163; d. February 27, 1167) or Robert Foliot (elected late April 1173; consecrated October 6, 1174; d. May 9, 1186). *Handbook of British Chronology*, 250.

55. This statement suggests that Walter's father had not presented a candidate. The prior's attorney could have demanded that Walter offer a charter evidencing the gift to his father, but the attorney did not do so, perhaps because he believed his argument that Walter was the heir of William to be stronger than the justices apparently concluded. It is possible that although Walter was William's heir, he had received no assets from him and thus was not held responsible for William's charter.

56. 11 CRR no. 1144, pp. 232–33 (Mich. 1223). Another case in which the plaintiff responded to a charter by alleging that he was not the donor appears in the plea rolls from Trinity Term 1205; however, it is less straightforward, in that a third party appeared and stated that the plaintiff was a bastard and the son of a priest, after which the justices ruled in favor of the defendant donee. 4 CRR 39–40 (Trin. 1205).

57. See, e.g., 2 RCR 200 (Pas. 1200) (offers charter of gift and confirmations in response to claim that plaintiff obtained advowson in court by chirograph); 2 RCR 259 (Pas. 1200) (charter of gift and confirmations offered in response to claim of last presentation); 1 CRR 385 (Hil. 1201); 4 CRR 75 (Hil. 1206) (both parties claim by gift, offering charters); 6 CRR 93 (Mich. 1210) (alleges gift from plaintiff's father); 6 CRR 170–71 (Mich. 1211) (offers charter of gift from father of plaintiff's ward, by whom plaintiff claimed advowson); 7 CRR 69 (Hil. 1214) (offers charter of gift from plaintiff's father).

58. In 1225, for example, the abbot of Missenden sought the advowson of Oulton (Norfolk) by writ of *quare impedit* from Hubert de Burgh, the royal justiciar. The abbot's attorney offered a charter of Walter fitz William of Penna, whom he called the patron of the church, giving the advowson to the abbey, along with a confirmatory charter of the bishop of Norwich. Hubert's attorney responded that the manor of Cawston, of which Oulton was a part, was the escheat of Henry II, who gave the manor of Cawston with all its members and appurtenances to William Longspee (the king's natural son) to be held at the king's will. The justiciar's attorney explained that William Longspee subsequently gave Oulton to William brother of Walter of Penna, but after the death of William Longspee, the manor of Cawston reverted to the king, and it was determined by the king's order that the manor of Oulton was a member of Cawston and that William of Penna only had a bailment. The justiciar's attorney continued that Walter fitz William of Penna, who had by that point presumably acquired the manor, was disseised of it, and Hubert had it by gift of King John. Since Walter did not have a fee, nor did any heir of his have or claim anything, the justiciar's attorney argued that the abbot's charter did not help him. The abbot's attorney responded that Walter held the land as his right and inheritance, which descended to him from his ancestors from the conquest of England, because William brother of Walter was seised of that land as of right, and William father of William in the same way. The abbot's attorney further stated that Hubert did not have that land by the king but rather held it of John of Ingworth, to whom Walter sold it. After further pleading, the court held that because no one had anything in the manor on the part of Walter, nor did Walter, who was supposed to have made the gift, present a clerk to the church, the abbot took nothing by the charter and was amerced. 3 BNB no. 1064,

pp. 92–93 (Hil. 1225). At no point did the justiciar's attorney argue that the justiciar was not the heir of Walter fitz William of Penna; the question was simply irrelevant.

59. "Inde ponet se super assisam, si curia consideraverit, vel super magnam assisam de jure."

60. The entry then notes that Gilbert the Chaplain, who was summoned to show by what patron he held himself in the church, came and said that he was there by gift of Jonah the Priest. A marginal notation notes that the justices were to speak with the bishop. 7 CRR 121–22 (Trin. 1214).

61. See *supra* chap. 3.

62. See, e.g., 1 CRR 279 (Mich. 1200) (alleges gift from plaintiff's ancestor around the time of the Conquest, followed by confirmation from that ancestor's son); 2 CRR 228 (Pas. 1203) (gift from ancestor of plaintiff's late husband, by whom she claimed the advowson); 8 CRR 357–58 (Pas. 1220) (gift from plaintiff's grandfather); 9 CRR 12 (Trin. 1220) (alleges gift from Henry II when plaintiff claims by gift from King John); 9 CRR 21 (Trin. 1220) (alleges gift from plaintiff's grandfather, by whom plaintiff claimed the advowson); 14 CRR no. 169, p. 33 (Trin. 1230) (gift from plaintiff's grandmother; offers her charter along with confirmations of plaintiff's father and uncle and various bishops); 16 CRR no. 2263, p. 453 (Pas. 1242) (gift from ancestor of plaintiff followed by quitclaim from plaintiff's grandfather); 19 CRR no. 1058, pp. 168–69 (Mich. 1249) (gift from grandfather of the person by whom plaintiff claims the advowson).

63. 1 RCR 391 (Trin. 1199) ("in quam ecclesiam ipsa nullam habet ingressum nisi per ablatorem suum"). The reference to "entry," of course, is reminiscent of the language used in writs of entry, which were being developed around the same time. See Joseph Biancalana, "The Origin and Early History of the Writs of Entry," *Law and Hist. Rev.* 25 (2007): 519–28.

64. Two churches remain in the vicinity today: Great Wymondley and Little Wymondley. One may have been a chapel of Hitchin, and the other a mother church. See *Guide to the Local Administrative Units of England: Southern England,* 245.

65. Presumably not William; perhaps Henry I.

66. 1 CRR 219, 248 (Trin. 1200); 1 CRR 450 (Pas. 1201); 2 CRR 96 (Mich. 1202); 2 CRR 159 (Hil. 1203); 4 CRR 91 (Pas. 1206); 4 CRR 273 (Mich. 1206); 5 CRR 129 (Hil. 1208); 5 CRR 166 (Pas. 1208).

67. 5 CRR 224, 226 (Trin. 1208).

68. See, e.g., 1 CRR 429 (Pas. 1201) (confirmatory charters of Henry I and Henry II); Lincs. no. 239, p. 39 (1202) (confirmatory charters of King John, the bishop of Lincoln, the archbishop of Canterbury, and two popes); 3 CRR 255 (Hil. 1205) (confirmations of a king and three archbishops); 5 CRR 145 (Hil. 1208) (confirmation of the archbishop of Canterbury); 5 CRR 146 (Hil. 1208) (confirmations of Henry II, Richard, and John); 7 CRR 102–3 (Hil. 1214) (confirmation of the archbishop of Canterbury); 3 BNB no. 1339, pp. 323–24 (Mich. 1217) (confirmations of Henry I and a pope); 12 CRR no. 1423, pp. 289–91 (Mich. 1225) (confirmations of two archbishops of York and Henry II).

69. For a particularly stark example, see 7 CRR 102–3 (Hil. 1214), where the plaintiff, the prioress of a nunnery, offered eight different charters, and the defendant responded with a curt statement that none of the charters were valid because a subsequent presentation had occurred. On the rule of subsequent presentation, see *infra*.

70. Many of these objections also applied to other charters, such as charters of institution offered to support a claim of plenarty.

71. See, e.g., 5 CRR 13 (Hil. 1207); 8 CRR 189 (Hil. 1220); 8 CRR 341–42 (Pas. 1220); 8 CRR 288 (Pas. 1220); 10 CRR 320 (Trin. 1222); 13 CRR no. 192, p. 43 (Pas. 1227).

72. See, e.g., 4 CRR 48 (Trin. 1205); 5 CRR 144 (Hil. 1208); 7 CRR 39 (Mich. 1213); 7 CRR 69–70 (Hil. 1214); 10 CRR 250–51 (Mich. 1221); 14 CRR no. 169, p. 33 (Trin. 1230); 17 CRR no. 1302, p. 248 (Hil. 1243). Parties also sometimes claimed that though the seal was genuine, the alleged donor was not in possession of his seal when the charter was made. See, e.g., 7 CRR 138 (Trin. 1214) (mother had access to father's seal and used it to seal charter of gift to beloved younger son).

73. Charter was made after donor's death: 5 CRR 145 (Hil. 1208); 10 CRR 70–71 (Pas. 1221). Alleged donor had become a monk or canon before the charter was made: 4 CRR 126 (Pas. 1206); 6 CRR 347–48 (Trin. 1212); 11 CRR no. 417, p. 78 (Hil. 1223); 17 CRR no. 1313, pp. 250–51 (Hil. 1243). These objections were essentially equivalent, because becoming a monk or regular canon was a form of civil death. Pollock and Maitland, I, 433.

74. 7 CRR 260 (Mich. 1214); 3 BNB no. 1570, pp. 452–53 (Hil. 1223); 14 CRR no. 169, p. 33 (Trin. 1230).

75. 6 CRR 93 (Mich. 1210); 7 CRR 322–25 (Hil. 1215); 11 CRR no. 632, p. 124 (Mich. 1223).

76. 6 CRR 170–71 (Mich. 1211); Yorks. no. 1151, pp. 425–26 (1218–19); 10 CRR 293–94 (Trin. 1222).

77. 7 CRR 285 (Mich. 1214). For this exception to be valid, the party had to show that the person who made the charter repudiated it after the duress ended. *Bracton*, f. 16b, II, p. 64; 15 CRR no. 1505, p. 360 (Trin. 1234–35).

78. For a case where several different objections were made to a series of charters, see 7 CRR 322–25 (Hil. 1215).

79. 1 CRR 239 (Trin. 1200).

80. 6 CRR 190–91 (Hil. 1212).

81. The earliest invocation of the rule may date to Hilary Term 1208, when the prior of Lenton sued the prior of the hospital of Saint John of Jerusalem to claim the advowson of Ossington (Notts). The prior of Lenton claimed to have been given the advowson by Hugh de Burun and offered Hugh's charter as well as confirmations from Hugh's son Roger de Burun and the archbishop of York. The prior of the hospital asserted that he had been given the church by Roger de Burun, and Roger had presented a parson after the prior of Lenton's charters but before his own. Both parties eventually put themselves on the jury as to whose *antecessor* (meaning, presumably, Hugh de Burun or Roger de Burun) presented the last parson. 5 CRR 141–42 (Hil. 1208). The jury came the following

term and said that Roger de Burun presented the last parson. 5 CRR 242–43 (Trin. 1208). While the entry from Trinity Term is denominated as an assize of darrein presentment, the Hilary entry shows that the case was begun by writ of *quare impedit.*

82. 7 CRR 69–70 (Hil. 1214).

83. The rule was also invoked in two other *quare impedit* suits from the end of John's reign; however, these suits involved parallel pleas of *quare impedit* and darrein presentment. See 7 CRR 54, 84–85 (Hil. 1214) (dispute between Richard Earl of Clare and the abbot of Notley); 7 CRR 57, 102–4 (Hil. 1214) (dispute between John of Bracebridge and the prioress of Markyate).

84. *Guide to the Local Administrative Units of England I: Southern England,* 437.

85. *Id.*

86. Maitland speculates that words may have been lost. 2 BNB p. 661, n. 7.

87. 2 BNB no. 853, pp. 660–62 (Pas. 1234).

88. 2 BNB p. 662, n. 2, citing the *Annals of Bermondsey.*

89. On the requirement of livery of seisin for gifts of land, see Pollock and Maitland, II, 83.

90. The rule of subsequent presentation is similar in this respect to the treatment of *pro omni servicio* charters, in which a lord agreed to accept certain services from a tenant "for all service" due from a particular tract of land. If the lord could show that greater services had nonetheless been received after the charter, the royal courts might hold the tenant to those greater services, even after the Statute of Marlborough of 1267 attempted to guarantee that the services would not be increased beyond those specified in the charter. See Paul Brand, *Kings, Barons and Justices: The Making and Enforcement of Legislation in Thirteenth-Century England* (Cambridge: Cambridge University Press, 2003), 189–90, 257–59.

91. For cases where a jury found in favor of the party claiming subsequent presentation, see 2 CRR 4 (Mich. 1201); 3 CRR 152 (Trin. 1204) and 170 (Mich. 1204); 6 CRR 190–91 (Hil. 1212); 7 CRR 200–201 (Trin. 1214); 2 BNB no. 636, pp. 488–89 (Mich. 1231). For cases where a jury found against the party claiming subsequent presentation, see, e.g., 7 CRR 178 (Trin. 1214) (jury finds that the presentation was subsequent to some of the charters but before others; party claiming by charter prevails); 8 CRR 357–58 (Pas. 1220) and 10 CRR 35 (Pas. 1221) (jury rejects subsequent presentation claim and other arguments made against the charter); 12 CRR no. 1412, p. 287 (Mich. 1225) and no. 2163, p. 438 (Pas. 1226) (jury rejects claim that the king presented after the charters were made); 13 CRR no. 76, p. 15 (Pas. 1227) (jury determines that the last parson was presented before the charter); TNA KB 26/160, m. 25, AALT no. 0079 (Mich. 1258), http://aalt.law.uh .edu/H3/KB26no160/aKB26no160fronts/IMG_0079.htm (accessed December 21, 2020) (court rejects vague claim of subsequent presentation because the plaintiff "nihil inde ostendit nisi simplex dictum suum").

92. From one perspective, however, the term "forgery" may be inappropriate when applied to "renewals of evidence which were intended to ensure that a monastic house was

adequately provided with charters to defend its patrons and saints against rivals." The distinction between "genuine" and "forged" might depend on "what interval of time between giving and writing . . . was generally considered allowable." M. T. Clanchy, *From Memory to Written Record: England, 1066–1307*, 2nd ed. (Oxford: Blackwell, 1993), 322–23.

93. *Bracton*, f. 54, II, pp. 162–63, allowing a limited exception if the gift was expressly made "to the donee and his heirs or to whom he wishes to give or assign" (donatorio et heredibus suis, vel cui dare vel assignare voluerit); *id.* ff. 242b–43, III, pp. 218–19; f. 246, III, pp. 227–28. *Bracton's* insistence on this rule was noted by Maitland, who called it "curious." Pollock and Maitland, II, 139.

94. 11 CRR no. 2780, p. 559 (Mich. 1224).

95. See 2 BNB no. 644, p. 495 (Mich. 1231).

96. Roger de Mohaut, the plaintiff in this case, seems to have been the son and heir of Robert de Mohaut. Cokayne, *Complete Peerage*, vol. 9, pp. 10–12. Robert, in turn, was the brother and heir of Ralph de Mohaut, who presented the last parson to the church of Elford, according to both parties. It seems, however, that Robert had another brother, Roger, whose granddaughter Agnes was Philip's ward. See *id.* at p. 11 n. (i), citing Harl. MS 2074 f. 70(d). Thus the plaintiff claimed the advowson through his uncle Ralph, while Philip claimed it by virtue of an agreement he made with the plaintiff's other uncle, the elder Roger, concerning the guardianship of Roger's granddaughter.

97. 13 CRR no. 245, p. 55 = 2 BNB no. 260, p. 213 (Trin. 1227). "Predictus Rogerus nichil ostendit quod advocacio excipiatur nec sectam producit nec cartam profert nec aliquid aliud nisi simplicem vocem suam, et preterea cognoscit quod Rogerus obiit seisitus de manerio illo cum pertiniciis et Leuca postea eodem modo, consideratum est quod Philippus recuperavit seisinam suam racione custodie predicte Agnetis, salvo iure ipsius Rogeri, si postea inde loqui voluerit."

98. *Id.*

99. We see an example of this in a case from Michaelmas Term 1250, although the lay parties in the surviving plea roll entry were the defendants, and the ancestor in the (presumably) forged charters was not particularly remote. The prioress of Harrold brought an assize of darrein presentment against Ralph Morin and Henry of Wengham concerning the church of Eythorne in Kent, claiming that the elder Ralph Morin, father of Ralph the defendant, had given her the advowson by his charter, which she offered. Ralph and Henry first defended on the grounds that Henry had previously brought an assize of darrein presentment against the prioress in the king's court, and the assize was taken by default after the prioress failed to appear. However, they then retracted this exception. Henry stated that he claimed nothing in the advowson except by enfeoffment from Ralph, who in turn asserted that (1) after the charter was made, he himself had successfully presented a certain William Rus to the church; (2) he had also successfully presented the last parson, a clerk also named Ralph, after the death of William; and (3) his father Ralph predeceased William. The prioress then responded that the elder Ralph had presented William, but claimed that he did so by consent of the former prioress, Egidia, and that

the elder Ralph had subsequently made a second charter of gift to the prioress. She alleged that after William took the habit of religion in Robertsbridge, the bishop collated the most recent parson, Ralph de Coquina, to the church during a dispute between the prioress and the younger Ralph, offering letters of the bishop to that effect. The prioress then put herself on the charter witnesses, as did Ralph. The witnesses reported that the elder Ralph did not present William Rus, having died before the death of William's predecessor Michael, nor did he make either of the charters to the nuns. Judgment was given in favor of Henry of Wengham, who had been enfeoffed by the younger Ralph, and the prioress was amerced. 20 CRR no. 1215, pp. 213–15 (Mich. 1250).

100. 1 PKJ no. 3475, p. 351 (Apr. 1199) ("ipsos monachos secundum consuetudinem regni inde iuste deducatis").

Chapter Five. Canon Law and Jurisdictional Competition

1. William M. Landes and Richard Posner, "Adjudication as a Private Good," *Journal of Legal Studies* 8 (1979): 235–84, at 254–55.

2. Daniel Klerman, "Jurisdictional Competition and the Evolution of the Common Law," *University of Chicago Law Review* 74 (2007): 1179–1226, at 1204–11.

3. Richard H. Helmholz, "Magna Carta and the *Ius Commune*," *University of Chicago Law Review* 66 (1999): 297–371, at 329–33, 357–58.

4. Joshua C. Tate, "Episcopal Power and Royal Jurisdiction," in *Studies in Canon Law and Common Law in Honor of R. H. Helmholz*, ed. Troy L. Harris (Berkeley, Calif.: Robbins Collection, 2015), 15–26, at 17.

5. Gratian's *Decretum* was written in two stages, a first and second recension; both recensions were apparently completed in Bologna between 1138 and 1150. Anders Winroth, *The Making of Gratian's "Decretum"* (Cambridge: Cambridge University Press, 2000), 144; Paolo Nardi, "Fonti canoniche in una sentenza senese del 1150," in *Life, Law and Letters: Historical Studies in Honour of Antonio García y García*, Studia Gratiana 29, ed. Peter Linehan (Rome, 1998), 661–70.

6. Landau, *Jus Patronatus*.

7. 3 Conc. Lat., c. 14 (1179), COD 219 = X 3.30.19; 4 Conc. Lat., c. 44 (1215), COD 254 = X 3.13.12.

8. 2 Conc. Lat., c. 1–2 (1139), COD 197. The term "simony" comes from Simon the sorcerer, who tried to buy the power of the Holy Spirit from the apostles. Acts 8:9–21.

9. There was a limited right to receive "tribute" when it was established by long custom, although some canonists held that the bishop's approval was required. Landau, *Jus Patronatus*, 130–36.

10. 7 CRR 138 (Trin. 1214) ("advocatio illius ecclesie est capud honoris sue"); 7 CRR 139 (Trin. 1214) ("advocatio[] . . . est capud hereditatis sue"); 7 CRR 323 (Hil. 1215) (plaintiff is concerned that by losing the advowson he will be "exheredatus de capite sue hereditatis").

11. See, e.g., 9 CRR 224 (Mich. 1220) (plaintiff claims to be damaged to the extent of twenty marks by the loss of his advowson).

12. See, e.g., 11 CRR no. 2666, p. 534 (Mich. 1224); 13 CRR no. 669, p. 150 (Pas. 1228); 14 CRR no. 676, p. 134 (Mich. 1230); 14 CRR no. 1336, p. 283 (Pas. 1231).

13. 3 CRR 341 (Pas. 1205).

14. N. Denholm-Young, *Seigniorial Administration in England* (Oxford: Oxford University Press, 1937), 2–3.

15. See Newman, "Greater and Lesser Landowners," at 281.

16. In the decretal *Quia clerici,* Alexander decreed that a clerk who obtained an advowson for the purpose of presenting a son or nephew to the benefice would forfeit the advowson in question. WH 46, 1 Comp. 3.33.8 = X 3.38.6 (1177). However, the pope did not specify whether it was the acquisition of the advowson for the purpose of nepotism, or merely the nepotism itself, that was impermissible. Another decretal, *Consulit nos,* provided that laymen could not "concede" churches to their sons "or to any others," but this could simply be a reference to lay institution without episcopal participation. WH 188, 1 Comp. 3.33.18 = X 3.38.15 (1159–81) ("non decet aliquatenus sustineri, ut . . . clerici ecclesias a parentibus suis fundatas propria auctoritate detineant, aut laici filiis vel aliquibus aliis ecclesias concedant easdem"). The *Glossa ordinaria* to the *Liber Extra* interpreted this decretal merely as requiring episcopal approval. Bernard of Parma, *Glossa ordinaria* to X 3.38.8, v. *concedant* ("sed episcopo presentare potest patronus filium"). Bernard's view was generally held among the decretalists. Landau, *Jus Patronatus,* 179. (Here and elsewhere, in referring to the *Glossa ordinaria* to the *Liber Extra,* I have consulted a 1479 Venetian printed edition available online from the website of the Bibliothèque nationale de France; see http://gallica2.bnf.fr/ark:/12148/bpt6k593240.)

17. See, e.g., 3 CRR 231 (Mich. 1204); 4 CRR 73 (Hil. 1206); 9 CRR 196 (Trin. 1220).

18. See, e.g., 1 RCR 142 (Pas. 1198); 4 CRR 49 (Trin. 1205); 4 CRR 233 (Mich. 1206); 7 CRR 190 (Trin. 1214); 8 CRR 41 (Mich. 1219); 13 CRR no. 82, p. 18 (Pas. 1227).

19. Pollock and Maitland, II, 268 (citing *Glanvill,* VII, 3, Woodbine pp. 101–4). On the distinction between tenure by knight's service and socage tenure, see Pollock and Maitland, I, 252–96. Whether the younger sons would inherit depended on the local custom with respect to land held in socage, but it would be necessary to prove this custom to persuade the court to depart from the usual rule of primogeniture. It was, of course, possible for the father to make an *inter vivos* gift to his younger sons (or daughters). For examples, see J. M. Kaye, *Medieval English Conveyances* (Cambridge: Cambridge University Press, 2009), 150–54.

20. 3 BNB no. 1352, pp. 328–29 (Mich. 1217). Nor is it clear how William was able to get out of his orders and become a knight, if his statement to that effect was indeed true; perhaps he was only in minor orders at the time. Episcopal registers from the thirteenth century show that many parish clergy remained in minor orders throughout their lives. See Moorman, *Church Life in England,* 34–37. For examples of royal lawyers making the switch from clergy to knighthood, see Jean Dunbabin, "From Clerk to Knight: Changing

Orders," in *The Ideals and Practice of Medieval Knighthood II: Papers from the Third Strawberry Hill Conference 1986,* ed. Christopher Harper-Bill and Ruth Harvey (Woodbridge: Boydell Press, 1988), 26, 37–39.

21. The *Summa Parisiensis* offered a different view. *Summa Parisiensis* gloss to C. 16, q.7, c.26, v. *Pie mentis,* in *The Summa Parisiensis on the Decretum Gratiani,* ed. Terence P. McLaughlin (Toronto: Pontifical Institute of Mediaeval Studies, 1952), 187 ("Non autem legitur quod ius istud repraesentandi transeat ad heredes, quamvis teneatur eos alere, ut tamen primo loco ministris suis necessaria deducat"). On the date of the *Summa,* see Kenneth Pennington, *Legal History Sources,* http://legalhistorysources.com/1140a-z.htm (accessed December 31, 2020).

22. "Patronatus autem transferri potest ad heredes sanguinis, non autem ad extraneos heredes. . . . Unde generaliter colligitur quod quicunque habet patronatum in aliqua ecclesia, non potest exceptis heredibus sanguinis transferre illum patronatum—neque per donationem neque per venditionem vel ex testamento vel ullo modo—ad alios, nec etiam ad aliam ecclesiam, nisi vel equalis vel maioris religionis; cui quidem donare poterit, vendere autem non poterit." Rufinus of Bologna, gloss to C.16 q.7 c.26, in *Summa decretorum,* ed. Heinrich Singer (1902; repr., Paderborn: Aalen, 1963), 369–70; Pennington, *Legal History Sources,* http://legalhistorysources.com/1140a-z.htm (accessed December 31, 2020).

23. On the views of other canonists who agreed with Rufinus, see Landau, *Jus Patronatus,* 51–53. Peter the Chanter, for example, wrote in his *Summa de sacramentis* that "the right of patronage passes by succession to the most closely related heirs" (Transit autem ius patronatus succession ad heredes proximos). Peter the Chanter, *Summa de Sacramentis et Animae Consiliis,* ed. Jean-Albert Dugauquier (Louvain: Éditions Nauwelaerts, 1954–67), vol. 3:2a, pp. 706–7.

24. "Indistincte loquitur canon nec distinguit inter heredes sanguinis et alios. . . . Nec ergo nos debemus distinguere. Potest ergo ius patronatus transire ad omnes heredes, nec assignari potest ratio quare potius transeat ad heredes sanguinis, quam ad alios." Huguccio, *Summa decretorum* (MS Admont 7), gloss to C.16 q.7 c.35, v. *Considerandum;* Pennington, *Legal History Sources,* http://legalhistorysources.com/1140a-z.htm (accessed December 31, 2020). On the later acceptance of Huguccio's theory, see Landau, *Jus Patronatus,* 56–57.

25. "Potest etiam donari et legari tam consanguineo quam extraneo." Huguccio, *Summa decretorum,* gloss to C.16 q.7 c.35, v. *Considerandum.*

26. See, e.g., 6 CRR 225 (Hil. 1212).

27. See, e.g., 15 CRR no. 947, pp. 202–3 (Trin. 1234); 17 CRR no. 2183, p. 439 (Pas. 1243).

28. *Glanvill,* VII, 1, Woodbine p. 98 ("solus deus heredem facere potest, non homo") (trans. Beames, p. 143).

29. "Si forte in plures partes fundatorum se vota diffuderint, ille praeficiatur ecclesie, qui maioribus iuvatur meritis et plurium eligitur et probatur assensu." 3 Conc. Lat. c. 17 (1179), COD 220 = X 3.38.3.

30. "Cum enim patroni dissentiunt in electione presbiteri, idem debet esse fieri enim, quod fit, cum clerici discordant in electione episcopi, scilicet ut obtineat sententia plurimorum. Si vero partes sint pares, ille de electis praeficiatur, qui maioribus meritis et studiis iuvatur. Si vero electi pares sint per omnia, credo quod forte lis sit dirimenda vel fiat gratificatio superioris." Huguccio, *Summa decretorum,* gloss to C.16 q.7 c.36, v. *reliquias sacras.* According to Landau, not only Huguccio but also Simon of Bisignano (taught at Bologna during 1170s), Bernhard of Pavia (taught at Bologna during 1170s; d. 1213), Alanus Anglicus (taught and wrote ca. 1190–1215), Godfrey de Trano (d. 1245), and Hostiensis (lived ca. 1200–1271) held this view. Landau, *Jus Patronatus,* 182–85. The relevant passage in Simon of Bisignano's *Summa,* however, does not appear in all manuscripts and may not have been part of the original text. See Simon of Bisignano, *Summa in Decretum,* ed. Pier Aimone (Fribourg, 2006), 326, http://www.unifr.ch/cdc/summa_simonis_2baende/summa_simonis_BAND_I.14.10.2007.pdf.

31. See Landau, *Jus Patronatus,* 184–85, discussing the *Summa decretalium Bruxellensis* (prob. early thirteenth century); the *apparatus glossarum Animal est substantia* (composed ca. 1206–10); and the *Glossa ordinaria* on the *Decretum* (composed 1216 by Johannes Teutonicus).

32. In a case from the 1230s, a defendant who had one-third of the advowson said that he refused to consent to the parson presented by the other patrons because he was not suitable. The court gave the plaintiffs a writ to the bishop to admit a clerk presented by the plaintiffs whether or not the defendant consented. 15 CRR no. 1198, pp. 295–96 (1234–35).

33. See, e.g., 14 CRR no. 381, p. 73 (Trin. 1230); 17 CRR no. 2183, p. 439 (Pas. 1243); 19 CRR no. 2338, pp. 395–96 (Pas. 1250).

34. 3 Conc. Lat. c. 17 (1179), COD 220 = X 3.38.3.

35. Landau, *Jus Patronatus,* 171–72. Alberigo's edition of the Third Lateran Council gives *tres menses* in the text, but *quattuor* and *duos* are listed as alternative possibilities. COD 220.

36. WH 380, 1 Comp 1.8.5 = X 3.38.22 (1179–81). Another portion of the decretal, excerpted in 1 Comp. 1.8.5, mentions the council, which led Holtzmann to assign a date of 1179–81.

37. Bernard of Pavia, *Summa Decretalium,* ed. E. Theodor Laspeyres (Graz, 1956), bk. III, tit. 33, § 9, pp. 122–23; Pennington, *Legal History Sources,* http://legalhistorysources.com/1140a-z.htm (accessed December 31, 2020).

38. See Landau, *Jus Patronatus,* 173 (discussing the French *apparatus glossarum Materia auctoris,* the *apparatus* of Vincentius on the *Compilatio III,* and the *Glossa ordinaria* on the *Decretum* of Johannes Teutonicus).

39. See *id.* The theory was developed in the *Glossa ordinaria* to X 1.31.4, v. *idoneae.* According to the *Glossa ordinaria,* because lay patrons could change their mind between the presentation and institution of a candidate, while clerical patrons could not, a shorter time limit ought to apply in general to presentations by laymen. Boniface VIII subsequently confirmed this interpretation in a decretal, without mentioning Bernard's rationale. See VI 3.19.un.; Landau, *Jus Patronatus,* 173–74.

40. In some circumstances, a different bishop might be able to exercise the right. In a 1253 case brought by Peter de Sabaudia against Saer de Freville concerning the advowson of Leake, it was determined that the archbishop of Canterbury instituted a parson "auctoritate concilii" while the see of Lincoln was vacant. TNA KB 26/149, m. 24_1 (Trin. 1253), http://aalt.law.uh.edu/H3/KB26_149/0024_1.htm (accessed December 21, 2020).

41. See, e.g., 12 CRR no. 379, p. 72 (Hil. 1225) ("episcopus . . . quia ecclesia vacavit ultra sex menses, ipse auctoritate concilii illam contulit . . . clerico suo"); 14 CRR no. 81, p. 13 (Trin. 1230) ("dominus Cantuariensis per lapsum sex mensium contulit ei ecclesiam illam auctoritate concilii"); 14 CRR no. 1227, p. 260 ("contulit ecclesisam illam . . . ratione concilii post lapsum vi. mensium").

42. Such pressure might have taken the form of the writ of *quare incumbravit,* a version of which was apparently in use as early as 1200. See 1 CRR 242 (Trin. 1200). It is puzzling, given the existence of this writ, that the bishops were able to follow the council at all. The early plea rolls, however, do not contain many such cases, suggesting that either the bishops ignored the writ, or Chancery was reluctant to grant it in light of the council. Further work needs to investigate the early history of *quare incumbravit.*

43. "Cum vero praebendas ecclesiasticas seu quaelibet officia in aliqua ecclesia vacare contigerit vel etiam si modo vacant, non diu maneant in suspenso, sed infra sex menses personis, quae digne administrare valeant, conferantur." 3 Conc. Lat. c. 8 (1179), COD 215 = X 3.8.2.

44. WH 380, 1 Comp 1.8.5 = X 3.38.22 (1179–81).

45. In the first decretal, *Cum seculum,* the pope prohibited the Templars and Hospitallers from making inappropriate use of advowsons they had acquired "as purchasers or other acquirers of fiefs" (ratione feudorum emptorum aliterve acquisitorum), thus implying that it was possible to purchase an advowson. WH 302, 1 Comp. 3.33.16 = X 3.38.13 (1175). The second decretal, *Ex litteris,* involved a lease of a particular vill by a convent to a layman; the pope determined that the advowson appurtenant to the vill was included in the lease because it was not specifically excepted. WH 422, 1 Comp. 3.33.9 = X 3.38.7 (1175–80). These decretals settled the previous dispute among the decretists, although it took some time for their significance to be appreciated. See Landau, *Jus Patronatus,* 111–13.

46. "Item transfertur [ius patronatus] ratione universitatis, sive illa universitas vendatur sive donetur sive infeudetur, vel alio modo aliter, nisi specialiter excipiatur, ut Alexander III Ex litteris, Cum seculum." Huguccio, *Summa decretorum,* gloss to C.16 q.7 c.26, v. *Pie mentis.*

47. Dig. 8.4.12 ("Cum fundus fundo servit, vendito quoque fundo servitutes sequuntur. aedificia quoque fundis et fundi aedificiis eadem condicione serviunt").

48. Landau, *Jus Patronatus,* 79–80. Several decretals of Alexander, for example, suggested that a bishop must consent for a gift of an advowson to be valid. See, e.g., WH 880, 1 Comp. 3.33.7 = X 3.38.5 (1179–81); WH 329, 1 Comp. 3.33.13 = X 3.38.11 (1160–76); WH 689, 1 Comp. 3.33.21 = X 3.38.17 (1159–81); WH 998, 1 Comp. 3.33.25 = X 3.38.20 (1177). In one decretal, however, Alexander suggested that a donation to a religious house might be valid even without episcopal authority (although a reference to episcopal

authority was interpolated in the *Liber Extra* by Raymond of Peñaforte). WH 184, 1 Comp. 3.33.23 = X 3.24.4 (1173–76). Another decretal of Alexander distinguished between the church, which could not be given without lay approval, and the advowson, which could freely be given to a religious house. WH 761, 1 Comp. 3.33.10 = X 3.38.8 (1177) ("laicus sine auctoritate episcopi nemini potest ecclesias dare, licet religioso loco ius patronatus conferendi liberam habeat facultatem"). Later canonists seized on actual or perceived inconsistencies in the decretals to defend their own views on the requirements for gifts. Landau, *Jus Patronatus*, 80–93.

49. Landau, *Jus Patronatus*, 86; Pennington, *Legal History Sources*, http://legalhistory sources.com/1140a-z.htm (accessed December 31, 2020).

50. "Possit donari etiam private persone, arg. in extra Continebatur, et etiam sine consensus et auctoritate episcopi, quod Alexander innuit in illo decreto Quamvis simus." Huguccio, *Summa decretorum*, gloss to C.16 q.7 c.26, v. *Pie mentis*.

51. Landau, *Jus Patronatus*, 89–90. For the dates of these canonists, see Pennington, *Legal History Sources*, http://legalhistorysources.com/1140a-z.htm (accessed December 31, 2020).

52. Bernard of Parma, *Glossa ordinaria* to X 3.38.8, v. *religioso* ("sive concedat ecclesiam, sive ius patronatus, necessaria est auctoritas episcopi"). The *Glossa ordinaria* was rewritten and revised several times between 1241 and Bernard's death in 1266. See Pennington, *Legal History Sources*, http://legalhistorysources.com/1140a-z.htm (accessed December 31, 2020).

53. Landau, *Jus Patronatus*, 90.

54. *Id.* at 94. The prohibition on sale appears in the first recension of Gratian's *Decretum* as well as in the decretals of Alexander III. See *Dictum post* C.16, q.7, c.30 ("fundatores ecclesiarum . . . non habent ius uendendi, uel donandi, uel utendi tamquam propriis"); WH 1061, 1 Comp. 3.33.20 = X 3.38.16 (1174–81) ("quum inconveniens sit et penitus inhonestum vendi ius patronatus, quod est spirituali annexum, contractum illum . . . irritum esse decernas"); Winroth, *The Making of Gratian's "Decretum,"* 216.

55. In Peter's view, because the advowson was a *ius corporale*, there was no reason why it could not be sold or mortgaged, provided that no creditor exercised the advowson without the patron's consent. Peter the Chanter, *Summa de Sacramentis*, vol. 3:2b, pp. 706–7 ("Credimus . . . quod ius patronatus merum sit corporale et vendi potest, et in perpetuum et ad tempus, et obligari pignori; tamen, si interim uacauerit beneficium aliquod, non debet creditor dare illud since licentia patroni, quia illud accederet preter sortem et esset usura"). Peter acknowledged, however, that others did not share his view, and he offered no textual support for his position, which later canonists rejected. Landau, *Jus Patronatus*, 98. On the intellectual approach of Peter the Chanter and its context, see Marcia L. Colish, *Medieval Foundations of the Western Intellectual Tradition, 400–1400* (New Haven, Conn.: Yale University Press, 1997), 287.

56. Landau, *Jus Patronatus*, 99–101. For the latter view, see Bernard of Parma, *Glossa ordinaria* to X 3.38.6, v. *spoliando* ("eo ipso quod imponitur pena emptori, et non venditori,

videtur remanere penes ipsum patronum ius patronatus; quia si voluisset privari, hoc dixisset").

57. See Joshua C. Tate, "Royal Privilege and Episcopal Rights in the Later Thirteenth Century: The Case of the Ashbourne Advowson, 1270–89," in *Law and Society in Later Medieval England and Ireland: Essays in Honour of Paul Brand,* ed. Travis R. Baker (Oxford: Routledge, 2018), 97–107, at 99, 106.

58. See 14 PRS 122–23 (September 1194) (no judgment); 7 CRR 280 (Mich. 1214) (no judgment); 9 CRR 15–16 (Trin. 1220) (case settled); 3 BNB no. 1570, pp. 452–53 (Mich. 1222); 11 CRR no. 2567, pp. 509–10 (Mich. 1224) (case settled); 2 BNB no. 644, pp. 495–96 (Mich. 1231) (donee loses).

59. See Tate, "Royal Privilege," at 99.

60. On the complex motivations for gifts to religious houses, see Stephen D. White, *Custom, Kinship, and Gifts to Saints: The "Laudatio Parentum" in Western France, 1050–1150* (Chapel Hill: University of North Carolina Press, 1988), 29–30.

61. Wood, *Proprietary Church,* 682–83; Newman, "Greater and Lesser Landowners," at 281.

62. 9 CRR 11 (Trin. 1220).

63. 4 CRR 126 (Pas. 1206); 6 CRR 348 (Trin. 1212); 11 CRR no. 417, p. 78 (Hil. 1223).

64. See Tate, "Royal Privilege," at 100.

65. 7 CRR 138 (Trin. 1214) ("ita tamen quod nulli domui religiose predictam ecclesiam conferat et ne aliquid fiat in preiudicium iuris heredum suorum").

66. See Tate, "Royal Privilege," at 100.

67. See *id.*

68. For the entries referencing the gifts, see 2 RCR 99 (Mich. 1199); 2 CRR 231–32 (Pas. 1203); 3 CRR 3 (Mich. 1203); 3 CRR 94 (Hil. 1204); 5 CRR 54 (Mich. 1207); 7 CRR 294–95 (Mich. 1214); Yorks. no. 1151, pp. 425–26 (1218–19); 8 CRR 241–42 (Hil. 1220); 8 CRR 287–88 (Pas. 1220); 9 CRR 26–27 (Trin. 1220); 9 CRR 107–8 (Trin. 1220); 2 BNB no. 172, pp. 139–40 (Pas. 1222); 2 BNB no. 182, pp. 148–49 (Pas. 1222); 11 CRR no. 768, p. 153 (Mich. 1223); 11 CRR no. 2733, p. 549 (Mich. 1224); 12 CRR no. 2641, p. 527 (Pas. 1226); 3 BNB no. 1813, pp. 621–22 (Norf. 1227); 3 BNB no. 1831, pp. 632–33 (Norf. 1227); 14 CRR no. 48, p. 7 (Trin. 1230); 16 CRR no. 1931, p. 394 (Pas. 1242); 19 CRR no. 1058, pp. 168–69 (Mich. 1249); 19 CRR no. 1079, p. 173 (Mich. 1249).

69. See, e.g., Lincs. no. 239, p. 39 (1202) (confirmatory charters of the bishop of Lincoln, the archbishop of Canterbury, and popes Lucius and Alexander); 2 BNB no. 34, pp. 28–29 (Pas./Trin. 1219) (confirmatory charter of Pope Alexander as well as bishop of Ely); 9 CRR 21 (Trin. 1220) (confirmatory charter of Pope Honorius offered along with confirmation of bishop of Lincoln).

70. A search of the published plea rolls for the period revealed thirty-nine instances of royal charters being offered to confirm a gift.

71. See Tate, "Royal Privilege," at 100.

72. See *id.*

73. 13 CRR no. 370, p. 85 (Trin. 1227) ("quidam Johannes filius Suani, qui habuit advocacionem tocius ecclesie, vendidit medietatem illius advocacionis Willelmo de Nevill', patri Sarre que fuit mater predicti Thome et cuius heres predictus Thomas est, et racione illius empcionis presentavit predictus Simon quondam vir ipsius Sarre; et aliam medietatem vendidit predictus Johannes Rogero de Montebegon', cuius heredes uxores Eudonis de Lungvillers et Gaufridi de Nevill' sunt").

74. *Id.*

75. Landau, *Jus Patronatus,* 207–10. See also R. H. Helmholz, *The Oxford History of the Laws of England,* vol. 1, *The Canon Law and Ecclesiastical Jurisdiction from 597 to the 1640s* (Oxford: Oxford University Press, 2004), 478–79 (citing X 2.1.3).

76. See F. Soudet, "Les Seigneurs patrons des églises normandes," in *Travaux de la semaine d'histoire du droit normand* (Caen, 1925), 321–26. Although a new procedure involving a mixed jury of priests and knights was approved for some cases involving churchmen, cases between laymen continued to be decided in Normandy under Philip Augustus as they had been under the Plantagenet kings. *Id.* at 323–24. On the situation in Austria, which recognized lay jurisdiction over advowsons in practice if not in theory, see Landau, *Jus Patronatus,* 210n740.

77. "De advocatione et presentatione ecclesiarum, si controversia emerserit inter laicos, vel inter clericos et laicos, vel inter clericos, in curia domini regis tractetur et terminetur." *Councils and Synods* I, pt. 2, 878–79.

78. *Id.* I, pt. 2, 877 ("facta est recordatio et recognitio cuiusdam partis consuetudinum et libertatum et dignitatum antecessorum suorum, videlicet regis Henrici avi sui et aliorum, que observari et teneri deberent in regno").

79. See Duggan, "Henry II, the English Church and the Papacy," at 171–75.

80. W. L. Warren, *Henry II* (London: Eyre Methuen, 1973), 524–31.

81. WH 775, 1 Comp. 2.1.5 = X 2.1.3 (1164–81). *Quanto* did not necessarily rule out any secular involvement in advowson litigation; it merely stated that such litigation should be *definiri et . . . terminari* in the church courts. Landau, *Jus Patronatus,* 206–7. For further discussion of the canon law of patronage, see *supra* chap. 2.

82. Gray, "Ius Praesentandi," at 481–509. Ecclesiastical courts continued to hear benefice disputes well into the fourteenth century, at least in the ecclesiastical province of York. See Charles Donahue Jr., "Roman Canon Law in the Medieval English Church: Stubbs vs. Maitland Re-examined after 75 Years in the Light of Some Records from the Church Courts," *Michigan L. Rev.* 72 (1974): 659, 661 (explaining that some of these cases involved an underlying dispute over the patronage); but see David Millon, "Ecclesiastical Jurisdiction in Medieval England," *University of Illinois L. Rev.* (1984): 624–25 (arguing that while benefice cases continued to be heard, "few, if any, cases appear to have exceeded the bounds of ecclesiastical jurisdiction as determined by the common law").

83. Eleanor Searle, ed. and trans., *The Chronicle of Battle Abbey* (Oxford: Clarendon Press, 1980), 76–79, 97–99, 224–35. For further discussion of this litigation, see Gray, "Ius Praesentandi," at 482–84.

84. Searle, *The Chronicle of Battle Abbey*, 224–25.

85. The discussion of Mildenhall in the chronicle omits the fact that the abbey of Bury Saint Edmunds also claimed the church and manor of Mildenhall by grant from Edward the Confessor. However, after the fall of Stigand, archbishop of Canterbury, in 1070, both the church and the manor passed into royal hands. William Rufus subsequently granted the church to Battle Abbey. By the end of the twelfth century, however, the church was once more in the possession of Saint Edmunds. Antonia Gransden, *A History of the Abbey of Bury St. Edmunds, 1182–1256* (Woodbridge: Boydell Press, 2007), 26–28. After a long lawsuit, Battle and Saint Edmunds arrived at a settlement whereby Battle no longer held the advowson but received a fixed annual pension from the church. C. R. Cheney and Mary G. Cheney, eds., *The Letters of Pope Innocent III (1198–1216) concerning England and Wales* (Oxford: Clarendon Press, 1967), no. 436, p. 71.

86. Searle, *The Chronicle of Battle Abbey*, 225 (trans. Searle).

87. *Id.* at 224–29.

88. The chronicle also mentions an earlier dispute concerning the same church in which the abbey sued the priest Roger, who held the church for a pension but refused to pay it. According to the chronicler, the abbey sued Roger in ecclesiastical court, and he sought pardon when he realized that he was bound to lose. *Id.* at 228–29.

89. Searle suggests that the king perhaps "was represented as being ultimate lord of a manor in ancient demesne, and himself presented the clerk as a favour to Hamo." *Id.* at 231n2.

90. *Id.* at 231 ("nunc a regia, nunc ab ecclesiastica curia iustitie plenitudinem sibi petit exhiberi, hinc super militis uiolentia conquerens, inde super clerici intrusione") (trans. Searle).

91. *Id.* at 233 ("qui auctoritate apostolica iampridem inde omnino amotus fuerat") (trans. Searle).

92. *Id.* at 229–35. See also R. C. van Caenegem, ed., *English Lawsuits from William I to Richard I,* Selden Society 107 (London, 1991), no. 445, pp. 476–79.

93. Searle, *The Chronicle of Battle Abbey*, 268–70.

94. *Id.* at 320; Charles Donahue Jr., "Gerard Pucelle as a Canon Lawyer," in *Grundlagen des Rechts: Festschrift für Peter Landau zum 65 Geburtstag*, ed. Jörg Müller et al. (Paderborn: Ferdinand Schöningh, 2000), 341.

95. On Pucelle's career, see Donahue, "Gerard Pucelle as a Canon Lawyer," at 333–40.

96. Searle, *The Chronicle of Battle Abbey*, 330 ("in rebus ecclesiasticis nichil iuris obtinet potestas secularis") (trans. Searle).

97. *Id.* at 330–32.

98. *Id.* at 332.

99. *Id.* at 335; Donahue, "Gerard Pucelle as a Canon Lawyer," at 347.

100. Richard de Belmeis I, bishop of London, was one of the two papal judges delegate in the Mildenhall case. Since Richard, who died in 1162, was unable to attend the hearing

concerning Mildenhall "because of sickness," it seems likely that the dispute was concluded toward the end of the bishop's life.

101. Gray, "Ius Praesentandi," at 482, 484; Searle, *The Chronicle of Battle Abbey*, 232–33n1. The papal judge delegate in the Thurlow case was Gilbert Foliot, who acceded to the see in March 1163, but the dispute over Thurlow continued for some time after the bishop's initial decision.

102. Searle, *The Chronicle of Battle Abbey*, 320–21n1.

103. According to Flahiff, the writs of prohibition probably date to the period 1165–70, although "proof positive of their use is not to be had before the early 1180's, and the first actual form of a writ of prohibition is to be found only in Glanvill's treatise a few years later." G. B. Flahiff, "The Writ of Prohibition to Court Christian in the Thirteenth Century [pt. 1]," *Mediaeval Studies* 6 (1944): 271–72.

104. G. B. Flahiff, "The Writ of Prohibition to Court Christian in the Thirteenth Century [pt. 2]," *Mediaeval Studies* 7 (1945): 232–49.

105. On the date and authorship of *Glanvill*, see *infra* chap. 3.

106. *Glanvill*, IV, 14, Woodbine p. 83 ("quia placita de advocationibus ecclesiarum ad coronam et dignitatem meam pertinent") (trans. Beames, p. 98). The treatise author and the rubric suggest that this writ was to be used as a follow-up when an initial writ of *indicavit* was not obeyed; however, since the *indicavit* deals with a dispute between clerks, this may not have been the original purpose of the other writ.

107. Flahiff, "The Writ of Prohibition [pt. 1]," at 275.

108. *Glanvill*, IV, 13, Woodbine p. 83 ("donec dirationatum fuerit in curia mea ad quem illorum advocatio illius ecclesiae pertineat") (trans. Beames, p. 97).

109. Flahiff, "The Writ of Prohibition [pt. 1]," at 269, 274.

110. This argument was being made by 1224. See 11 CRR no. 2666, p. 535 (Mich. 1224); 13 CRR no. 669, p. 150 (Pas. 1228). See also *Bracton*, ff. 402b–403, IV, pp. 253–54, discussed in *Select Cases from the Ecclesiastical Courts*, 95 Selden Soc. 78. A case from Easter Term 1221 illustrates the difficulty the royal courts faced in policing the boundary between litigation concerning tithes and advowson disputes. Warin de Muntchanesy sued the prior of Hereford in a plea of *quare secutus est placitum contra prohibitionem*, arguing that the prior wrongly impleaded his clerk concerning the advowson of Painswick. The prior responded that he sued the clerk not concerning the advowson but rather concerning a portion of the tithes to which the prior was entitled by gift of Warin's ancestors: namely, two parts of the tithes of Warin's demesne and of one additional virgate. Warin conceded that the prior was entitled to that portion of the tithes, but argued that the prior had instead impleaded Warin's clerk concerning the whole church. The prior defended by compurgation. 10 CRR 104 (Pas. 1221). Perhaps this case and others like it led to the development between 1221 and 1224 of a special writ of *indicavit* for tithes.

111. Probably a younger brother or cousin of Oliver II de Aincourt, Lord of Blankney. See I. J. Sanders, *English Baronies: A Study of Their Origin and Descent, 1086–1327* (Oxford: Clarendon Press, 1960); see also 8 CRR 239 (Hil. 1220) (land dispute between Oliver and John).

112. A suit before papal judges delegate involved a papal commission to the delegates, usually granted because the case brought to the pope's attention involved a factual dispute. On papal judges delegate, see Jane E. Sayers, *Papal Judges Delegate in the Province of Canterbury, 1198–1254* (Oxford: Oxford University Press, 1971), 54. The late twelfth and early thirteenth centuries "witnessed the high-water mark of Roman jurisdiction in England." *Id.* at 238. The term *breve de intrusione* may have been developing into a technical term for this type of action in the ecclesiastical courts.

113. 8 CRR 74–75 (Mich. 1219) = 2 BNB no. 62, p. 55.

114. The ecclesiastical courts could also hear disputes over whether a particular house of worship was a chapel pertaining to another church. In Michaelmas Term 1250, for example, Geoffrey of Titsey, parson of Warlingham, in Surrey, was summoned before the king's court by the prior of Bermondsey to explain why he brought a plea in an ecclesiastical court concerning the advowson of the church of Chelsham in the same county. Geoffrey explained that he brought no plea concerning the advowson but rather impleaded William, the parson of Chelsham, to claim the tithes of Chelsham as a chapel belonging to Geoffrey's church of Warlingham. The prior claimed that in fact it was Warlingham that was a chapel dependent on Chelsham, and not the other way around. The parties put themselves on a jury as to which was the chapel and which was the mother church, and the jury reported that Chelsham was the chapel, belonging to Warlingham. The court gave Geoffrey a writ to the elect of Winchester to cause him to have full seisin of the church of Chelsham as a chapel pertaining to his church of Warlingham, noting that it would clearly be unjust if Geoffrey was not able to seek the church of Chelsham as a chapel pertaining to his church in an ecclesiastical court and that no one should be defrauded of his right in the royal court ("manifeste esset contra justiciam si predictus Galfridus non posset petere predictam ecclesiam de Chelesham tanquam capellam pertinentem ad ecclesiam suam de Werlingham in foro ecclesiastico, necque in curia regis nec aliquis debet defrauderi iure suo"). 20 CRR no. 1742, pp. 300–301 (Mich. 1250).

115. Gray, "Ius Praesentandi," at 491.

116. Helmholz, *Canon Law and Ecclesiastical Jurisdiction,* 485–86.

117. 7 CRR 43 (Mich. 1213). Thomas also offered letters of the archdeacon of Suffolk testifying that he knew that Ralph was canonically instituted in the church, along with a charter of the bishop of Norwich (John of Gray) attesting to the admission of Ralph at Thomas's presentation. William of Coleville, the plaintiff, responded that if Ralph was admitted, it was done unjustly and over his appeal, since, shortly after the last parson died, William presented his clerk and appealed for his right. In a later hearing, Thomas offered an earlier charter of the bishop of Norwich attesting that a certain Adam had been instituted parson of the church by presentation of Roger fitz Walerian, the patron of the church. This last charter, the relevance of which is unclear, was older than the others, being made by John *quondam Norwicensis episcopi* (i.e., John of Oxford, d. 1200) rather than John of Gray, the current bishop. The parties were sent away without day on the

grounds that the church was not vacant. The plea roll does not specify whether the basis for this was the last charter offered by Thomas or the documentation in the earlier hearing, although the latter seems more likely.

118. 7 CRR 291 (Mich. 1214) ("venit et appellavit, ne quid fieret contra libertatem prebende sue"). Philip asserted that he held the prebend of Yetminster and that the prebend had the liberty that when a church pertaining to it became vacant, the patron of that church would present a candidate to the canon having the prebend, and the canon would make the inquisition. When the church of Clifton Maybank became vacant, Philip explained, the plaintiff (William Maubanc) presented his clerk to the bishop rather than to Philip. The bishop held an inquisition. After Philip appealed, William responded that he ought to present to the church as pertaining to his own prebend. William subsequently withdrew this claim and was amerced; Philip prevailed and obtained a writ to the bishop.

119. 4 CRR 92 (Pas. 1206) ("convocavit clericos suos ut faceret quod facere deberet").

120. *Id.* ("non ausus fuit personam super personam admittere").

121. After the bishop made his defense, the canons argued before the royal court that had they been present when Cecily's assize was taken, they would have shown that it should not have proceeded. *Id.* In a subsequent entry, the canons argued that they were parsons by gift of Cecily's grandfather William, offering William's charter and a charter of the bishop of Hereford confirming the gift. The canons asserted that they had brought a royal writ to postpone Cecily's assize until they could make their claim. The sheriff confirmed that he had received that writ but said that the assize was taken after the day granted to the canons by the king. The canons paid forty shillings to have a writ summoning a jury of attaint, and the writ was granted. 4 CRR 230 (Mich. 1206). The jury's verdict is not recorded, but a subsequent entry shows that Cecily was amerced. 5 CRR 38 (Mich. 1207).

122. See Helmholz, *Canon Law and Ecclesiastical Jurisdiction,* 479.

123. See Joshua C. Tate, "Competing Institutions and Dispute Settlement in Medieval England," in *Law and Disputing in the Middle Ages: Proceedings of the Ninth Carlsberg Academy Conference on Medieval Legal History 2012,* ed. Per Andersen et al. (Copenhagen: DJØF Publishing, 2013), 235–44, at 238.

124. The data on the number of benefices come from Sarah Davnall et al., "The Taxatio Database," *Bulletin of the John Rylands Library* 74 (1992): 89–108, at 101–8. The diocese of Rochester and the Welsh dioceses are omitted from this table, as they did not produce any royal court cases from 1194 to 1199. Churches in Wales were, however, occasionally the subject of litigation in the royal courts. See 10 CRR 178 (Mich. 1221) (advowson of Skenfrith in the diocese of Llandaff); 11 CRR 484 no. 91 (advowson of Llantilio Crossenny, also in the diocese of Llandaff).

125. The percentage of the 1291 valuation is based on table 3 in Bruce M. S. Campbell, "Benchmarking Medieval Economic Development: England, Wales, Scotland, and Ireland, c. 1290," *Econ. Hist. Rev.* 61 (2008): 896–945, at 903.

126. *Id.* at 240. In some instances, sufficient information exists to determine that a religious house was involved on one side of a lawsuit, but the surviving information does not

allow one to determine the order of the religious house. Such instances are counted in tables 2 and 3 but not table 4.

127. Henrietta Leyser, "Hugh the Carthusian," in *St. Hugh of Lincoln,* ed. Peter Mayr-Harting (Oxford, 1987), 1–18, at 2.

128. David Hugh Farmer, "Hugh of Lincoln, Carthusian Saint," in *De Cella in Seculum: Religious and Secular Life and Devotion in Late Medieval England,* ed. Michael G. Sargent (Cambridge, 1989), 9–15, at 9.

129. H. E. J. Cowdrey, "Hugh of Avalon, Carthusian and Bishop," in Sargent, *De Cella,* 41–57, at 50–51.

130. Nicholas Vincent, "The Court of Henry II," in *Henry II: New Interpretations,* ed. Christopher Harper-Bill and Nicholas Vincent (Woodbridge: Boydell Press, 2007), 278–334, at 307 (quoting the *Life of St. Hugh*).

131. Karl Leyser, "The Angevin Kings and the Holy Man," in Mayr-Harting, *St. Hugh,* 49–73, at 56–57.

132. K. Leyser, "The Angevin Kings," 58–60.

133. Christopher Harper-Bill, "John of Oxford, Diplomat and Bishop," in *Medieval Ecclesiastical Studies in Honour of Dorothy M. Owen,* ed. Michael J. Franklin and Christopher Harper-Bill (Rochester, N.Y., 1995), 83–105, at 83–86.

134. Harper-Bill, "John of Oxford," 91–93.

135. W. Warren, *Henry II* (London: Eyre Methuen, 1973), 553.

136. Harper-Bill, "John of Oxford," 94.

137. Richard Mortimer, "Religious and Secular Motives for Some English Monastic Foundations," in *Religious Motivation: Biographical and Sociological Problems for the Church Historian,* ed. Derek Baker (Oxford, 1978), 77–85 (discussing the foundations of Ranulf de Glanville, the justiciar, among others).

138. Harper-Bill, "John of Oxford," 98.

139. Everett U. Crosby, *Bishop and Chapter in Twelfth-Century England: A Study of the "Mensa Episcopalis"* (Cambridge, 1994), 191–92.

140. Harper-Bill, "John of Oxford," 99–100.

141. David Knowles and R. Neville Hadcock, *Medieval Religious Houses: England and Wales,* 2nd ed. (New York, 1971), 137–45.

142. Tate, "Competing Institutions," at 243.

143. 1 CRR 44 (Pas. 1198); 1 RCR 141 (Pas. 1198); Knowles and Hadcock, *Medieval Religious Houses,* 96.

144. 14 PRS 22 (Trin. 1194).

145. Tate, "Competing Institutions," at 243.

146. 14 PRS 7 (Trin. 1194).

147. 14 PRS 10 (Trin. 1194).

148. 14 PRS 28 (Trin. 1194).

149. Tate, "Competing Institutions," at 244.

150. See Tate, "Episcopal Power and Royal Jurisdiction in Angevin England," at 19.

151. 1 CRR 442 (Pas. 1201).

152. 2 CRR 179 (Hil. 1203).

153. 5 CRR 231 (Trin. 1208).

154. Tate, "Episcopal Power and Royal Jurisdiction," at 19.

155. See, e.g., 3 CRR 193 (Mich. 1204) (party excused from appearance); 7 CRR 297 (Mich. 1214) (losing party pardoned of an amercement).

156. Doris Mary Stenton, "King John and the Courts of Justice," in 67 PKJ 86.

157. "Nulli vendemus, nulli negabimus aut differemus rectum vel justiciam." Great Charter of 1215, clause 40.

158. David Knowles, *The Religious Orders in England,* vol. 3, *The Tudor Age* (Cambridge: Cambridge University Press, 1959), 62.

159. Davnall, "The *Taxatio* Database," at 102, 108. These percentages include the Welsh dioceses and Rochester and are thus slightly lower than those in table 1, which includes only the dioceses that sent cases to the royal courts from 1194 to 1199.

160. Tate, "Competing Institutions," at 238.

161. Out of fifty-two advowson cases that first appear in the surviving rolls from Trinity Term and Michaelmas Term 1214, nine involved churches in the diocese of Lincoln. The highest number of cases, twelve, came from the diocese of Norwich, and the remaining cases were spread out more or less evenly among other dioceses.

162. Tate, "Competing Institutions," 240–44.

163. 7 CRR 135 (Trin. 1214) (Milton); 7 CRR 221 (Trin. 1214) (Ingham); 7 CRR 278 (Mich. 1214) (Asgarby); 7 CRR 302 (Mich. 1214) (Harby); 7 CRR 305 (Mich. 1214) (Morton).

164. 7 CRR 118 (Trin. 1214) (Barningham); 7 CRR 165 (Trin. 1214) (Bilton and Healaugh); 7 CRR 177 (Trin. 1214) (Attenborough); 7 CRR 260 (Mich. 1214) (South Kirkby); 7 CRR 261 (Mich. 1214) (Elvaston); 7 CRR 280 (Mich. 1214) (Adel).

165. 7 CRR 132 (Trin. 1214) (Burnham); 7 CRR 259 (Mich. 1214) (Stanninghall); 7 CRR 286 (Mich. 1214) (Barney); 7 CRR 297 (Mich. 1214) (Randworth).

166. 7 CRR 129 (Trin. 1214) (Englishcombe); 7 CRR 164 (Trin. 1214) (Stanton); 7 CRR 196 (Trin. 1214) (Brean).

167. See Tate, "Episcopal Power and Royal Jurisdiction," at 22.

168. The time frames in tables 5 and 6 are of unequal length to compensate for the differential survival of rolls from different time periods.

169. It is possible that some of the trends here might reflect a general increase in litigation in the royal courts. Counting the number of nonadvowson civil cases in the plea rolls might shed light on that issue but would be a monumental task that I have not attempted for the present analysis.

170. David M. Smith, "The Rolls of Hugh of Wells, Bishop of Lincoln, 1209–35," *Bulletin of the Institute of Historical Research* 45 (1972): 155.

171. Gray, "Ius Praesentandi," at 491–94.

172. Smith, "Rolls of Hugh of Wells," at 157–60.

173. Smith, "Rolls of Hugh of Wells," at 160.

174. "Magister T. de Tyrintona presentatus per abbatem et conventum de [Thorney] ad ecclesiam de Stibbingtona, ad eam est admissus et institutus in eadem. . . . Et facta fuit prius inquisitio per episcopum, in ipsa ecclesia presentem, quod fuit sine controversia et de advocatione dictorum Abbatis et conventus." 1 RHW 5–6.

175. 1 RHW 2–9 (entries referring to inquests by the dean of Lincoln, archdeacons of Northampton, Oxford, Bedford, and Buckingham, and official of Northampton).

176. "Willelmus de Cennora, clericus, presentatus per abbatissam et conventum de Godestow ad ecclesiam de Esindone . . . cum omnia per inquisitionem per Archidiaconum Oxoniensem factam essent liquida . . . admissus est et in persona institutus." 1 RHW 16 (membrane 4).

177. See, e.g., 1 RHW 12 (membrane 3); 1 RHW 63 (membrane 9).

178. Tate, "Episcopal Power and Royal Jurisdiction," at 24.

179. David M. Smith, "Wells, Hugh of (d. 1235)," in *Oxford Dictionary of National Biography* (Oxford: Oxford University Press, 2004), http://www.oxforddnb.com/view/article/14061.

180. See Tate, "Episcopal Power and Royal Jurisdiction," at 25.

181. Roy Martin Haines, "Gray, John de (d. 1214)," in *Oxford Dictionary of National Biography* (Oxford: Oxford University Press, 2004), http://www.oxforddnb.com/view/article/11541.

182. 2 CRR 163 (Hil. 1203).

Chapter Six. Conclusion

1. The other three key attributes, according to Rogers, are complexity, trialability, and observability. Rogers, *Diffusion of Innovations,* at 211.

2. Brand, "*Multis Vigiliis Excogitatam,*" at 102.

3. Milsom, *Historical Foundations,* 1.

4. Robert C. Palmer, *Selling the Church: The English Parish in Law, Commerce, and Religion, 1350–1550* (Chapel Hill: University of North Carolina Press, 2002), 20–22.

5. Blackstone, *Commentaries,* vol. 3, p. 246. The later action of *quare impedit* differed from the writ of the early plea rolls in that not only the "pseudo-patron" but also his clerk and the bishop were joined as defendants. *Id.* at 248. The essence of the action, however, was the same.

6. John Mallory, *Quare impedit* (London: E. and R. Nutt, R. Gosling, and J. Shuckburgh, 1737).

7. 3 and 4 Will. 4, c. 27, § 36.

8. Common Law Procedure Act, 23 and 24 Vict., c. 126, § 26.

SELECT BIBLIOGRAPHY

Manuscript Sources

Admont, Stiftsbibliothek MS 7: Huguccio, *Summa decretorum*.

National Archives of the United Kingdom: Court of Common Pleas and King's Bench, and Justices Itinerant: Early Plea and Essoin Rolls (KB 26), Anglo-American Legal Tradition, http://aalt.law.uh.edu.

Norfolk Record Office (Norwich, England): DN/EST 5/6 (1220). Confirmation by William, prior of Norwich, of the impropriation by Bishop Pandulf to Saint Benet's Abbey of the church of Ludham.

Printed Primary Sources

English Plea Rolls

Bracton's Note Book. Edited by F. W. Maitland. 3 vols. London, 1887.

Curia Regis Rolls Preserved in the Public Record Office. 20 vols. London, 1922–2006.

The Earliest Lincolnshire Assize Rolls, 1202–1209. Edited by Doris M. Stenton. Lincoln Record Society 22 (1926).

The Earliest Northamptonshire Assize Rolls, 1202–1203. Edited by Doris M. Stenton. Northamptonshire Record Society 5 (1930).

Memoranda Roll for the Tenth Year of King John [etc.]: "Curia Regis Roll 5 (1196)" and "Curia Regis Roll 8B (1198)." Edited by R. Allen Brown. Pipe Roll Society, New Series 31 (1955), pp. 69–118.

Pleas before the King or His Justices, 1198–1202. Edited by D. M. Stenton. 4 vols. Selden Society 67, 68, 83, and 84. London, 1952–67.

Rolls of the Justices in Eyre at Bedford, 1202. Edited by G. H. Fowler. Bedfordshire Historical Record Society 1 (1913), pp. 133–247.

Rolls of the Justices in Eyre for Gloucestershire, Warwickshire, and Staffordshire [Shropshire], *1221–1222*. Edited by D. M. Stenton. Selden Society 59. London, 1940.

Rolls of the Justices in Eyre for Lincolnshire, 1218–1219, and Worcestershire, 1221. Edited by D. M. Stenton. Selden Society 53. London, 1934.

Rolls of the Justices in Eyre for Yorkshire, 1218–1219. Edited by D. M. Stenton. Selden Society 56. London, 1937.

Rotuli Curiae Regis. Edited by Francis Palgrave. 2 vols. London, 1831.

Rotuli Hugonis de Welles, Episcopi Lincolniensis A.D. MCCIX–MCCXXXV. Edited by W. P. W. Phillimore. Lincoln Record Society, 1913.

Staffordshire Suits Extracted from the Plea Rolls, temp. *Richard I and King John*. Edited by G. Wrottesley. William Salt Archaeological Society 3 (1882), pp. 25–163.

Three Rolls of the King's Court in the Reign of King Richard the First, 1194–1195. Edited by F. W. Maitland. Pipe Roll Society 14 (1891).

Edited Selden Society Volumes (excluding Plea Rolls)

Brevia Placitata. Edited by G. J. Turner. Selden Society 66. London, 1951.

The Earliest English Law Reports. Edited by Paul A. Brand. 4 vols. Selden Society 111, 112, 122, and 123. London, 1995–2007.

Early Registers of Writs. Edited by Elsa de Haas and G. D. G. Hall. Selden Society 87. London, 1970.

English Lawsuits from William I to Richard I. Edited by R. C. van Caenegem. 2 vols. Selden Society 106–7. London, 1990–91.

The Liber Pauperum of Vacarius. Edited by Francis de Zulueta. Selden Society 44. London, 1927.

Royal Writs in England from the Conquest to Glanvill. Edited by R. C. van Caenegem. Selden Society 77. London, 1959.

Select Cases from the Ecclesiastical Courts of the Province of Canterbury, c. 1200–1301. Edited by Norma Adams and Charles Donahue Jr. Selden Society 95. London, 1981.

Select Cases of Procedure without Writ under Henry III. Edited by H. G. Richardson and G. O. Sayles. Selden Society 60. London, 1941.

The Teaching of Roman Law in England around 1200. Edited by Francis de Zulueta and Peter Stein. Selden Society Supp. Series 8. London, 1990.

English Treatises (Common Law)

Beames, John. *A Translation of Glanville.* London: A. J. Valpy, 1812.

Blackstone, William. *Commentaries on the Laws of England.* 4 vols. Chicago: University of Chicago Press, 1979. Facsimile of the first edition, 1765–69.

Hall, G. D. G., ed. and trans. *The Treatise on the Laws and Customs of the Realm of England Commonly Called Glanvill.* Oxford: Clarendon Press, 2002. Reprint of the 1965 edition.

Mallory, John. *Quare impedit.* London: E. and R. Nutt, R. Gosling, and J. Shuckburgh, 1737.

Thorne, Samuel E., trans., and George E. Woodbine, ed. *Bracton on the Laws and Customs of England.* 4 vols. Cambridge, Mass.: Harvard University Press, 1968–77.

Woodbine, George E., ed. *Glanvill de Legibus et Consuetudinibus Regni Angliae.* New Haven, Conn.: Yale University Press, 1932.

Ecclesiastical Histories and Monastic Chronicles

The Cartulary of Carisbrooke Priory. Edited by S. F. Hockey. Southampton: Camelot Press, 1981.

Early Charters of the Cathedral Church of St. Paul, London. Edited by Marion Gibbs. London: Royal Historical Society, 1939.

The Chronicle of Battle Abbey. Edited by Eleanor Searle. Oxford: Clarendon Press, 1980.

Liber Controversarium Sancti Vincentii Cenomannensis. Edited by A. Chédeville. Paris, 1968.

Liber Eliensis. Edited by E. O. Blake. Woodbridge: Boydell, 1962.

Manuscripts from St. Alban's Abbey, 1066–1235. Edited by Rodney M. Thompson. Woodbridge: D. S. Brewer, 1982.

Register of the Abbey of St. Benet of Holme, 1020–1210. Edited by R. West. Norfolk Record Society 3 (1932).

Canon Law Sources and Collections

Bernard of Parma. *Glossa ordinaria ad decretales.* In *Decretalium libri V cum glossa.* Venice: Nicolai Jenson, 1479.

Bernard of Pavia. *Summa Decretalium.* Edited by E. Theodor Laspeyres. Graz, 1956.

"*Collectio Wigorniensis.*" Edited by Hans-Eberhard Lohmann. *Zeitschrift der Savigny-Stiftung für Rechtsgeschichte, Kanonistische Abteilung* 22 (1933): 36–187.

Conciliorum Oecumenicorum Decreta. Edited by Giuseppe Alberigo et al. Bologna: Edizioni Dehoniane, 1991.

Corpus Iuris Canonici. Edited by Emil Friedberg. 2 vols. Leipzig, 1959. Reprint of the 1879–81 edition.

Councils and Synods with Other Documents Relating to the English Church. Edited by D. Whitelock, M. Brett, and C. N. L. Brooke. 2 vols. Oxford: Clarendon Press, 1964–81.

Grosseteste, Robert. *The Letters of Robert Grosseteste, Bishop of Lincoln.* Edited and translated by F. A. C. Mantello and Joseph Goering. Toronto: University of Toronto Press, 2010.

Innocent III, Pope. *The Letters of Pope Innocent III (1198–1216) concerning England and Wales.* Edited by C. R. Cheney and Mary G. Cheney. Oxford: Clarendon Press, 1967.

Johannes Teutonicus. *Apparatus glossarum in Compilationem tertiam.* Edited by Kenneth Pennington. Vatican City: Biblioteca Apostolica Vaticana, 1981.

John of Salisbury. *The Letters of John of Salisbury.* Rev. ed. Edited by W. J. Millor, S.J., and H. E. Butler, rev. by C. N. L. Brooke. Oxford: Clarendon Press, 1986.

John of Salisbury. *The Statesman's Book of John of Salisbury.* Edited by John Dickinson. New York: A. A. Knopf, 1963.

Papsturkunden in England. Edited by Walther Holtzmann. Berlin: Weidmannsche Buchhandlung, 1935.

Peter the Chanter. *Summa de Sacramentis et Animae Consiliis.* Edited by Jean-Albert Dugauquier. 5 vols. Louvain: Éditions Nauwelaerts, 1954–67.

Quellen zur Geschichte der Römisch-Kanonischen Processes im Mittelalter. Edited by Ludwig Wahrmund. 5 vols. Innsbruck: Waguer, 1915–31.

Rufinus of Bologna. *Summa decretorum.* Edited by Heinrich Singer. Paderborn: Aalen, 1963. Reprint of the 1902 edition.

Simon of Bisignano. *Summa in Decretum.* Edited by Pier Aimone. Fribourg, 2006.

The Summa Parisiensis on the Decretum Gratiani. Edited by Terence P. McLaughlin. Toronto: Pontifical Institute of Mediaeval Studies, 1952.

"*Ulpianus.*" *Incerti auctoris ordo iudiciorum (Ulpianus de edendo).* Edited by Gustav Hänel. Leipzig: B. G. Teubneri, 1838.

Sources of Ancient Roman Law

Corpus Iuris Civilis. Edited by Theodor Mommsen, Paul Krüger, et al. 3 vols. Berlin, 1954. Reprint of the 1895 edition.

Justinian's Institutes. Translated by Peter Birks and Grant McLeod. London: Duckworth, 1987.

Other Sources

Johnson, John. *The Clergyman's Vade-Mecum.* London: Robert Knaplock and Sam. Ballard, 1731.

Smith, Thomas. *De Republica Anglorum: A Discourse on the Commonwealth of England.* Edited by L. Alston. Cambridge: Cambridge University Press, 1906. Originally published 1583.

Secondary Sources

Addleshaw, G. W. O. *Rectors, Vicars, and Patrons in Twelfth and Early Thirteenth Century Canon Law.* London: St. Anthony's Press, 1956.

Alexander, J. J. G., and M. T. Gibson, eds. *Medieval Learning and Literature: Essays Presented to Richard William Hunt.* Oxford: Clarendon Press, 1976.

Amt, Emilie. *The Accession of Henry II in England: Royal Government Restored, 1149–1159.* Woodbridge: Boydell Press, 1993.

Arnold, Morris S. "Book Review." *Harvard Law Review* 91 (1977): 517–21.

Baker, J. H. *An Introduction to English Legal History.* 4th ed. Bath: LexisNexis, 2002.

Barton, John L. "The Mystery of Bracton." *Journal of Legal History* 14 (1993): 1–142.

Barton, John L. *Roman Law in England. Ius Romanum Medii Aevi* pt. V.13a. Milan: Giuffrè, 1971.

Benson, Robert L. *The Bishop-Elect: A Study in Medieval Ecclesiastical Office.* Princeton, N.J.: Princeton University Press, 1968.

Berman, Harold J. *Law and Revolution: The Formation of the Western Legal Tradition.* Cambridge, Mass.: Harvard University Press, 1983.

Biancalana, Joseph. "For Want of Justice: Legal Reforms of Henry II." *Columbia Law Review* 88 (1988): 433–536.

Biancalana, Joseph. "The Origin and Early History of the Writs of Entry." *Law and Hist. Rev.* 25 (2007): 513–56.

Blumenthal, Uta-Renate. *The Investiture Controversy: Church and Monarchy from the Ninth to the Twelfth Century.* Philadelphia: University of Pennsylvania Press, 1988.

Boyle, Leonard E. "The Beginnings of Legal Studies at Oxford." *Viator: Medieval and Renaissance Studies* 14 (1983): 107–31.

Boyle, Leonard E. "Canon Law before 1380." In *The History of the University of Oxford,* edited by J. J. Catto, vol. 1, 531–64. Oxford: Clarendon Press, 1984.

Brand, Paul. "The Age of Bracton." *Proceedings of the British Academy* 89 (1996): 65–89.

Brand, Paul. "Ireland and the Literature of the Early Common Law." In *The Making of the Common Law,* by Paul Brand, 445–63. London: Hambledon Press, 1992.

Brand, Paul. *Kings, Barons and Justices: The Making and Enforcement of Legislation in Thirteenth-Century England.* Cambridge: Cambridge University Press, 2003.

Brand, Paul. "Legal Education in England before the Inns of Court." In *Learning the Law: Teaching and the Transmission of Law in England, 1150–1900,* edited by Jonathan A. Bush and Alain Wijffels, 51–84. London: Hambledon Press, 1999.

Brand, Paul. *The Making of the Common Law.* London: Hambledon Press, 1992.

Brand, Paul. " '*Multis Vigiliis Excogitatam et Inventam*': Henry II and the Creation of the English Common Law." In *The Making of the Common Law,* by Paul Brand, 77–102. London: Hambledon Press, 1992.

Brand, Paul. "The Origins of English Land Law: Milsom and After." In *The Making of the Common Law,* by Paul Brand, 203–25. London: Hambledon Press, 1992.

Brand, Paul. *The Origins of the English Legal Profession.* Oxford: Blackwell, 1992.

Brand, Paul. " 'Time Out of Mind': The Knowledge and Use of the Eleventh- and Twelfth-Century Past in Thirteenth-Century Litigation." In *Anglo Norman Studies XVI: Proceedings of the Battle Conference 1993,* edited by Marjorie Chibnall, 37–54. Woodbridge: Boydell, 1994.

Brini, Giuseppe. *Possesso delle Cose e Possesso dei Diritti nel Diritto Romano.* Rome: G. Bretschneider, 1978. Reprint of the 1906 edition.

Buckland, W. W. *A Textbook of Roman Law from Augustus to Justinian.* Rev. ed. Edited by Peter Stein. Cambridge: Cambridge University Press, 1963.

Buckland, W. W., and Arnold D. McNair. *Roman Law and Common Law: A Comparison in Outline.* 2nd rev. ed. Edited by F. H. Lawson. Cambridge: Cambridge University Press, 1952.

Burger, Michael. *Bishops, Clerks, and Diocesan Governance in Thirteenth-Century England.* Cambridge: Cambridge University Press, 2012.

Bush, Jonathan A., and Alain Wijffels, eds. *Learning the Law: Teaching and the Transmission of Law in England, 1150–1900.* London: Hambledon Press, 1999.

Campbell, Bruce M. S. "Benchmarking Medieval Economic Development: England, Wales, Scotland, and Ireland, c. 1290." *Econ. Hist. Rev.* 61 (2008): 896–945.

Carey Miller, David L. "Property." In *A Companion to Justinian's Institutes*, edited by Ernest Metzger, 42–79. Ithaca, N.Y.: Cornell University Press, 1998.

Carey Miller, David L., and Reinhard Zimmermann, eds. *The Civilian Tradition and Scots Law.* Berlin: Duncker and Humblot, 1997.

Carpenter, D. A. *The Reign of Henry III.* London: Hambledon Press, 1996.

Catto, J. J., ed. *The History of the University of Oxford.* Vol. 1. Oxford: Clarendon Press, 1984.

Cheney, C. R., and Mary G. Cheney, eds. *The Letters of Pope Innocent III (1198–1216) concerning England and Wales.* Oxford: Clarendon Press, 1967.

Cheney, Mary. "The Litigation between John Marshal and Archbishop Thomas Becket in 1164: A Pointer to the Origin of Novel Disseisin?" In *Law and Social Change in British History,* edited by J. A. Guy and H. G. Beale, 9–26. London: Royal Historical Society, 1984.

Cheney, Mary. "*Possessio/proprietas* in Ecclesiastical Courts in Mid-twelfth Century England." In *Law and Government in Medieval England and Normandy: Essays in Honour of Sir James Holt,* edited by George Garnett and John Hudson, 245–54. Cambridge: Cambridge University Press, 1994.

Chibnall, Marjorie, ed. *Anglo Norman Studies XVI: Proceedings of the Battle Conference 1993.* Woodbridge: Boydell, 1994.

Clanchy, M. T. *From Memory to Written Record: England, 1066–1307.* 2nd ed. Oxford: Blackwell, 1993.

Clanchy, M. T. "Magna Carta, Clause Thirty-Four." *English Historical Review* 79 (1964): 542–48.

Cohen, Morris R., and Felix S. Cohen. *Readings in Jurisprudence and Legal Philosophy.* New York: Prentice Hall, 1951.

Cokayne, George Edward. *The Complete Peerage of England, Scotland, Ireland, Great Britain, and the United Kingdom.* 13 vols. London: St. Catherine's Press, 1910–59.

Colish, Marcia L. *Medieval Foundations of the Western Intellectual Tradition, 400–1400.* New Haven, Conn.: Yale University Press, 1997.

Cowdrey, H. E. J. "Hugh of Avalon, Carthusian and Bishop." In *De Cella in Seculum: Religious and Secular Life and Devotion in Late Medieval England,* edited by Michael G. Sargent, 41–57. New York: Boydell and Brewer, 1989.

Crosby, Everett U. *Bishop and Chapter in Twelfth-Century England: A Study of the "Mensa Episcopalis."* Cambridge: Cambridge University Press, 1994.

Davnall, Sarah, et al. "The Taxatio Database." *Bulletin of the John Rylands Library* 74 (1992): 89–108.

Denholm-Young, N. *Seigniorial Administration in England.* Oxford: Oxford University Press, 1937.

Denton, J. H. *English Royal Free Chapels, 1100–1300: A Constitutional Study.* Manchester: Manchester University Press, 1970.

Donahue, Charles, Jr. "The Civil Law in England." *Yale L.J.* 84 (1974): 167–81.

Donahue, Charles, Jr. "Gerard Pucelle as a Canon Lawyer: Life and the Battle Abbey Case." In *Grundlagen des Rechts, Festschrift für Peter Landau zum 65 Geburtstag,* edited by Jörg Müller et al., 333–48. Paderborn: Ferdinand Schöningh, 2000.

Donahue, Charles, Jr. "*Ius Commune,* Canon Law, and Common Law in England." *Tulane Law Review* 66 (1992): 1745–80.

Donahue, Charles, Jr. "Roman Canon Law in the Medieval English Church: Stubbs vs. Maitland Re-examined after 75 Years in the Light of Some Records from the Church Courts." *Michigan Law Review* 72 (1974): 647–716.

Dondorp, Harry. "*Ius ad Rem* als Recht, Einsetzung in ein Amt zu Verlangen." *Tijdschrift voor Rechtsgeschiedenis* 59 (1991): 285–318.

Duggan, Anne J. "Henry II, the English Church and the Papacy, 1154–76." In *Henry II: New Interpretations,* edited by Christopher Harper-Bill and Nicholas Vincent, 154–83. Woodbridge: Boydell Press, 2007.

Duggan, Charles. "Reginald fitz Jocelin (c. 1140–1191)." In *Oxford Dictionary of National Biography.* Oxford: Oxford University Press, 2004.

Dunbabin, Jean. "From Clerk to Knight: Changing Orders." In *The Ideals and Practice of Medieval Knighthood II: Papers from the Third Strawberry Hill Conference 1986,* edited by Christopher Harper-Bill and Ruth Harvey, 26–39. Woodbridge: Boydell Press, 1988.

Ewald, William. "Comparative Jurisprudence (II): The Logic of Legal Transplants." *American Journal of Comparative Law* 43 (1995): 489–510.

Eyton, Robert William. *Court, Household, and Itinerary of King Henry II.* London: Taylor and Co., 1878.

Farmer, David Hugh. "Hugh of Lincoln, Carthusian Saint." In *De Cella in Seculum: Religious and Secular Life and Devotion in Late Medieval England,* edited by Michael G. Sargent, 9–15. New York: Boydell and Brewer, 1989.

Finzi, Enrico. *Il Possesso dei Diritti.* Milan: A Giuffrè, 1968. Reprint of the 1915 edition.

Flahiff, G. B. "The Writ of Prohibition to Court Christian in the Thirteenth Century [pt. 1]." *Mediaeval Studies* 6 (1944): 271–72.

Flahiff, G. B. "The Writ of Prohibition to Court Christian in the Thirteenth Century [pt. 2]." *Mediaeval Studies* 7 (1945): 229–90.

Forrest, Ian. *Trustworthy Men: How Inequality and Faith Made the Medieval Church.* Princeton, N.J.: Princeton University Press, 2018.

Fowler-Magerl, Linda. Ordines Iudiciarii *and* Libelli de Ordine Iudiciorum *(From the Middle of the Twelfth to the End of the Fifteenth Century)*. Turnhout, Belgium: Brepols, 1994.

Fryde, E. B., et al. *Handbook of British Chronology*. 3rd ed. Cambridge: Cambridge University Press, 1986.

Garnett, George, and John Hudson, eds. *Law and Government in Medieval England and Normandy: Essays in Honour of Sir James Holt*. Cambridge: Cambridge University Press, 1994.

Gordon, William M. "A Comparison of the Influence of Roman Law in England and Scotland." In *The Civilian Tradition and Scots Law*, edited by David L. Carey Miller and Reinhard Zimmermann, 135–48. Berlin: Duncker and Humblot, 1997.

Gransden, Antonia. *A History of the Abbey of Bury St. Edmunds, 1182–1256*. Woodbridge: Boydell Press, 2007.

Gransden, Antonia. *Legends, Tradition, and History in Medieval England*. London: Hambledon Press, 1992.

Gray, J. W. "The Ius Praesentandi in England from the Constitutions of Clarendon to Bracton." *English Historical Review* 67 (1952): 481–509.

Guy, J. A., and H. G. Beale, eds. *Law and Social Change in British History*. London: Royal Historical Society, 1984.

Haines, Roy Martin. "Gray, John de (d. 1214)." In *Oxford Dictionary of National Biography*. Oxford: Oxford University Press, 2004. http://www.oxforddnb.com/view/article/11541.

Harper-Bill, Christopher. "John of Oxford, Diplomat and Bishop." In *Medieval Ecclesiastical Studies in Honour of Dorothy M. Owen*, edited by Michael J. Franklin and Christopher Harper-Bill, 83–105. Rochester, N.Y., 1995.

Harper-Bill, Christopher. "Oxford, John of (d. 1200)." In *Oxford Dictionary of National Biography*. Oxford: Oxford University Press, 2004.

Harper-Bill, Christopher. "Thomas de Blundeville (d. 1236), Bishop of Norwich and Papal Legate." In *Oxford Dictionary of National Biography*. Oxford: Oxford University Press, 2004. https://doi.org/10.1093/ref:odnb/2717.

Harper-Bill, Christopher, and Ruth Harvey, eds. *The Ideals and Practice of Medieval Knighthood II: Papers from the Third Strawberry Hill Conference 1986*. Woodbridge: Boydell Press, 1988.

Harper-Bill, Christopher, and Nicholas Vincent, eds. *Henry II: New Interpretations*. Woodbridge: Boydell Press, 2007.

Hartridge, R. A. R. *A History of Vicarages in the Middle Ages*. Cambridge: Cambridge University Press, 1930.

Helmholz, R. H. *The* Ius Commune *in England: Four Studies.* Oxford: Oxford University Press, 2001.

Helmholz, R. H. "Magna Carta and the *ius commune.*" *University of Chicago Law Review* 66 (1999): 297–371.

Helmholz, R. H. *The Oxford History of the Laws of England.* Vol. 1, *The Canon Law and Ecclesiastical Jurisdiction from 597 to the 1640s.* Oxford: Oxford University Press, 2004.

A History of Hampshire and the Isle of Wight. 5 vols. Victoria History of the Counties of England. London, 1973. Reprint of the 1900–1912 edition.

Holdsworth, William Searle. *A History of English Law.* 3rd ed. London: Methuen, 1923.

Holt, J. C. *Colonial England, 1066–1215.* Rio Grande, Ohio: Hambledon Press, 1997.

Hudson, John. *The Formation of the English Common Law: Law and Society in England from King Alfred to Magna Carta.* 2nd ed. London: Routledge, 2018.

Hudson, John. *Land, Law, and Lordship in Anglo-Norman England.* Oxford: Oxford University Press, 1994.

Hudson, John. *The Oxford History of the Laws of England.* Vol. 2, *871–1216.* Oxford: Oxford University Press, 2012.

Ibbetson, David. *Common Law and* Ius Commune. London: Selden Society, 2001.

Jaffé, Philip. *Regesta Pontificium Romanorum.* Leipzig, 1888.

Joliffe, J. E. A. *Angevin Kingship.* London: A. and C. Black, 1955.

Jolowicz, H. F., and Barry Nicholas. *Historical Introduction to the Study of Roman Law.* 3rd ed. Cambridge: Cambridge University Press, 1972.

Kamali, Elizabeth Papp. *Felony and the Guilty Mind in Medieval England.* Cambridge: Cambridge University Press, 2019.

Karn, Nicholas. "Geoffrey de Burgh (*d. 1228*), Bishop of Ely." In *Oxford Dictionary of National Biography.* Oxford: Oxford University Press, 2004. http://www.oxforddnb.com/view/article/95140.

Kaye, J. M. *Medieval English Conveyances.* Cambridge: Cambridge University Press, 2009.

Klerman, Daniel. "Jurisdictional Competition and the Evolution of the Common Law." *University of Chicago Law Review* 74 (2007): 1179–1226.

Knowles, David. *The Religious Orders in England.* Vol. 3, *The Tudor Age.* Cambridge: Cambridge University Press, 1959.

Knowles, David, and R. Neville Hadcock. *Medieval Religious Houses: England and Wales.* London: Longman, 1971.

Kurze, Dietrich. *Pfarrerwahlen im Mittelalter.* Cologne: Böhlau, 1966.

Kuttner, Stephan, ed. *Proceedings of the Third International Congress of Medieval Canon Law.* Vatican City: Biblioteca Apostolica Vaticana, 1971.

Kuttner, Stephan, and Eleanor Rathbone. "Anglo-Norman Canonists of the Twelfth Century: An Introductory Study." *Traditio* 7 (1949–51): 279–358.

Landau, Peter. *Jus Patronatus: Studien zur Entwicklung des Patronats im Dekretalenrecht und der Kanonistik des 12. und 13. Jahrhunderts.* Cologne: Böhlau, 1975.

Landau, Peter. "Zum Ursprung des 'Ius ad rem' in der Kanonistik." In *Proceedings of the Third International Congress of Medieval Canon Law,* edited by Stephan Kuttner, 81–102. Vatican City: Biblioteca Apostolica Vaticana, 1971.

Landes, William M., and Richard Posner. "Adjudication as a Private Good." *Journal of Legal Studies* 8 (1979): 235–84.

Lawrence, C. H. "The English Parish and Its Clergy in the Thirteenth Century." In *The Medieval World,* 2nd ed., edited by Peter Linehan, Janet L. Nelson, and Marios Costambeys, 746–69. Abingdon: Routledge, 2018.

Lewis, Charlton T., and Charles Short. *A Latin Dictionary.* Oxford: Oxford University Press, 1879.

Leyser, Henrietta. "Hugh the Carthusian." In *St. Hugh of Lincoln: Lectures Delivered at Oxford and Lincoln to Celebrate the Eighth Centenary of St. Hugh's Consecration as Bishop of Lincoln,* edited by Peter Mayr-Harting, 1–18. Oxford: Clarendon Press, 1987.

Leyser, Karl. "The Angevin Kings and the Holy Man." In *St. Hugh of Lincoln: Lectures Delivered at Oxford and Lincoln to Celebrate the Eighth Centenary of St. Hugh's Consecration as Bishop of Lincoln,* edited by Peter Mayr-Harting, 49–73. Oxford: Clarendon Press, 1987.

Linehan, Peter, ed. *Life, Law and Letters: Historical Studies in Honour of Antonio García y García.* Studia Gratiana 29. Rome, 1998.

Linehan, Peter, Janet L. Nelson, and Marios Costambeys, eds. *The Medieval World.* 2nd ed. Abingdon: Routledge, 2018.

Macnair, Mike. "Vicinage and the Antecedents of the Jury." *Law and Hist. Rev.* 17 (1999): 537–90.

Masmejan, Lucien. *La protection possessoire en droit romano-canonique médiéval (XIIIe–XVe siècles).* Montpellier: Société d'histoire du droit et des institutions des anciens pays de droit écrit, 1990.

Masschaele, James. *Jury, State, and Society in Medieval England.* New York: Palgrave Macmillan, 2008.

Mayr-Harting, Peter, ed. *St. Hugh of Lincoln: Lectures Delivered at Oxford and Lincoln to Celebrate the Eighth Centenary of St. Hugh's Consecration as Bishop of Lincoln.* Oxford: Clarendon Press, 1987.

McSweeney, Thomas J. *Priests of the Law: Roman Law and the Making of the Common Law's First Professionals.* Oxford: Oxford University Press, 2019.

Metzger, Ernest. "Actions." In *A Companion to Justinian's Institutes,* 208–28. Ithaca, N.Y.: Cornell University Press, 1998.

Metzger, Ernest. *A Companion to Justinian's Institutes.* Ithaca, N.Y.: Cornell University Press, 1998.

Midmer, Roy. *English Medieval Monasteries (1066–1540): A Summary.* Athens: University of Georgia Press, 1979.

Millon, David. "Ecclesiastical Jurisdiction in Medieval England." *University of Illinois Law Review,* no. 3 (1984): 621–38.

Milsom, S. F. C. *Historical Foundations of the Common Law.* 2nd ed. London: Butterworths, 1981.

Milsom, S. F. C. *The Legal Framework of English Feudalism.* Cambridge: Cambridge University Press, 1976.

Milsom, S. F. C. "Legal Introduction" to *Novae Narrationes.* Selden Society 80. London, 1963.

Milsom, S. F. C. *A Natural History of the Common Law.* New York: Columbia University Press, 2003.

Moorman, John R. H. *Church Life in England in the Thirteenth Century.* Cambridge: Cambridge University Press, 1955.

Mortimer, Richard. "Religious and Secular Motives for Some English Monastic Foundations." In *Religious Motivation: Biographical and Sociological Problems for the Church Historian,* edited by Derek Baker, 77–85. Oxford: Basil Blackwell, 1978.

Müller, Jörg, et al., eds. *Grundlagen des Rechts: Festschrift für Peter Landau zum 65 Geburtstag.* Paderborn: Ferdinand Schöningh, 2000.

Nardi, Paolo. "Fonti canoniche in una sentenza senese del 1150." In *Life, Law and Letters: Historical Studies in Honour of Antonio García y García,* Studia Gratiana 29, edited by Peter Linehan, 661–70. Rome, 1998.

Newman, J. E. "Greater and Lesser Landowners and Parochial Patronage: Yorkshire in the Thirteenth Century." *English Historical Review* 92 (1977): 280–308.

Palmer, Robert C. "The Feudal Framework of English Law." *Mich. L. Rev.* 79 (1981): 1130–64.

Palmer, Robert C. "The Origins of Property in England." *Law and Hist. Rev.* 3 (1985): 1–50.

Palmer, Robert C. *Selling the Church: The English Parish in Law, Commerce, and Religion, 1350–1550.* Chapel Hill: University of North Carolina Press, 2002.

Pennington, Kenneth. *Legal History Sources.* Electronic database. http://legalhistorysources.com/1140a-z.htm.

Pollock, Frederick, and F. W. Maitland. *The History of English Law before the Time of Edward I.* 2 vols. 2nd ed. Cambridge: Cambridge University Press, 1968. Reprint of the 1898 edition.

Pound, Roscoe. *The Formative Era of American Law.* New York: Peter Smith, 1950.

Pounds, N. J. G. *A History of the English Parish.* Cambridge: Cambridge University Press, 2000.

Rathbone, Eleanor. "Roman Law in the Anglo-Norman Realm." *Studia Gratiana* 11 (1967): 255–71.

Rogers, Everett M. *Diffusion of Innovations.* 3rd ed. New York: Free Press, 1983.

Round, J. H. "The Date of the Grand Assize." *English Historical Review* 31 (1916): 268–69.

Round, J. H. *Geoffrey de Mandeville: A Study of the Anarchy.* London: Longmans, Green, 1892.

Ruffini, Francesco. *L'actio spolii: Studio storico-giuridico.* Rome: L'Erma di Bretschneider, 1972. Photographic reprint of the 1889 edition.

Sanders, I. J. *English Baronies: A Study of Their Origin and Descent, 1086–1327.* Oxford: Clarendon Press, 1960.

Sargent, Michael G., ed. *De Cella in Seculum: Religious and Secular Life and Devotion in Late Medieval England.* New York: Boydell and Brewer, 1989.

Savigny, Friedrich Carl von. *System des heutigen Römischen Rechts.* 8 vols. Berlin: Veit, 1840–49.

Sayers, Jane E. *Papal Judges Delegate in the Province of Canterbury, 1198–1254.* Oxford: Oxford University Press, 1971.

Schulz, Fritz. *Classical Roman Law.* Oxford: Clarendon Press, 1951.

Seipp, David J. "Roman Legal Categories in the Early Common Law." In *Legal Record and Historical Reality: Proceedings of the Eighth British Legal History Conference Cardiff 1987,* edited by Thomas G. Watkin, 9–36. London: Hambledon Press, 1989.

Senior, W. "Roman Law in England before Vacarius." *Law Q. Rev.* 46 (1930): 191–206.

Senior, W. "Roman Law Mss. in England." *Law Q. Rev.* 47 (1931): 337–44.

Sherman, Charles P. "The Romanization of English Law." *Yale L.J.* 23 (1914): 318–29.

Smail, Daniel Lord. *The Consumption of Justice: Emotions, Publicity, and Legal Culture in Marseille, 1264–1423.* Ithaca, N.Y.: Cornell University Press, 2003.

Smalley, Beryl. *The Becket Conflict and the Schools: A Study of Intellectuals in Politics.* Totowa, N.J.: Rowman and Littlefield, 1973.

Smith, David M. "The Rolls of Hugh of Wells, Bishop of Lincoln, 1209–35." *Bulletin of the Institute of Historical Research* 45 (1972): 155.

Smith, David M. "Wells, Hugh of (*d.* 1235)." In *Oxford Dictionary of National Biography*. Oxford: Oxford University Press, 2004. http://www.oxforddnb.com/view/article/14061.

Smith, Peter M. "The Advowson: The History and Development of a Most Peculiar Property." *Ecclesiastical L.J.* 5 (2000): 320–39.

Soudet, F. "Les seigneurs patrons des églises normandes." In *Travaux de la semaine d'histoire du droit normand*, 313–26. Caen, 1925.

Southern, R. W. "Master Vacarius and the Beginning of an English Academic Tradition." In *Medieval Learning and Literature: Essays Presented to Richard William Hunt*, edited by J. J. G. Alexander and M. T. Gibson, 257–86. Oxford: Clarendon Press, 1976.

Steimer, Bruno, ed. *Lexikon der Kirchengeschichte*. Freiburg im Breisgau: Herder, 2001.

Stein, Peter. "Vacarius (*c.* 1120–*c.* 1200)." In *Oxford Dictionary of National Biography*. Oxford: Oxford University Press, 2004.

Stenton, Doris M. *English Justice between the Norman Conquest and the Great Charter, 1066–1215*. Philadelphia: American Philosophical Society, 1964.

Stenton, Doris M. "King John and the Courts of Justice." In *Pleas before the King and His Justices*. 67 Selden Society 86.

Stickler, Alfons Maria. *The Case for Clerical Celibacy: Its Historical Development and Theological Foundations*. San Francisco: Ignatius Press, 1995.

Stutz, Ulrich. *Die Eigenkirche als Element des mittelalterilich-germanischen Kirchenrechts*. Darmstadt: Wissenschaftliche Buchgesellschaft, 1955. Reprint of the 1895 edition.

Sutherland, Donald W. *The Assize of Novel Disseisin*. Oxford: Clarendon Press, 1973.

Taliadoros, Jason. *Law and Theology in Twelfth-Century England: The Works of Master Vacarius (c. 1115/1120–c. 1200)*. Turnhout, Belgium: Brepols, 2006.

Tate, Joshua C. "Competing Institutions and Dispute Settlement in Medieval England." In *Law and Disputing in the Middle Ages: Proceedings of the Ninth Carlsberg Academy Conference on Medieval Legal History 2012*, edited by Per Andersen et al., 235–44. Copenhagen: DJØF Publishing, 2013.

Tate, Joshua C. "Episcopal Power and Royal Jurisdiction." In *Studies in Canon Law and Common Law in Honor of R. H. Helmholz*, edited by Troy L. Harris, 15–26. Berkeley, Calif.: Robbins Collection, 2015.

Tate, Joshua C. "Glanvill and the Development of the English Advowson Writs." In *Texts and Context in Legal History: Essays in Honor of Charles Donahue*, edited by Sara McDougall, Anna di Robilant, and John Witte Jr., 129–43. Berkeley, Calif.: Robbins Collection, 2016.

Tate, Joshua C. "The Origins of Quare Impedit." *Journal of Legal History* 25 (2004): 203–19 .

Tate, Joshua C. "Ownership and Possession in the Early Common Law." *American Journal of Legal History* 48 (2006): 280–313.

Tate, Joshua C. "Royal Privilege and Episcopal Rights in the Later Thirteenth Century: The Case of the Ashbourne Advowson, 1270–89." In *Law and Society in Later Medieval England and Ireland: Essays in Honour of Paul Brand,* edited by Travis R. Baker, 97–107. Oxford: Routledge, 2018.

Tate, Joshua C. "The Third Lateran Council and the *Ius Patronatus* in England." In *Proceedings of the Thirteenth International Congress of Medieval Canon Law: Esztergom, 3–8 August 2008,* edited by Peter Erdö and Sz. Anzelm Szuromi, 589–600. Vatican City: Biblioteca Apostolica Vaticana, 2010.

Teubner, Gunther. "Legal Irritants: Good Faith in British Law, or How Unifying Law Ends Up in New Divergences." *Modern L. Rev.* 61 (1998): 11–32.

Thibodeaux, Jennifer D. *The Manly Priest: Clerical Celibacy, Masculinity, and Reform in England and Normandy, 1066–1300.* Philadelphia: University of Pennsylvania Press, 2015.

Thomas, Hugh M. *The Secular Clergy in England, 1066–1216.* Oxford: Oxford University Press, 2014.

Tullis, Sarah. "*Glanvill Continued:* A Reassessment." In *Law in the City: Proceedings of the Seventeenth British Legal History Conference, London, 2005,* edited by Andrew Lewis et al. Bodmin, Cornwall: MPG Books, 2007.

Turner, Ralph V. *The English Judiciary in the Age of Glanvill and Bracton, c. 1176–1239.* Cambridge: Cambridge University Press, 1985.

Turner, Ralph V. "Roman Law in England before the Time of Bracton." *Journal of British Studies* 15 (1975): 1–10.

Victoria History of the County of Rutland. 2 vols. Edited by William Page. London, 1975.

Vincent, Nicholas. "The Court of Henry II." In *Henry II: New Interpretations,* edited by Christopher Harper-Bill and Nicholas Vincent, 278–334. Woodbridge: Boydell Press, 2007.

Vincent, Nicholas. "Pandulf (*d.* 1226), bishop of Norwich." In *Oxford Dictionary of National Biography.* Oxford: Oxford University Press, 2004. http://www.oxforddnb.com/view/article/2717.

Vincent, Nicholas. "William de Warenne (*d.* 1240), Fifth Earl of Surrey." In *Oxford Dictionary of National Biography.* Oxford: Oxford University Press, 2004. http://www.oxforddnb.com/view/article/28739.

Warren, W. L. *Henry II.* London: Eyre Methuen, 1973.

Watkin, Thomas G., ed. *Legal Record and Historical Reality: Proceedings of the Eighth British Legal History Conference Cardiff 1987*. London: Hambledon Press, 1989.

Watson, Alan. *Legal Transplants: An Approach to Comparative Law*. 2nd ed. Athens: University of Georgia Press, 1993.

Whatley, Charlotte. "Edward III and the Fight for the Benefices of Exeter." In *Fourteenth Century England VIII*, edited by J. S. Hamilton, 59–81. Woodbridge: Boydell Press, 2014.

White, Stephen D. *Custom, Kinship, and Gifts to Saints: The "Laudatio Parentum" in Western France, 1050–1150*. Chapel Hill: University of North Carolina Press, 1988.

Whitman, James Q. *The Legacy of Roman Law in the German Romantic Era*. Princeton, N.J.: Princeton University Press, 1990.

Winroth, Anders. *The Making of Gratian's "Decretum."* Cambridge: Cambridge University Press, 2000.

Wood, Susan. *The Proprietary Church in the Medieval West*. Oxford: Oxford University Press, 2006.

Wormald, Patrick. *The Making of English Law: King Alfred to the Twelfth Century*. Vol. 1, *Legislation and Its Limits*. Oxford: Blackwell, 1999.

Young, Charles R. *The Making of the Neville Family in England, 1166–1400*. Woodbridge: Boydell Press, 1996.

Zimmermann, Reinhard. "Der europäische Charakter des englischen Rechts." *Zeitschrift für Europäisches Privatrecht* 1 (1993): 4–51.

Zimmermann, Reinhard. *The Law of Obligations: Roman Foundations of the Civilian Tradition*. Oxford: Clarendon Press, 1996. Originally published 1990.

INDEX

Page numbers in *italics* indicate illustrations. Page numbers followed by *table* indicate a table.